THE
BOTTOM LINE
CATECHISM
for
Contemporary Catholics

THE
BOTTOM LINE
CATECHISM
for
Contemporary Catholics

by
Andrew M. Greeley

THE THOMAS MORE PRESS
Chicago, Illinois

Material in this book appeared in different format in the newsletter Bottom Line, also published by the Thomas More Association.

ISBN 0-88347-135-3

Contents

Chapter One

The Bottom Line of the Bottom Line

What is the Bottom Line of the Christian Faith?

WHEN all is said and done, when all the scholars have been consulted, all the Roman documents read, all the textbooks pondered, all the wise men from ages past examined, all the qualifications entered, all the uncertainties underscored, all the new opinions considered, all the references to Hans Kung and Karl Rahner and the documents to Vatican II checked out, what do you *have* to believe?

That is the bottom-line question of Christian faith, and it is to that "bottom line" that this book is addressed.

Mind you, I don't like the way the bottom line is worded. I would much prefer to say not, "What do we *have* to believe?" or "What must we believe?" but "What *may* we believe?" Even better, "What are we lucky enough to believe?" Best of all "What are we *privileged* to believe?" But the immediate past of Catholic religious teaching is still upon us, and many folk—bishops, priests, *Catechetical Directory* authors, and ordinary (as well as extraordinary) laity—still want to know what *must* they believe. So we will take that bottom-line wording and see what we can do with it.

There are two short, quick, and simple answers to the bottom-line question, what must we believe? The first answer is, "Not much"; the second answer is, "Everything." Both answers are true, depending on how you choose to look at religious reality.

7

The "not much" answer is true because when push comes to shove, there are only a couple of things that are at the core of the Christian message. It may be only one thing really: God is love. All the other doctrines and dogmas, teachings and regulations, principles and rules, rituals and practices, are only various ways of articulating that fundamental truth.

What about less basic beliefs—all those things above the bottom line?

EVEN among the handmaiden teachings that cluster around that central one, there are grades of importance. The resurrection of Jesus, for example, even by old standards, is more important than the proper way to address a cardinal ("Your Eminence" "Mr. Cardinal?" "Lord Cardinal?" or, simply "Cardinal?").

There are only three or four major implications of the basic insight that God is love that constitute the mind and the heart of the Christian heritage. Not one of them should put any great strain on our credulity if we accept the basic insight to begin with. All the doctrines and dogmas that one can sort out of the various editions of Denzinger's collection of doctrinal pronouncements (H. Denzinger and A. Schonmetzer, *Enchiridion Symbolorum, Defintionum et Declarationum de Rebus Fidei et Morum.* Freiburg: Herder, 1976) are merely commentaries and reflections on the basic insight and its immediate implications.

One may view, then, the insight and its basic implications as a vast array of reflections that have grown up through the centuries as a test, an intellectual obstacle course through which one must pass in order to be certified as a believing, practicing Catholic Christian. One may elect to describe things that way. One does so, though, at the risk of missing entirely the point of the mission of Jesus and the reason for the existence of the church.

There are not all that many things we in fact *have* to assent to. Once we buy the core insight that God is love, all the others ought to come easily. That may sound like a strange assertion, because it would seem relatively easy to believe that God is love and relatively difficult to believe that there are three persons in God. In fact, however, the doctrine of the Trinity is rudimentary compared to the wildly romantic and well-nigh incredible proposition that God is love.

On the other hand, it is often true that we must believe virtually everything. There is a practical implication to human life and love contained in the assertion that God himself *is* love without limitation. To put the matter somewhat differently, if one is prepared to accept the notion that the sentiment which we call love is the best experience we have of what God is, then our lives ought to be so utterly and totally transformed that we become totally different persons than those who cannot subscribe to such an assertion. To accept the idea that God is love is to accept everything; if we are willing to believe that God is love, then we are willing to believe almost anything else.

To accept that love defines God and then deny the existence of angels is ridiculous. I am not asserting either that one has to believe in the existence of angels or that there are angels (I would be terribly disappointed, however, if there were not); I am simply saying that the existence of angels is not worth getting upset about if you believe that God is love—nor is the possibility of miracles, the inerrancy of scripture, the infallability of the pope, or anything else for that matter.

What is the real relationship of religious truth to life?

PART of our difficulty in working our way to the bottom line and understanding how, on the one hand, it requires us to believe "not much" and, on the other hand, "practically everything," is that we have been educated by methods that incline us to completely misunderstand the relationship of religious truth to human life. We come away from such educational experiences with the notion that there exists somewhere a collection of religious truths, or, if we are more up to date, religious symbols which have gathered together—perhaps in the "deposit of faith" (one gets the image of an underground vault somewhere beneath the apostolic palace of the Vatican)—and are to be applied to the human condition.

This collection of religious truths has come from some place—presumably "revelation—and has an independent existence of its own over against human experience and by which human experience is to be interpreted, judged, explained, and validated. Religious questions, in other words, are asked out of our experience of life, and the religious answers are imposed from the outside on that experience. Revelations, we were taught implicitly, provided absolute, safe, and certain answers to life's questions.

What such a perspective overlooked were the profound psychological, sociological, and linguistic truths (emphasized especially by the great scientist and philosopher Michael Polanyi) that far more critical than the answers were the questions themselves. The wording of the question already implies the answer. The answers to most of our religious questions are in fact implicit in the questions, or at least in our ability to ask the questions.

Religious truth grows out of human experience,

achieves a reality of its own when it is first of all articulated in stories or in symbols and then, only later, in philosophical propositions. Then it "bounces back" to provide explicit answers and detailed interpretations for those human experiences that are already inchoately explained and interpreted in the fact of experience itself. Religion, to put the matter in somewhat different words, confirms our hunch that our wildest dreams will come true; and it ultimately takes its strength from our profound internal conviction that the hunch is right.

All this may sound new or radical or even heretical. At least it seems to be untraditional. In fact, it is quintessentially traditional. All good religious teaching (the parables of Jesus, for example) take such a perspective for granted.

But I'd still better explain. Or at least illustrate.

Let us take the renewal experience of reconciliation in which two lovers (any kind of lovers), after a long, bitter, and angry quarrel, take hesitant and stumbling first steps, then impulsive and hurried strides toward the rebirth of love. Such an experience of sorrow, forgiveness, renewal, reconciliation, and the rebirth of a more durable love are almost as intrinsic to the human condition as breathing.

If one has gone through even a few such experiences, one must begin to ask whether the reality of hatred or the reality of forgiveness and reconciliation is more powerful. Is what forgiveness stands for more powerful than that for which anger stands? Is what reconciliation stands for more powerful than that for which hatred stands? The person who has been through the renewing experience of reconciliation has not the slightest doubt. Rebirth is stronger than death, love is stronger than hate, forgiveness stronger than anger.

From that conviction—a fundamental and basic reli-

gious insight—arises our suspicion that the universe itself is animated by forgiveness, renewal, and rebirth.
The religious symbol, from whatever symbol tradition,
is then invoked (for the first time when a tradition
begins or subsequently by those who inherit it) to articulate, confirm, reinforce, and validate the meaning of
this intimate explanation, this "rumor of angels," this
"signal of the transcendent," this sacrament (note the
small "s") of God's love.

What did Jesus come into this world to reveal?

TO put the matter in the terminology of Christian revelation, Jesus did not come into the world to reveal for
the first time that renewal, rebirth, reconciliation were
possible, for humankind had suspected that possibility
from the beginning—though we humans had encountered enormous difficulty fulfilling the possibility. Jesus
came to reveal in a definitive, unimpeachable, irrefut-
able way that the hints we had experienced since becoming human were not only possibilities but were in fact
true. We could safely trust our hunches, our instincts,
our inclinations and believe those hints, living as though
they were true.

Jesus added nothing to the repertory of human religious symbols. Death and resurrection, rebirth and reconciliation, forgiveness and renewal were all there
before Jesus came. The role of Jesus was to make the utterly definitive, wildly spectacular interpretation of
these symbols: "Eye has not seen, nor has ear heard,
nor has it entered the heart of man those things that God
has prepared for the ones who love him."

The coming of Jesus, then, was not intended to re-
place, contradict, or supplement our natural experiences
of grace, but rather to reinforce, validate, and enrich

them. "Grace is everywhere," as Karl Rahner once wrote, because we know Jesus. We do not so much see grace that was not there before but have our vision sharpened so that we may recognize the presence of grace that is always there.

What convinces us to believe in religious truths?

RELIGION does not begin in church, it begins with the human race and its species, with the great religious traditions of humankind, and in our own individual biographies and our experiences of grace, or gratuity, of giftedness, the experiences of the transcendent which lurk in everyday life. These experiences not only raise the basic religious questions, such as what does out life mean, but articulate in an inchoate way the answers to them, answers that emerge not as prose propositions but as symbols, rituals, and stories, which, in turn, serve to validate and reinforce subsequent experiences of grace. "Church religion" or "Sunday religion" serves to draw together our daily experiences of grace, integrates them, and then heightens our sensitivity to the experiences of grace which will happen tomorrow, the next day, or next week.

So the bottom line of the bottom line is that we believe not in things which we are afraid are not true, but we believe things we know in the depths of our heart are true—at least in things whose truth (however tentatively, however hesitantly) we have already experienced. We believe in the death and resurrection of Jesus and our own eventual death and resurrection because experiences of death and resurrection happen to us all the time. Faith is not any easier because it is a commitment to Truths (or Persons) which (or whom) we have already experienced; but faith thus perceived is not commitment to something extrinsic to or on the surface of our lives. It is rather a commitment to the goodness (or Goodness) that we have already experienced at the core of our lives.

Is it realistic to hope in a gracious God?

RELIGION is related to two capabilities of the human organism—the necessity to hope and the capacity to periodically experience renewals of hope. Hope is structured into the human personality, the result of biological and genetic programming, according to anthropologist Lionel Tiger, or the inevitable result of human culture and social structure, according to other scholars. Research about death and dying indicates that in the final moments of our life, hope increases in strength instead of growing weaker, so that at the end of life all that remains, it seems, is hope.

The *bottom line* religious question is whether our propensity to hope and our experiences of grace are revelatory or deceptive, either cruel tricks of a capricious or arbitrary universe, or else the hint of an explanation. Hence the *bottom line* religious question is not, do you believe in God? but rather is reality gracious? (Or, if one wants to put it a slightly different way, is Reality gracious?) Either choice, as John Shea notes in his *Stories of Faith,* represents an act of faith, a leap beyond conclusive evidence to an existential rather than an intellectual stance. We either believe that reality is gracious and commit ourselves to a life based on that assumption, or we reject graciousness and try to commit ourselves to a life in a universe that is absurd and in which we are definitely alone.

The latter choice is more difficult to make not because, as some of its proponents would have us believe, it is the more tough-minded, realistic, objective choice

—for there is no more objective evidence to support such a position than its reverse—but because the human organism refuses to give up hope even when the human intellect orders it to do so. The brave stoicism of the agnostic, the posture of living as though there were hope when there is in fact no hope is merely hope sneaking in the back door.

Is God a force or a person?

IN our moments of grace (or moments of "wonder") we intuit "otherness" or, as John Shea calls it, the "mysterious." There is "something else" which intrudes into our life with a sudden, dramatic crash, perhaps, or with a gentle touch like a spring breeze, demanding, either noisily or faintly, to be recognized.

In the religious experience itself, be it major or minor, that which is encountered is "otherness." It is only after the experience is over and we reflect upon it that we begin to think about what "otherness" or "the mysterious" or the "sacred" is like. In the Western world such reflection often leads to the conclusion that the "otherness" encountered in the experience is an "Other" or "The Other." It is, indeed, a "Thou."

The tiresome discussion about whether one believes in a "personal" God is irrelevant and should be rephrased: is the graciousness we encounter a "Thou," a someone or a Someone with whom we can interact? Those who say they believe in God but not a personal God seem to think that some sort of impersonal "life force" is morally or intellectually superior to a God who is a "person." By this they seem to mean a God who has human characteristics. Such a perspective seems utterly innocent of the natural propensity for analogy among humans when they try to describe their experiences of grace. That which is encountered in such experiences is similar to us and can be addressed as "Thou," but it is also different from us in that its "Thouness" is not limited or constrained the way human thouness is limited and constrained. One may, if one wishes, call "Thou" impersonal, but only in the sense that it is more than a human person rather than less.

How are we to understand the nature of God?

OUR primordial notions of God are based on our experiences of the graciousness of reality, an ambiguous graciousness, indeed, because in reality good is experienced as mixed with evil. God is the symbol, or the construct, or, finally, the notion that summarizes our feelings and ideas about the other that (or whom) we have experienced. To say that "God" is a symbol, a construct, or an idea is not to deny that there exists a Reality that corresponds to the term; it is rather to indicate that the term and the pictures and ideas which cluster around it are at best limited and inadequate descriptions of the Reality.

The Canadian Catholic philosopher Leslie Dewart suggested that the term "God" be dropped from the discussion because so many extraneous, false, superstitious, and negative emotions are stirred up by its use. But, as Gertrude Stein might have said, "A God is a God is a God." It matters much less what we call "The Other" than that we have experienced it (or him or her). We come to know the nature of the Other by reflecting on our experiences of grace. We encounter it through its "sacraments," through those creatures that seem to reveal him/her to us. While we sense that the Other is encountered in some fashion directly in the experience triggered by the "sacrament," the Otherness that is encountered is in a strict sense ineffable, that is, beyond description.

So we fall back on a description of the creature (or "sacrament") that seems to reveal the Other. As the sun shatters the darkness of the night and reveals to us a Light that goes beyond light, then we say that the Other is the rising sun (by which we mean, of course that he/she is like the rising sun).

Do we feel that we have encountered Otherness in the overflow of joy and happiness which comes from a human love experience? Then we say that the Other is an aroused and implacably faithful spouse (which means that the Other is like, or has some of the characteristics of, an aroused and implacably faithful spouse). We come to know the nature of the Other by studying his/her footprints.

To put the matter in a quasi-parable, it is as though we are standing in a room by ourselves looking out the window and watching the flow of pedestrians along the street. We are suddenly aware that someone else is in the room with us; we turn around just in time to see the door swing closed. Whoever was there is gone, but there is a great big gift-wrapped package in the center of the room with tissue paper and multicolored ribbons. We rush to open the package and inside it find the rising sun, or a smiling toddler, or an aroused and implacably faithful lover. We say to our selves, "Aha, where there is a gift like this there must be a giver." To have given us such a splendid gift the giver must be like his/her gift, for otherwise how could he/she have thought it up? Still he/she must be different from the gift, because he/she gave a gift, not himself/herself.

What was unique about the Hebrew experience of God?

HUMANKIND'S experiences of the Other are variegated. Hence the images of God that recall, resonate, and articulate these experiences are multitudinous. One way to arrange these experiences is according to how they respond to the mystery of evil, against which our hopefulness needs to be renewed. Paul Ricoeur summarized it by saying that the worldview that can be drawn out of the symbol of God may be optimistic or pessimistic or fatalistic or hopeful.

The Egyptians were optimists. Believing that evil resulted from the inattention of the god, they addressed themselves to their gods with reminders of the promises they had made, pleas that the gods awaken from their inattention and discipline errant nature, the Nile River. (Many traces of this influence may be found in the Hebrew scriptures, particularly in prayers and in the Psalms.)

The Babylonians took the opposite view. Evil seemed to triumph over good most of the time, and the gods were contentious, difficult, crotchety beings who had to be placated. Easy to offend, quick to anger, punctilious in their demands, the gods of the Babylonians could only be approached from a propitiatory stance. Again, in the Hebrew scriptures there are many pleas to Yahweh that he come down and be appeased, that he forgive his poor, stupid, offending people instead of rampaging around the cedars of Lebanon tearing things up in his fury.

In Greece the mystery of evil was attributed to the fact that daily human existence was governed by the fates, blind, unreasoning forces which cared nothing for the humans that were doomed by their inevitable destinies. The thin sliver of hope that was kept alive was justified by the possibility that Chronos, the sleeping father God, might arise, blind the fates, discipline the unruly Olympians, and bring some goodness and some peace back to human existence.

The mystery of evil, then, was resolved in Egypt by

pleading with the gods to remember their promises, to awaken from their inattention; in Mesopotamia evil was averted by propitiating the anger of the gods; and in Greece, a world controlled by irrational fates was faced by Stoic bravery or indulging in Dionysian escape. The God of the Hebrews, however, was something else altogether.

When the ragtag collection of desert tribes gathered under the shadow of Sinai and experienced that they were a people and that their God had constituted them a people, it was a strikingly different encounter for them than for those others of the ancient world. While the other gods stood aloof on their mountaintops waiting for the people to come to them, Yahweh came down off the mountain and intervened directly in human affairs. He announced peremptorily, "I am Yahweh your God."

Period, Paragraph. End of revelation.

What is the basic Christian experience of God and the meaning of existence?

YAHWEH, in effect, dismissed the mystery of evil. He said in effect, "Whatever else may happen, I am still implacably faithful to you. I have freed you, I have brought you out of the land of Egypt, I have made you a people. Isn't that enough to demonstrate my love for you? Leave the rest to me, for I am a passionate God, and I do not want a frigid people." And then he quickly added, "You may go off and whore with false gods if you want. I don't like it, because I am a passionate God; but do not think that you can escape from me. You cannot. I do not repent of the promises I made, and nothing will shake my fidelity."

The God of the Hebrews and the God of the Christians (your God and my God) is therefore a God of implacable fidelity. Our hope comes not from the possibility of reawakening the gods to their promises or calming down the gods' anger, or the eventual return of Chronos. Our hope rests in God's love—wholly, completely, totally. It may not be a God you particularly wish to believe in; lots of folks haven't. But the only good reason for breaking with the Yahwistic tradition is that the picture of a God who falls in love with his creatures and commits himself to permanent affection for them is a God who is too much altogether (as the Irish would say).

In *Stories of Faith* John Shea says that our experience of God in the Yahwistic tradition is one of non-abandoning love. We must carefully note that this experience is not limited to the Yahwistic heritage. Indeed, the perception of "otherness" as non-abandoning love may be almost universal in the human condition.

What is unique about the Yahwistic heritage is not the discovery of such an experience but rather the making of it into the central experience, the "privileged" experience of the heritage, and the conviction that non-abandoning love is the "essence" of God, and hence the ultimate explanation of human existence and of the cosmos of which we are a part. To the question of whether Reality is gracious, Jewish and Christian followers of Yahweh respond, "Reality is as gracious as non-abandoning love." And what can be more gracious than that?

The *bottom line* question, then, is really far more difficult than whether you believe in God. It is, rather, do you believe that reality is (gracious-like) non-abandoning love? Or, more concretely, do you believe that the experiences of faithful love that you have had during your life are the best hints available to us of what our existence is all about?

Chapter Two

The Son & the Spirit

Is Jesus Divine?

THE bottom-line question is not whether you believe that Jesus is divine, but whether you believe the gospel Jesus preached. The issue of the divinity of Jesus was not raised in his own time and was only implicitly and indirectly raised in the Scriptures. It became an issue when Christianity shifted from a Jewish to a Hellenistic world, and it became necessary to define Jesus in terms that were pertinent for Hellenistic experience and philosophy.

I am not suggesting that the issue of Jesus as divine/human or human/divine is unimportant, much less irrelevant, for we are intellectual and spiritual descendants of the Hellenistic world. I am suggesting that the issue of the gospel of Jesus is prior to the issue of the nature of Jesus (or, if one wishes, the natures). Many modern Catholic theologians are suggesting that soteriology (the study of salvation) precedes the issue of christology both in the church's historical experience and in the quest for understanding of Jesus on which we Christians are necessarily embarked. The early Christians encountered salvation both in the words and in the person of Jesus, and then they began to ask what kind of a man was this Jesus in whom they could experience such an incredible salvation.

It was the "trajectory" of that question filtered through the Hellenistic atmosphere that pointed the way toward the definitive, though not necessarily exhaustive, solutions at the Councils of Chalcedon and Ephesus in the two nature-one person christology, which has been paradigmatic for the church ever since. The question of the divinity of Jesus, in other words, was necessary and inevitable, and the solutions posed by the great ecumenical councils were appropriate for their time and place, *given the early church's experience of Jesus as savior.* But the question rose out of the savior experience, which was prior historically and psychologically.

What was it that Jesus preached?

WHAT then was the gospel of Jesus? What was the salvation he preached both by word and by the example of his life? At one level we can say that it is nothing more than a renewal of the revelation of Yahweh on Sinai—the gospel of non-abandoning love. The God of the Old Testament for many centuries was a God who related to a corporate personality, to a people—Israel— rather than to individual members of a nation.

However, as the Hebrew religion evolved, Yahweh became not only the God of Israel but the God of each individual Israelite, demanding not merely a corporate response but, by the time of the prophets, a response of the individual person. Yahweh was "married" to his people from the beginning, but by the time of Osee, Ezekiel, and Jeremiah, he had also established a liaison, which was a passionate romance, with the individual person.

A religion which had begun as a tribal cult (although an advanced and sophisticated cult) changed into a universalistic world religion so subtly that it is hard to say when the transition occurred precisely. But by the time the Israelites returned from captivity, the personalism and the universalism of their religion was firmly established, and the belief began to emerge that Yahweh's love was stronger even than death and that no power could break the loving affection between God and the individual person to whom he had committed himself.

The change, then, from Sinai to the Second Temple era (when Jesus was born) was enormous, though in some sense logical, once the human race discovered (at about the same time in Greece, Asia, and China) the importance of the individual human person. Jesus' immediate predecessors, the so-called Pharisees of love, had developed firm beliefs in the resurrection of the body and love as central to human ethical choice and in the importance of love of God and love of neighbor as central to religious belief.

The more we learn about the religious environment into which Jesus came, the more clear it becomes that he was very much a part of his time. His unique contribution was not the revelation of new doctrines or new truths but a deepening and enriching and validating of tentative insights and intuitions toward which the most generous of existing religious impulses were already moving.

If Jesus was not the first to preach resurrection or to preach that God is love and to demand love of neighbor, what is special or unique about his message?

THERE are two responses: First of all, Jesus claimed to have a special intimacy, a special insight, a special awareness of the nature of God. He could call him "Papa," *Abba,* a term of intimate and playful familiarity which came dangerously close to being disrespectful. "I know the Father," Jesus said, "and his love for us is such that it is not only all right but appropriate to address him by a name like 'Daddy' or even 'Daddy-o.'"

The second aspect of the specialness of Jesus is really a development of the first. God, who is the Father of Jesus (the Daddy-o of Jesus) is also our Father. He relates to us in the same intimate familiarity with which he relates to Jesus. (A later theology, concerned with precision, would change "same" to "similar." That is valid, no doubt, but it loses some of the shock value of the original formulation.)

Of what nature is this God with whom Jesus claimed to have such intimacy, and who also sought intimacy with us? He is a father who outrageously spoils wayward children, an employer who pays people a day's wage for hardly working at all, a farmer who refuses to tear up weeds, a king who throws a party for disreputable people, a bishop who forgives sinful women even before they have admitted their sorrow, a wealthy man who urges his servants to recklessness with the goods he has left in their charge, a traveler who risks his life by taking care of a sworn enemy, a fisherman who does not reject worthless fish.

What kind of God is that? The only answer is that it is a God who by human standards is a bit crazy, something of a lunatic, a God whose love has blinded him/her to sensible reality, a God whose behavior if imitated would lead to arrest and incarceration on the grounds that those who behaved in such ways were seriously disturbing the peace. The Father of Jesus, in other words, is a God who has fallen hopelessly in love with his people. Non-abandoning love, indeed, but also passionate, reckless, headstrong, wild. One might almost say, half-mad non-abandoning love characterizes this God.

The unique contribution of Jesus to human religious thought is that he pushed the image of God's love as far as it could be pushed. It is fashionable in some theological circles to say that Jesus is the "uniquely adequate representation of God's love." That statement is strictly and literally true, but it is utterly impossible to present a picture of God's love as more total, more generous, more passionate, or more committed than Jesus presented. "I know the Father," Jesus said in effect, "and the Father's love goes beyond even the wildest extent of the love that has been hitherto revealed to you. You are saved, you are free, you are reconciled to one another and to the Father not because you particularly deserve it but because of the Father's manic, passionate love."

What is the only "catch" in Jesus' claim that the Father loves us passionately?

ONE may well wish not to accept the above view of things, but one ought not and cannot deny that it was Jesus' view of things. The parables, those core products of the religious imagination of Jesus, do indeed present such a picture of God. That kind of Good News may be too good to be true, too good, too wildly, insanely hopeful to be taken seriously by sober, respectable, thoughtful, and responsible human beings. But the only reason for finally rejecting the message of Jesus of Nazareth is not that one has some doubts about the divinity of Jesus or is not able to accept the intricate formulations of the first four councils.

The only reason for rejecting Jesus that makes any sense at all is to reject him because you don't believe his story of God, you don't believe his claim to intimacy with his Father in heaven, and you don't believe in a God whose love is so wild, so passionate, so utterly and completely committed, so totally and absolutely non-abandoning.

There is a catch, of course, and the catch is not that

Jesus imposes a set of harsh and rigorous rules; the catch is that Jesus, in the name of the Father, demands a response. "The Father loves you," he says in effect, "you must love the Father in return, and then you must love one another as the Father loves you. Don't expect to be perfect at it, don't even expect to be very good at it, and don't feel that a flawless response is the price you have to pay to earn my Father's love. He has given that love as a free gift by thrusting you into existence. He won't take it back, he simply wants you to respond!

As long as we live (at least) the possibility for response is still there. The marvelous ethical vision of the Sermon on the Mount, therefore, is not so much a description of a new moral imperative as it is a description of the kind of love that becomes possible (though scarcely in its fullness and perfection) for those who are ready to lose themselves in a trusting and loving response to an overwhelming, passionate love which has already been offered them.

What exactly is Jesus' unique relationship with God?

AGAIN, one may well wish to dismiss the vision of a passionately loving God as absurd. There is a touch of the absurd about it. But the question is not whether it sounds absurd, the question is whether God is really that way. Jesus claimed he was, and that was the name of his game, his gospel, his special and unique contribution to human religious thought.

We can now deal somewhat more easily with questions of christology. For what kind of person would dare such intimacy with the Father and portray the Father in such dazzling and outrageous terminology save a person who had a special and unique relationship with the Father, a relationship that enabled him to know the Father as he really is.

Jesus claims this special relationship was based on his ability to specially "comprehend" the Father, a comprehension which implies some fundamental equality with the Father. It was a long way intellectually from the apostles' experience of Jesus as someone who had a unique "comprehensive" unity with the Father to the precise formulations of the first four gospels, a way that struggled through the complex thicket of Greek philosophical issues which are no longer very pertinent to us.

Catholic Christians are committed to the paradigm of the divine person and the human and divine nature of Jesus because that paradigm sustains the experience of Jesus by the apostles and the early Christians as one who had unique access to and a unique vision of the Father. There may be other modalities of expression of these experiences, which, while certainly not denying the value of the formularity of the Council of Chalcedon, may more accurately and effectively articulate the blend of the divine and the human in Jesus than the 1400 year-old formula of the early church.

It must be said candidly, however, that contemporary Catholic theological efforts to restate the mystery of the Incarnation, of the unity of the divine and human in Jesus, have yet to be particularly successful. At present we must be content with the assertion that Jesus was both human like us and also united to the Father in heaven in some absolutely unique way which enabled him to reveal the Father and the Father's love not only accurately but "comprehensively."

What of the relationship between the Father and the Holy Spirit?

FOR our practical religious life, however, the bottom line is not the philosophical and theological explanation for the Incarnation that we may be able to fashion; the bottom line is whether we are willing to believe in the madly loving and implacably faithful love which Jesus revealed to us as the nature of the Father—a vision of God's goodness and affection that pushes humankind's brightest explanations and its faintest hopes as far as they could ever be pushed. "Imagine," Jesus tells us, "the most wildly loving God possible, and then when your imagination ends, the reality of my heavenly Father only begins."

The Old Testament knew of Yahweh's "Spirit," the Shekinah of Yahweh. It hovered over the Ark of the Covenant and preceeded the Israelites on their pilgrimage. It was Yahweh and yet was distinctive from Yahweh. It was "the presence" of Yahweh that hovered above those about whom Yahweh was concerned even when Yahweh himself was absent. Of course, Yahweh could never be absent, so the Shekinah was both distinct and not distinct from him.

The Shekinah was not a metaphysical concept, it did not anticipate the development of our doctrine of the Trinity, at least not logically. Psychologically and historically there was a connection, for in the Second Temple Judaism from which Christianity emerged there was a readiness to imagine Someone going forth from Yahweh who protected and cared for his people.

Some students of biblical archaeology and Middle Eastern literature are convinced that at one time in the pre-Sinai Yahweh tradition the Shekinah was in fact the spouse of Yahweh, a female consort, who played a characteristic maternal role over against Yahweh's paternal role. A similar, or at least parallel person, also emerged in both the folk Judaism of Palestine and some variants of the official Yahwehism which flourished in the Diaspora. Reconstruction of the pre-Sinai Yahweh tradition, as well as variants that survived into the Second Temple era, has only just begun.

The most one can say now is that the Shekinah, the Spirit of Yahweh, was thought of to some extent and by some people as a maternal or feminine aspect or component of the deity. Minimally, a certain maternal strain of meaning seemed to be attached to the term when it was appropriated for Christian usage. It is too much to say that the Holy Spirit in early Christianity was thought of as a "feminine" personage in the Trinity, but it would not be so wrong to think that there was a feminine component in the meaning of the word.

Just as the Scriptures contain a trajectory toward the early ecumenical councils and a clear, preliminary statement of christology, so there is a trajectory in the Scriptures pointing toward the later trinitarian definition and the explicit specification of the current Catholic doctrine of the Holy Spirit.

How did the doctrine of the Trinity evolve?

THE men who preached the Christian message and wrote the Scriptures were not interested in metaphysical doctrine (which is not to say that such an interest is invalid). For them the Holy Spirit was the one whom the Father and the Son sent to continue the work of Jesus —the teacher, the comforter, the encourager, the reassurer who called the Christian community and the individual Christian to continue what Jesus had begun.

The New Testament experience of the Trinity can be simply summarized: the Father sends Jesus to reveal himself; the Father and the Son send the Spirit (after the Son returns to the Father) to inspire those who come after Jesus to respond to the invitation to love that he brought from the heavenly Father. It is in this early

Christian experience of God's dealing with them that we find the beginning of the trajectory that leads to greater conciliar precisions and definitions.

This early Christian experience of diverse "functions" of God resonates with a more general human intuition that "Otherness" both sends and calls, both orders and invites, both creates and attracts. The Father is the "Creator God," the Spirit the "Attracting God." The Father is the Alpha, the Spirit is the Omega.

What is the "function" of the Holy Spirit?

THE early Christians also had a vivid understanding (not metaphysically developed) of how the Spirit worked. Paul summarized this early Christian image when he said, "the Spirit speaks to our spirit." The calling principle in God speaks to that aspect of our personality which is most outgoing, most responsive, most generous, uniquely and specially us. The Spirit is God calling to the spark of the divine in our personality, inviting that which is divine in us to come home to that which is Altogether Divine.

Some modern Catholic religious thinkers have reflected the same insight when they say that if the Other is the principle of unity in the universe, then the Holy Spirit is the principle of diversity precisely because he/she does appeal to our spirit and calls forth from us that which is unique and special to us and by so doing multiples the amount of human variety.

Moreover, he/she also speaks to us, calls to us, invites us, yes, even seduces us through the splendid variety of creatures which are "sacraments" and stories of God. The Spirit especially resides in other human beings who call forth from us the most generous, the most creative, the most noble, the most self-giving and thus the most self-fulfilling dimensions of our personhood. The Spirit seduces us most effectively through other human beings. The God who calls, the God who invites, the God who attracts does this with special effect through his human agents. Where charity and love are, there, too, is the Spirit, the consoling, the reassuring, the comforting, the attractive God.

What is the Bottom Line of belief in the Holy Spirit and the Trinity?

THE bottom line seems to be whether we believe in a God who, in addition to being non-abandoning love, is also permanent attractiveness, a God who wants to win us, one might even say wants to seduce us into responding generously to his love, particularly as it is offered to us through other human beings. It is a different question. One can accept a Creator God, the Unmoved Mover, the Source of all Love, as being a not unreasonable concept; one can accept the non-abandoning God, a God of implacable fidelity as a wonderful and fantastic ground for hope and confidence.

But the God who calls, the God who excites, the God who invites adds something more to the picture. It is God not merely implacable in his promises and relentless in his pursuit; he/she is also clever in his/her enticement, adroit in her/his invitation, tricky in his/her appeal. The Hound of Heaven who is chasing us is also the fair maiden (or magic prince) who waits for us in the tower. A God who pursues us may be difficult to believe in, a God who tries to seduce us with his/her beauty and his/her love may be even more difficult to believe in.

Yet in our experiences with hope, in our encounters with Otherness, and in our moments of grace we do indeed meet the Spirit. In fact, in the interludes when hope is renewed, it is precisely the Holy Spirit who is the one we are most likely to bump into. The Christian doctrine of the Holy Spirit is one more reconfirmation, revalidation, re-enforcement of something that humankind half-suspected to be true all along.

The doctrine of the Trinity, classically formulated as a doctrine of one God and three divine persons, reveals to us when we come to the bottom line that the deity relates to us in many different ways. He/she is the one who sends, who reveals, the one who attracts. It is of his/her very nature to behave with this "multiple" strategy. God can't help himself/herself. He/she who creates must reveal, must attract, if he/she is to do anything at all. The Trinity is not an option for God. God by his/her very nature is power, knowledge, and love.

Chapter Three

Sin

What is wrong with human nature?

MARTIN Marty, the Protestant historian and theologian, once remarked that original sin is the only Christian doctrine for which there is unanswerable empirical evidence. One merely has to read the front page of the morning newspaper to know how right St. Paul was when he said "I can will what is right, but I cannot do it. For I do not do the good I want, but the evil I do not want is what I do."

We are curiously flawed, capable of extraordinary good but also capable of terrible evil. We can eliminate plagues, build cathedrals, write magnificent symphonies, devote our lives generously to others, and yet also commit genocide, napalm innocent villagers, build concentration camps, and stand silently by while millions starve.

Furthermore, each of us need only to look at our own lives to realize how many opportunities for goodness have been missed and how many cruelties, infidelities, betrayals are on our consciences. Even in our warmest and most generous relationships, we are frequently nasty, defensive, critical, punitive.

There is something wrong with human nature—not only human nature in particular. It is not merely enough to say that we *do* wrong, though that surely is true; we also seem to be wrong. We are certainly flawed, if not depraved.

Is human nature basically good?

THE question of what is wrong with human nature has bothered secular thinkers as well as religious thinkers. Such giants of secular thought as Rousseau, Marx, and Freud have found the fundamental flaw not in the human personality as such but in the social order, the system of economic ownership, or in the repressed conflicts of childhood. Rearrange society, redistribute the means of production, release the hostilities and conflicts carried over from childhood and the natural goodness of human nature will flourish. (Freud was in this respect not nearly so optimistic as some latter-day liberal Freudians like Erich Fromm, for example).

Is there crime in the street? The criminals are not responsible, society is, or the poor distribution of wealth, or bad childrearing practices, or lack of proper education. If we can eliminate poverty, injustice, concentration of power, or patriarchal childrearing, crime will diminish and eventually disappear. Such was the liberal faith which dominated much of American scholarly and popular thinking for a long time.

More recently, however, in the wake of the atomic bomb, the Vietnam War, the Watergate scandals, the disasters of the 1960s (and, though they probably don't realize it, the most shattering blow of all to the liberal faith, World War I), many people have abandoned this optimistic view of human nature. They now tell us that human nature is not basically good. Evolution, one man wrote, made a horrendous, self-destructive mistake when it produced *Homo Sapiens* a couple million years ago (or the hominid that was to evolve into *Homo Sapiens*). We are fundamentally evil, self-destructive, and cosmos-destroying. We will do ourselves in, and deserv-

edly, either by nuclear holocaust or environmental disaster. We have an aggressive instinct which is incorrigi-
ble. We are the only animal, besides giraffes, that kill
our own kind. We are, in short, up to no good and never
have been.

It is not, you see, that we are almost as bad as the animals; we are much worse. For the beasts of the jungle do
not kill for the fun of it, and they rarely kill their own
kind. They kill for food, and while they may engage in
aggressive conflict with others of their species for
dominance, this conflict is rarely to the death. The other
species have built-in inhibitors against destroying their
own kind. Human nature does not have such built-in in-
hibitions.

Some observers even point out how far superior animal sexuality is to human sexuality. Animal sex is
limited and episodic; it occurs only at a certain period
each month when the female of the species is receptive.
It interferes not at all with the social life of the animal
community at other times. If animals are pair-bonded
(as are some birds), they are invariably faithful for life.
They are, like the baboons and gorillas, organized into
harems or, like the chimpanzees, practice free love, doing so without guilt, without inhibition, without neurotic prudery.

We humans, it is said, are the only animals for whom
sexuality has become an obsession. Aggressive and destructive by instinct, disorderly and puritanical in our
sexuality (the only animal that must cover its private
parts with clothes because of shame), human nature is
obviously fouled-up, depraved, intrinsically evil, unsalvageable. How to explain human depravity?

Some see a fundamental flaw in a genetic adaption
that turned us from food-gatherers into hunters. Others,

somewhat less pessimistic, see it in the cultural adaptation that turned us from hunters into farmers. Still others see it in the technological adaptation that turned us from farmers into machine-builders. The latter two explanations see human evil as acquired, not innate. Occasionally they take comfort in the discovery of primitive tribes in the jungles of New Guinea or the Philippines that do not seem to be so corrupted.

Nowadays, among the critics of human nature, there is little optimism that we would be brave enough to return to the simple life of such food-gathering societies and recover our primitive virtue.

Whatever the explanation, even in the absence of any religious language, pessimists of human nature remain profoundly convinced of our sinfulness. It is worth noting that the pessimists do not have all the scholarly evidence on their side. Most humans, for example, do not kill other humans; the other animals are not nearly so innocent as some of their enthusiastic admirers would suggest; and there is increasing evidence that human nature possessed built-in genetic programmings for both cooperation and love before it could evolve from pre-hominid to *homo sapiens.*

Whether we have an instinct for aggression or not, we certainly have powerful predispositions for love and affection. Despite all the attempts to prove how similar we are to animals, it still is true that we study the animals, they don't study us; we teach chimpanzees how to communicate on our terms; they don't teach us on theirs.

What is the bottom line about original sin?

THE Catholic Christian bottom line on original sinfulness is often stated in terms of Adam and Eve, the eating of the apple, the transmission of guilt from our first

parents to us. But such a statement of the issues is in fact
a mistaken approach. It applies the tools of rational historical analysis inappropriately to a religious story and
misses the point completely.

Most Catholic discussions of original sin fail to perceive any link between this doctrine and the current discussion of human nature. What kind of clothes Adam
and Eve might have worn, whether the serpent was
really a serpent or not, whether Adam and Eve were individuals or a group are not prime questions. The paradise story, adapted from many other Middle Eastern
creation myths, is designed to convey basic truths,
neither science nor history. The basic truth it conveys is
one that many scientists and historians today would reject even though their scholarly disciplines do not give
them solid reasons for such a rejection.

What Yahweh created is good. Human nature in its
origin is good. If there is evil in the world, it is the result
of human sinfulness; but that sinfulness, while it may
weaken human nature, does not destroy its goodness.
This was the bottom line for the writer of the book of
Genesis, and it is the bottom line for us today.

What is the Christian tradition concerning sin and evil?

THE Catholic Christian tradition, interpreting the
Genesis story and subsequent Jewish and Christian beliefs, says that human nature has fallen, perhaps, but it
is not evil; it is deprived, perhaps, but not depraved;
prone to doing bad things, but also capable of doing
good things.

To put the matter somewhat differently, the Catholic
tradition is that on the whole, most of the time, when
human beings are not afraid, they are marginally more
likely to do good than evil. They are a little less than

angels, perhaps—indeed, substantially less than angels
—but still substantially more than demons. Human nature may be "wounded," but it is not perverse.

Note that in recent years the Catholic Christian tradition has had to take on a different set of enemies. For a
long time its adversaries were the disciples of Rousseau,
Marx, and Freud who thought that a quick social, economic, or psychological fix would restore paradise.
These were the disciples of the ancient Celtic monk
Pelagius (360?-420) who thought that human nature was
basically good and that humankind could, by its own
unaided effort, straighten out the mess it was in. Now
the liberals have been routed. Belief in science, progress,
technology, liberal democracy has folded—perhaps too
soon.

The new adversaries are those who are convinced of
the fundamental evil of human nature, the intellectual
and spiritual descendants of the Manichees, those other
adversaries of St. Augustine (who also fought the Pelag-
ians) who were convinced that human nature was irredeemably sinful. Almost without warning the Catholic
heritage and human sinfulness has had, so to speak, to
move its fleet from one ocean to another, to worry more
about those who deny human goodness than about
those who deny human sinfulness.

The moderate Catholic position on the sinfulness of
humankind has been especially abhorrent to certain
mainline Protestant thinkers who have been convinced
that Catholics are not sufficiently pessimistic about human nature. When the late Reinhold Niebuhr, a great
political and social liberal, said that the Catholic
doctrine of human nature as represented by Thomas
Aquinas was "semipelagian," he was expressing the
mainline Protestant dissatisfaction with Catholics for

not being nearly so pessimistic about human evil as Martin Luther was.

What is the contemporary position on human sinfulness?

AT the time of the Reformation the Catholic tradition had to fight with those who believed in the basic corruption of humankind; for the last 200 years it has had to fight those who believed in the basic perfectability of humankind. The name of the new pessimism may be different, but the old Reformation argument is once more center stage. The ordinary Catholic who reads the magazines and the Sunday supplements, as well as the scholarly Catholic who reads philosophy and ecology books, must once again insist that for all the depravity humans do, we are not basically depraved.

What, then, is the matter with us? What is the nature of our sinfulness? It is much easier to repeat the tradition and to point out how deeply rooted it is in the Scripture than it is to provide a philosophical explanation that is pertinent and intelligible to those who, on the one hand, are concerned about the contemporary articulation of the human nature problem, and also to satisfy those who, on the other hand, are more concerned about some of the traditional and theological conflicts and the terms and categories in which these conflicts have been presented.

Thus, in the contemporary world, the question of whether our basic flaw is *transmitted* from our primal ancestors is not of great moment. They are obsessed, rather, with the nature of the flaw and its causes —though both those who see it as the result of a genetic adaptation and those who see it as the result of a cultural adaptation would surely have no difficulty in conceding that the flaw is passed on from parents to children. On the other hand, Catholic theologians, and to some extent spokesmen for the magisterium, have been more concerned with the transmission of sinfulness than about its nature.

The bottom line for Catholics, however, must still be that God created us good, and despite our sinfulness we continue to be good. God has fallen in love with us; he continues to love us despite the evil we do and despite the enormous burden of past evil, the inheritance to which each of us is born.

In other words, the Catholic conviction is that while something terrible has gone wrong in the course of human history, this momentous flaw in our personalities and in our species is not utterly uncorrectable, even though on the face of it there is little reason to think we can correct it ourselves. We are selfish, frightened, defensive, hateful creatures, proud, stubborn, envious, vindictive. Try as we might, our own efforts fall short of curing these vices. Still, the vices are not, in principle, incurable.

What is sin?

ONE of the more satisfying explanations of human sinfulness derived by Catholic teachers suggests that our fundamental weakness is to be found in our finitude, our contingency, our limits. As a self-reflecting animal, we know our hunger for total love, existence without end, and power and knowledge without limit. We also know that these hungers cannot be satisfied because we are bound to die. Our sinfulness consists of our refusal to accept our finitude, our limitations, our contingency, our mortality.

Sin is our rebellion against our fate, and in this rebellion we turn to all the sinful acts in which we engage. We pile up pleasures, power, wealth as though by so doing we can become infinite, unlimited, uncontingent, and immortal.

Not only are we born into the world with this propensity to rebel against our limitations, we also inherit the awful burden of past rebellions throughout the tragic, bloody story of humankind. We are born with the physical, psychological, cultural, ethnic, and religious weakness, rigidities, ignorance, and mistakes that have been made by our ancestors. We are born, in other words, not only with sinful propensities but into a sinful condition, a horrifying inheritance of evil that results from the immoral acts that have gone before us.

Are we born guilty—responsible for our sinful inheritance?

THIS is one of the most debated and argued questions in the Christian churches. Like so many hotly debated questions, it is one that misses the point.

If the question means to imply that are we personally responsible for our inherited burden of evil that was done by our predecessors, the same way we are responsible for our own acts of evil, the answer must obviously be no. It is no personal moral fault of ours that we were born with our hunger for immortality; nor is it any personal fault of ours that our predecessors, haunted by this hunger, did all kinds of evil things to create the evil, messy, sinful world into which we make our appearance.

If, however, one means by the question, are we "stuck" with this fundamental flaw and with the evil world to which we are heirs, the answer must be yes.

And there isn't much we can do about it. Whether we like it or not, we emerge as part of a species that is badly flawed.

If we are Catholic Christians, we will quickly add that we are not so flawed as to be incurable. But the cure is a long, arduous, uncertain process that will only finally come to an end in the acts of mercy and love that mark the end of our life and the end of the human era.

If one wishes to come to the core of the fundamental human flaw, might one not suggest that it is fear, a flaw, primal terror of nonbeing? We do not want to be destroyed; we are afraid that we will be destroyed. We are incapable of trusting the processes that have brought us into existence. Our sinfulness, at its root, is a refusal to trust that the powers who produced us care sufficiently about us to respond to our hunger for existence and love.

Is salvation possible?

ONE overcomes slowly and always imperfectly one's own sinfulness by learning to trust the Love which thrust us into existence. The species finds salvation, to the extent that it finds it at all, by gradually giving itself over in collective response to the Love which it perceives, however dimly, to animate all that is.

To the pessimist, then, the Catholic Christian heritage says that human nature is not so depraved as to be unsalvageable—even if the salvage job is a slow, cumbersome one that human kind cannot embark upon unaided. (The latter part of the assertion is, of course, empirically verifiable from a study of human history, as well as being theological doctrine.)

To the optimist the church says that the problems of

human nature are not merely problems of society, economic structure, ignorance and personality disorder, though these all are serious and important parts of the problems. The basic flaw in human nature, however, is more the cause than the effect of such evils in society; it is the flaw that affects a creature who is self-conscious about its mortality and tries to deal with the terrors that mortality brings by seeking salvation in its own power, wealth, and pleasure.

To the pessimist the Catholic says salvation is possible, and it is not merely an extrinsic salvation in which God blinds himself, as it were, to human evil. To the optimist the Catholic Christian says that salvation, while possible, cannot be achieved merely by the reform of institutions and structures, not by unaided human effort —however much humans are bound to seek reform of the structures and institutions in their lives.

How do original sin and personal sin differ?

ARE we sinful by nature? The Catholic Christian replies that yes, we are sinful by nature, but our nature is not fundamentally sinful, not unsalvageably sinful, not irredeemably sinful. We are not cheery optimists about human nature, but neither have we despaired.

In the Catholic theological and catechetical tradition, sharp distinction is made between "original sin" and "personal sin," a distinction that is much sharper in the Catholic tradition than in the Protestant tradition. In the latter, the confession, "I am a sinner," covers both the fundamental flaw in human nature and the personal flaws for which I am responsible because of my fundamental flaw.

Perhaps there is no greater occasion for misunderstanding between Protestants and Catholics in their ordinary conversation than this frequently overlooked difference. Protestants confess guilt indiscriminantly, willing to assume responsibility not only for the things which they, as individuals, have done wrong but also for the more general sinfulness of human nature and for the sinful deeds that have been done in the past. Given the Protestant perspective on the nature of human nature, such confession of guilt is understandable. What else can a fundamentally depraved creature do except confess guilt for all the evil in sight?

In the Catholic heritage, however, the individual person is held to be more or less responsible for his or her individual acts but not for the propensities that come with his/her nature or his/her inheritance as a member of the human species. If we start out with a couple of strikes against us when somebody else was batting, then the strikes aren't "our fault," even though we may have to put up with them.

Thus, the term "sin" has an analogous meaning for Catholics when it is applied to original sin and personal sin. Both sets of sin are moral burdens that we must carry through our lives, but one is a burden that we have added of our own free will and the other is one that we are "stuck with," and while they are similar, they are also strikingly different.

Are there degress of responsibility for our sins?

IN the Catholic perspective we are not responsible for original sin and we are responsible for personal sin. God may forgive them both, and he may forgive them both out of his loving generosity; but from the Catholic point of view they are still different matters. A lover may forgive his/her beloved the weakness with which he/she is born and also the affronts and offenses against the lover which he/she commits.

But the lover, from the point of view of the Catholic heritage, distinguishes between the things the beloved can help and what the beloved can't help. Both sets of offenses are forgiven because of love, but it is love operating in different modalities. In the first instance love says, "I forgive you because I love you and it wasn't your fault anyway." In the second instance love says, "All right, it was your fault, but I don't care, I still love you."

In recent centuries Catholicism has also distinguished between mortal and venial sin, the former being a total turning away from God and the latter being only a "partial" turning away. The distinction between the two kinds was not explicitly known for more than 1,000 years of Catholic Christianity, though, obviously, before a distinction was made, Catholics realized that some sins were more serious than others.

Catholic moral theology in recent centuries has stressed the three conditions that are necessary for the "gray" area of mortal sins: serious matter (a moral offense of major importance); sufficient reflection (a realization by the person that what he or she is doing is indeed a monstrous evil); and full consent of the will (the availability of a sufficient amount of freedom not to perform the act, so that the act itself becomes a matter of full and free human choice).

Recent Catholic moral theology, integrating our new psychological understandings of the limitations on human freedom, tends to wonder how often in the course of a human life all three conditions are present. It

seems safe to say that full-fledged mortal sin may be a
good deal less frequent than we normally thought.

What is the Bottom Line on sin?

CONTEMPORARY Catholic thought is more interested in the basic orientation and thrust of a person's
life, whether it is marked by openness to other human
beings and God, or by narrowness, rigidity, and a refusal to respond to offers of love. We will be judged, according to this view of things, not so much by a specific
individual act (like the person who was doomed for all
eternity in the last second of his life, as in some of our
old catechetics), but by the patterns of love and hatred
that characterize the entire course of our life. Of course,
such patterns result from the repetition of individual
acts and from the habits we acquire by the repetition of
these acts. So this new so-called fundamental option approach does not deny the importance of individual
moral decisions but stresses, rather more emphatically
than some past moral approaches, the patterns of our
moral responses.

Finally, the bottom line on the subject of sin for the
Catholic Christian is not sin at all but God's forgiveness.
We are sinful by nature, we commit sins by our personal
actions, we form sinful patterns in our lives. God still
loves us and still forgives us when, like the prodigal son
or the woman taken in adultery, we make the slightest
movement in his direction.

Chapter Four

Salvation

Do we need salvation?

VIRTUALLY all the world's religions have salvation myths, stories which presume the possibility of a fresh beginning, a new start for the species or the individual or for both. In some religions, such as that of ancient Greece, the possibility of salvation is remote. Perhaps Kronos will awaken and begin the great cycle of time again. Until then, however, the best humans can do is cope with life's fatalism by losing themselves in revelry and life's pleasures, by seeking out the truth of philosophy, or by grimly facing life's troubles with stoic bravery. The world will not be renewed (or is not likely to be renewed), but at least the individual human can adjust wisely, or bravely, or pleasurably to the absurdity of his or her own existence.

Most renewals in the world's religions are cyclic. Human events are seen as part of a great turning wheel, so that what has happened now has happened before and will happen again. The new beginning will occur when the great wheel of the heavens spins finally to the First Time, and all starts again. (In some versions of things, the Great Renewal commences with the Age of Aquarius, the first of the celestial months.)

In a few religions (most notably, Yahwism) the new world and the new humanity are not the result of a mechanical turn of the heavenly wheel but rather the dramatic interventions of God in human history. They are not oft-repeated human events, but "once and for all" interventions. First it was on Sinai with the old covenant between God and his people, and second, and more dramatically, on Calvary with the new covenant —and, presumably, the first covenant.

The stories of salvation rearticulate and re-present three fundamental human insights: (1) We are not that which we might be (an awareness of our sinfulness, discussed in a previous section). (2) Intermittently, however, we can break out of the bonds and the chains that tie us to begin again. (3) Our new beginnings almost always require some kind of outside help.

Humankind, in other words, profoundly understands that it needs salvation, and that salvation, theoretically, at least, is possible. Each time we make a new beginning in our lives—reconciliation after a quarrel, the return of love after hatred, a fresh start after discouragement or depression, a new beginning after failure—we understand how profoundly we have been separated from our own best instincts as well as from others and the world of which we are a part; also, how strained and limited we are by our weaknesses, our flaws, our habits, our ignorance. Nonetheless, we are still capable of making new beginnings. We need salvation and salvation is possible.

What did salvation mean to Jesus' followers?

SALVATION is precisely what the followers of Jesus experienced in the Easter event. Alienation was replaced by reconciliation, captivity by liberation. Humanity was born again with a new Adam, humanity was reconciled with God and with itself, humanity was liberated again by a new Moses, freed from the slavery not of Egypt but of sin and death.

The life, death, resurrection of Jesus meant salvation

to his early apostles, salvation from the fundamental human flaws and weaknesses that we call sinfulness and from the evil effects of our own personal sin. We are liberated from sin, reconciled to God—dead to the old man, alive in Christ Jesus.

Yet this salvation was clearly not complete. The apostles were still to some extent bound by human weakness and frailty; they still had to die. They were still partially alienated and unreconciled from other human beings and from the natural forces of the universe and even from the Father in Heaven.

Sin had been defeated in the resurrection of Jesus, the apostles believed; yet, that defeat was not complete and final on the face of it. Of what nature was that salvation then, which was experienced on Easter but experienced simultaneously as full and partial, as fulfillment and promise, as complete and still just beginning, as already but also not yet?

The apostles had two challenges, challenges which have faced Christian teachers and preachers ever since. They had to explain how Jesus was salvation and why salvation still seemed incomplete. Much of the theological controversy that has gone on since the Reformation has been concerned with the former question —usually in terminology that includes such words as "justification," which now seems archaic and meaningless to most people.

The second question, the "incompleteness" (as far as application) of salvation—a question modern Christians would be much more concerned about—has been put on the back burner. Christian teachers and preachers have been content to say that the evil effects of sin and death, defeated in principle by the saving action of Jesus, will be fulfilled only in the life of the resurrection, only after the return of Jesus.

How did the early church experience Jesus as savior?

CHARCTERISTICALLY we have argued about a controversy which no longer interests people much—how did Jesus save?—and ignored the question that does interest people today—if we are saved, why are we still so bad?

As the apostles strove to answer the first question, they searched, as all religious teachers must, for stories that would have meaning in their culture, that would convey the experience they felt on Easter. Three stories emerged: (1) the liberation of the slave (or the ransoming of the captive), (2) the reconciliation of enemies, (3) the healing of sickness.

Did human nature experience itself as trapped, bound, constrained, limited? Jesus was the liberator who set us free. Did human nature experience itself as alienated, isolated, separated? Jesus was the reconciler and ended the conflict between us and God. Did human nature experience itself as wounded, sick, battered, and bruised? Jesus was the divine physician who healed us.

The first two stories seemed to be more effective in apostolic times and received much greater emphasis in the New Testament—quite possibly because physicians weren't all that good at healing people in those days. All three, however, contain the basic theme that through Jesus humankind had a new beginning. It was renewed, given a chance to start over again; it was reborn. With Jesus the past was wiped out and a new start could be made.

The writers of the epistles and gospels and the early

Christian prachers made a good deal out of the liberation of the captive and the reconciliation of enemies stories. The death of Jesus was the "price" that had to be paid—sometimes to the Father in heaven and sometimes to the devil—in order that we might be free. The sufferings of Jesus appeased God's anger because of our sinfulness, and he accepted the self-sacrifice of Jesus as the "price" for forgiving our sinfulness.

Both stories are stories of "satisfaction," of debts being paid, of economic exchange. The early Christian writers were rough and ready theologians, storytellers, really, more than they were theologians. The "economic" approach to salvation they used was illustrative rather than definitive. They intended to convey the experience of liberation and reconciliation rather than elaborate a precisely specified and analytical theory of how it happened.

Do we have a proper understanding of Jesus' salvation experience?

UNFORTUNATELY for us, many later Christian preachers and teachers proceeded to take the satisfaction stories literally, twisting them so that God's love, instead of seeming gracious, actually appears to be monstrous. Jesus died, many of us were told in grammar school, so that the gates of heaven might be opened. His precious blood was the "price" that had to be paid to appease God's anger so that he would swing open the gates he had locked shut in righteous outrage at the time of Adam's sin.

I was asked by Phil Donahue one morning what kind of a loving God it was who would sternly demand the terrible death through crucifixion of his only son as recompense for his offended dignity? Such a question represents the satisfaction theory pushed to its ultimate —and erroneous—logical conclusion.

But that Mr. Donahue would ask it and that the members of his audience were not offended by it indicates how often the satisfaction story is pushed to its logical absurdity and how, therefore, the glorious good news of liberation and reconciliation becomes utterly lost in a false story of a monstrous God demanding a false price.

Karl Rahner rightly remarked that while the satisfaction story is assumed by much of Catholic theologizing and teaching, it has never been defined as such by the church. It may well be that in an era that does not know slavery or blood feuds the story is less well suited to convey the Christian experience of salvation than it once was (which does not mean, incidentally, that I am suggesting it should be abandoned). But the story of Jesus as physician healing sickness would be more useful for modern people simply because they have had more experience with sickness and being healed than they have had either with being slaves who are liberated or with blood feuds being settled by a blood price.

How do we explain our salvation through Jesus' life, death and resurrection?

FOR a Catholic Christian today the bottom line is that Jesus did save us, he did reconcile us to God and our fellow human beings; he did liberate us from our sinfulness; he did open up to us the possibility of new life; he did heal us from our wounds. To those stories we must hold with all the fierceness of our faith.

We must also believe that Jesus *really* did do this through life, death, and resurrection, that something actually happened in the objective world outside, something beyond a mere change in human attitudes and perception. There was a real objective—if one wishes to use the word, "metaphysical"—transformation in the human condition and in the nature, if not in the human nature, then in the relationship of human nature, to the God who created us.

The explanation of how these things happened, while important, is not as important as our conviction, indeed our faith, that they *did* happen. Jesus *did* justify us (to use the old term). He did communicate God's Grace (and note the capital G) to us. That is the bottom line.

What follows is a tentative explanation of how this occurred, an explanation culled from contemporary Catholic writings, offered to the reader for whatever use he or she may make of it for his or her own prayerful reflection about the meaning of salvation. It is not offered as a definitive statement of a theology of salvation.

Jesus came into the world to demonstrate God's love for us. He told us about it in his parables, he revealed it in his own person, he demonstrated it in his relationships with other human beings, and, above all, in the courage and fidelity with which he went to his death in the name of that love. Jesus' conviction of God's non-abandoning love was confirmed and validated definitively and irrevocably in his resurrection.

Note that there are two statements implicit in this "story:" (1) The love that Jesus experienced was so powerful that he could go confidently to death because of that love. One might call this an indirect revelation of the nature of God's love, because we see that love as it affected the behavior of Jesus.

(2) The behavior of Jesus also directly reveals God's love, because that love takes possession of him and is

united to Jesus by "dying for us." Jesus reveals the dizzying love of God the Father, who would if he could, go even to death for us, his creatures.

Furthermore, by his life and death, Jesus also demonstrates the possibilities of life for those who have a sense similar to his of the nature of God's love. Jesus, in other words, revealed both the love of God—a love which, as it applies to us and affects us, is properly called Grace —and he also reveals a model of human responsiveness to that love.

Note well that the love of God revealed in Jesus is not a new thing. It has been "out there" since God created us. It would be utterly wrong to depict God as having loved us once and then stonily sulking behind the closed gates of heaven until Jesus came along to "win" that love for us once again. Jesus does not reveal in his parables, in his faith, or in his death that the heavenly father does not confirm, validate, in the resurrection a new love; it was love that was always there, occasionally, desperately hoped for by humankind but never seen with quite the brilliant clarity with which it was illustrated in the life, death, and resurrection of Jesus.

Grace did not come with Jesus, it was always there. Jesus did not "create" Grace, nor did he earn it. Grace is an utterly free gift of an utterly loving God. More precisely, it is the utterly free love of God, not earned by anything any of us does, demanding only response. Jesus demonstrated for us the possibility of response, a model for such response and a vision of the depths of response of which human nature is capable.

To put the matter somewhat differently: to the agonized human question, "Is there someone out there who will save us?" the reply, through the life, death, and resurrection of Jesus is, in effect, "Yes, there is someone out there who will save you. He has always been in the process of saving you because he has always loved you. Now that through me you know more clearly the nature of the saving, healing, liberating, reconciling love, you also have available a model for responding to that love. You are saved in a decisively different way than you were before.''

This explanation says in effect that Jesus redeemed us, liberated us, bought us back, ended the blood feud between us and God precisely because his life, death, and resurrection manifested to us the height and the depth, the length and the breadth of God's love. The passion of Jesus was not a blood price to end a blood feud but rather the ultimate way of revealing to us how much God loves us, how we should respond to that love, and how he finally will respond to our response—which is the love that on Easter Sunday was manifested as being "stronger than death."

What is the difficulty in reaching a contemporary understanding of salvation?

SOME Catholics react negatively against this "story" of reconciliation. As several writers complained to me after the Donahue program, I am reducing the redemption to merely a "good example." But such a reaction, it seems to me, betrays on the one hand an unnecessary and quite possibly a radical commitment to a "blood price" explanation of salvation; and, on the other hand, a narrow and stilted view of the nature of the human personality.

"Good example" is a narrow and trivial phrase, a bloodless and empty piety in a certain kind of Catholic catechetics. To say that someone provides us with a "model for life" or a "pattern for living" is not, however, to say that he has done something trivial, but rather that he has done something extraordinarily important. Human kind has always sought desperately for such models and patterns.

Part of the problem of dealing with an explanation of salvation which on the one hand is true to the tradition and on the other hand means something to contemporary humans is that those catechism teachers who passed the tradition on to many of us had a rather different notion of what is "objective," "real," "actual." In the old catechetical mentality something was "only hard" if it was external, extrinsic, metaphysical. The communication of knowledge about God's love and a pattern for response to that love is "soft," that is to say, not real, not actual, not metaphysical.

To the modern mentality, however, the acquisition of new knowledge and the understanding of new patterns of behavior is "hard." It does affect the basic structure of the personality. It does represent not only an "existential" but also a "metaphysical" chain, metaphysical precisely because existential.

Someone who, for example, has gone through intensive psychotherapy and emerges with greater confidence in himself or herself and greater ability to love others has not, to the modern way of thinking, undergone merely an extrinsic or "moral" or "soft" change. There has been a basic restructuring of his or her personality, a basic renewal of the life force, a fundamental and very "hard" change in personal posture vis-a-vis the world. Indeed, the modern mind would argue that the profound personality change that comes from knowledge and love and the acquisition of a pattern of responding to love is far more intrinsic, far "harder" than the often legalistic, not to say certified public accounting approach of some of the old explanations of redemption.

Do we earn salvation and grace?

BY showing us God's love and by demonstrating the possibility of response to that love, Jesus did indeed (so this explanation contends) profoundly alter the nature of the human condition. This alteration is indeed objective, it indeed "wins" for us Grace, it indeed frees us from sin, and it indeed does reconcile us to the Father in heaven—not that he needed the reconciliation, but we did.

Thus the revelation of Jesus and Jesus as revelation "accomplishes" our redemption and conveys to us God's Grace ("justifies" us, if one wishes) through its extraordinary impact on the perceiving, responding, understanding dimensions of the human personality. That impact profoundly changes the human condition, renews and recreates the human race, and sets forth in the world a new humanity.

It must be insisted that both the Grace itself and the salvation which makes that Grace available to us in a spectacularly new way are utterly gratuitous—as love is always utterly gratuitous. One no more "earns" salvation and Grace than one earns any other kind of love. One responds to a gift that has been given. Salvation is no more something we can win by ourselves than we can be created by ourselves. For both salvation and creation are acts of God's love. (Different kinds of love or the same love? Love is love. Especially when it is God's love.)

This is not the appropriate context to enter into the Reformation controversies, especially since Catholic and Lutheran theologians seem to be reconciling most of the differences. However, it is worth noting that the Lutheran insistence on the utter gratuity of God's love and our inability by ourselves to remake ourselves is something with which all Catholic theologians would today agree.

For example, with the "self-help" propaganda of the various psychological salvations which are being offered (particularly from the center of such salvations—southern California), one must, if one is a Catholic Christian, respond. However useful or however insightful the techniques of such salvations may be, they will inevitably fail to provide the salvation they promise if the devotee thinks he can remake himself by himself.

We can no more overcome our fundamental fear by trusting in psychotherapeutic security any more than we can overcome our basic fear (that is to say our basic sinfulness) by trusting in power or pleasure or wealth. We must, of course, do all that we can; we must not be irresponsible in facing and coping with our own problems.

The bottom line for Catholic Christians is that all the other things will only begin to work when we cast ourselves with complete and total and helpless trust into the arms of the loving God who thrust us into existence and who revealed his love uniquely, adequately, definitively, and efficaciously in the life, death, and resurrection of Jesus. Only such a total surrender to the Goodness Which Is can assure salvation. That is the bottom line.

The sinfulness of human nature, in other words, can only be counteracted by surrender to God's love. We overcome our fear—just as Jesus overcame his fear in the garden—by committing ourselves utterly and completely to the Goodness that created us and which renewed us by revealing Itself in Jesus.

How is God's saving love brought to fulfillment in us?

WHAT does it mean to say that at baptism original sin is forgiven and we receive God's Grace? Obviously God loves a little child even more than the child's parents do before baptism. Just as obviously, after baptism, the child is as prone to the fundamental frailties of human nature as he or she was before baptism.

In baptism, however, the love of God is solemnly and efficaciously revealed (the word "sacrament" means "revelation") to the child. Through membership in the church a child receives and will continue to receive a revelation of both God's love and of the possibilities of response to that love, which were initially revealed in Jesus. Thus a child becomes "graced" in a way in which it was not before, precisely because now the child possesses and will continue to possess a revelation about the depths of God's love and the possibility of human response which fundamentally alters the life possibilities of a child and thus fundamentally restructures the child's personality.

Does this Graciousness "really" change the child? The answer has to be that yes, of course it does, because now possibilities of knowledge and love are open to the child which were not previously present, save for in a much more remote way.

Does the child really receive a new life? The answer is yes, of course the child receives a really new life. The child is really renewed because now the child has the capacity for a life that can be and indeed will be very different precisely because of the contact with the saving action of Jesus that comes through membership in the church.

One of the major advantages of this explanation of salvation is that it puts us in a much better position for responding to the second question about salvation: If we are saved, why not yet completely saved?

We are saved because Jesus has "won" for us God's love in the sense that we now know about that love and have available a model for a response to it in ways hitherto not available to us, save, perhaps, in dim anticipation. The fundamental flaw of human fearfulness is not eliminated, but the effective antidote to it is now at our disposal. We are still flawed creatures, but we have the possibility of coping with our flaw by committing ourselves in utter trust to God's love.

This commitment, however, must be endlessly renewed in the course of a life and endlessly renewed in the history of the human species and the church (which is nothing more than the human species in contact with God through Jesus). The conquest of sin and death, in other words, has begun through the life, death, and resurrection of Jesus; it can be brought to fulfillment only in God's good time when the work that Jesus so notably advanced is finally brought to completion.

The "secret" (sacrament, symbol, revelation, story) is out; but the secret must ferment in the life of the individual and in the life of the species until finally it bears the fullness of its fruit.

Chapter 5

The Church

What is the "Church"? How do people experience it?

THE church we experience in our daily life is very different from the church of the catechisms and the textbooks. The church we know is the parish, the buildings, the parking lot, the priests, religious, and lay staff members. The church in the catechism is the one holy Catholic and apostolic church, made up of popes, bishops, and curial officials, and a worldwide institutional network of dioceses and national hierarchies.

The church we experience early in our lives is often as much a part of our environment as the block on which we live and the air which we breathe. We see it solidly embodied in the church building, so much so that children equate the church with the church building and have a hard time grasping the distinction between the institution and the building on the corner a couple of blocks away.

One, holy, apostolic church we never see. The bishop who represents it in our city we may see on occasion; the pope who presides over it in Rome we see even more rarely (until John Paul II, at any rate).

The question, "Do you believe in the church?" is normally taken to refer to the institution we never see—the worldwide, one, holy, Catholic and apostolic church—and not to the local parish. This, however, may be a misplaced instructional emphasis. For it takes belief out of the realm of the concrete and the experiential, placing it in the realm of the intellectual and the abstract.

61

If we begin our search for bottom line beliefs about the church with the parish, with the local, experiential, religious community, we may find the bottom line more easily, and also understand better what the church really is.

The research my colleagues and I have been doing on American Catholicism over the past decade-and-a-half leaves little doubt that the most important factor in determining the religious behavior of American Catholics—once one has taken into account the enormous importance of family of origin and family of procreation—is the local parish.

If people are satisfied with the work their pastor does, if they are enthusiastic about sermons, if they think their clergy are sympathetic to human problems, if they think the laity are taken seriously in their parish, then they are much more likely to be devout and much more likely to have good feelings about the "Catholic church."

Whatever they believe intellectually, in other words, most people equate the church, for all practical purposes, with the local parish. The experience of church in the local community is so powerful that other considerations, positive or negative, become unimportant by comparison.

If we stop for a moment to think about it, it should be clear to us why this is so. We are all creatures of time and space. Even in this communication satellite, jet-powered age, we tend to have roots and to sink them very quickly when we settle into a place. The physical and interpersonal surroundings in which we find ourselves might not affect archangels, but we are part of a world of concrete geography and concrete relationships and not in a world of abstract organizational charts.

**How does our experience of local church affect
our belief in the universal church?**

HELL, the French existential philosopher Jean Paul
Sartre said, is other people. Doubtless it is, but then so is
heaven and so is the church.

If we approach the church from a worm's eye view, so
to speak, a number of things about it become immediately obvious.

First of all, it is made up of people, the good and the
not so good, the young and the old, the bright and the
not so bright, big sinners and little sinners and occasionally a saint or two; factions and feuds, loves and hates,
ups and downs, joys and sorrows, births, marriages and
death—the dilemmas, poignancies, the disappointments
and joys of the human condition abound there.

Because it is made up of people the church tends to be
a mess. Masses don't start on time, the roof leaks, there
are conflicts over first communion ceremonies, the sing-
ing is in disarray, sometimes the snow doesn't get shov-
eled, people leave after communion, some projects get
more attention than others, nothing is done perfectly, a
fair number of things aren't done all that well, and some
things are disasters.

We may not like the messiness of a local parish. The
confusion, the conflict, the uncertainty, and the frustration are galling, but they don't shake our faith when we
know that the priest and the laity, the deacons, the
parish staff members are human beings like us, and that
the parish will bumble and stumble along as does any organization made up of human beings.

The third aspect of our experience of the local church
is that it is made up of friends—not everybody, of

course, but those of our neighbors who are Catholic and go to the same church we do. We see them coming in and out of school or religious instruction class, we meet them in the back of the church after mass on Sunday, we pass them on the street going to midnight mass at Christmas or to the Easter vigil, we play basketball with them in the parish yard. Perhaps we go to the teen club dances with them. We attend the baptisms and first communions of their children, we celebrate their marriages, and, perhaps, eventually, we may marry them ourselves.

The local parish, in other words, is not merely the parish building and grounds; it is also a collection of networks. Indeed, it may even be the occasion of new friendship networks as we get to know people better precisely because we belong to the same parish.

So in the local parish we experience the messy, human network of friendship relationships—flawed, fallible, frustrating, but also frequently responding to what we need. If we are asked whether we "believe" in the local parish, the question may seem absurd at first. What are we supposed to believe? That it's perfect? That it doesn't make any mistakes? That it has all the answers to our problems? Obviously not. It would be ridiculous to believe such things.

The local parish, if it is anything at all, is nothing more than a group of people trying to worship God together, trying to respond to the gospel of Jesus together, trying to pass on their faith to their children, trying to preach the gospel, however poorly, to one another. It is the place where most of us encountered the Christian heritage as children, where we still practice our Christian worship and strive to go forward in our faith and commitment to that heritage while we try to pass on that heritage to those who come after us.

It is not hard to believe that this is what the local

parish is for, because this is what it is patently about. If we were to be asked whether we encounter Jesus in the local parish community, our puzzled response is likely to be, "Well, where in the world else would we encounter him, for that's where we pray, that's where we worship, that's where we receive the sacrament, that's where we were baptized, married, and where the funeral mass is said for us."

Obviously Jesus isn't limited to the local parish, but it is the primary and principal place where, de facto, we do encounter him in our lives.

Now that is the Catholic church. Indeed, for most Catholics in the course of human history it is the only church they knew, because they saw their bishops hardly at all and were only barely aware of the existence of the pope in Rome. They knew no elaborate ecclesiological doctrines or theories; they knew only the concrete reality of the local community.

We survived a millenium and a half without having to provide the faithful with any theology beyond their experience in the local community. Furthermore, before the church became anything else it was a local community made up of a messy, disorganized network of friends who were the apostles and disciples of Jesus.

The church, in other words, began as a small religious community and is still experienced most of the time by most of its members as a local friendship network setting. Surely our ecclesiologies do not stop at the boundaries of the parish, but if they are to make sense to people, it seems to me they have to start there.

How would one best describe the church?

UNFORTUNATELY, much of our religious instructions about the church start out with the pope, international institutions, and all the characteristics and attributes, rights and privileges and protections of that institution—most of which make very little difference to the ordinary person.

Then, only at the end of our instruction do we find time to describe the local religious community and the church as a response in a friendship network to the gospel. We emphasize the church that most people don't know and ignore the church that most people do know. Belief in the church becomes equated with belief in the proposition about the attributes and quality of the Universal Church and its leadership which have little impact on or importance for people, while little is said about their relationship with other members of their own parishes who can, and usually do, have enormous impact on their lives.

Belief in infallibility, for example, may or may not be an enormous intellectual challenge. There is a much more important question, however, for most people about whether the church they experience is, for all its defects and fallibility, the best set of relationships and resources available to respond to the gospel. Normally the answer to that question is not difficult.

The local parish may not be very good but it's the only one we have. It's where we first encountered the Lord, where we first heard the gospel and still hear it preached, however poorly, and where the sacraments are administered to us, where we can sometimes find comfort and solace in crisis and difficulty. It isn't a very good church, perhaps, but where will we find another? It is, I suspect, the answer Bartholomew would have given had someone said to him, "Do you believe in that bunch?" He might very well have replied, "Where am I going to find another church?"

This may seem like a minimalist approach to ecclesiology, but it surely is not; for it emphasizes the humanity of the church, its uniqueness, and its primary functions: the preaching of the gospel and the organizing of our collective and supportive response to it. That's why the church exists—not to provide a series of propositions that test our faith or a setting where ecclesiastical authority can exercise the marvelous powers it claims to enjoy.

At the local community level it is impossible to make the mistake of thinking the priests and the nuns are the parish. Clearly they are not, even though sometimes, they have tried to exercise authority as though they were. We know that the parish is us. It requires our money, our work, our attendance, our support, our consent.

At the local neighborhood level the church is clearly made up of its people. It has its faults, its frailties, its fallibilities precisely because it is made up of people.

Is the church subject to human limitations?

IF someone should come and ask you why your parish is not perfect, you would be utterly astonished. With all those guys in it, how could anyone expect it to be perfect? And if we were in an especially humble mood, we might add, "If they let somebody like me in, it's certainly not going to be perfect."

Much of our religious education has spoken of the church in such a way that the result is a kind of "angelism" in which perfection is demanded of or expected from the church as proof that it is the church of Jesus—despite overwhelming historical evidence that even at the very beginning the church was substantially less than angelic.

The angelism of the right refuses to acknowledge any

imperfections in the church or churchmen and women, while the angelism of the left demands perfection of the church as a condition for membership or acceptance. Both varieties seem to think that somehow once you get beyond the parish the church undergoes an enormous transformation, no longer made up of human beings.

I was astonished by the reaction of many people to my study of the papal elections. They were shocked, offended, and scandalized that I would suggest that the election of a pope was a political process. Somehow or other, the Holy Spirit had to be at work to cancel out the ordinary processes of human elections, to make "politics" unnecessary.

It was as though their "faith" required them to believe that the Holy Spirit came down and whispered in the ears of the cardinals, that there simply could not be conflicts and differences about the fundamental problems that faced the church, that there couldn't be caucuses and campaigns around those issues. Such things may be all right in parish school board elections, for example, but God forbid that they should happen in the College of Cardinals. At that level, it would appear, it is necessary to think that the church is not made up of human beings but seraphim.

Such naivete, I confess, shocked me, as much as my realistic account of how the pope is elected shocked them. It simply can't be that way in the church, they said, meaning of course, that the church can't be made of up human beings.

Sometimes I would ask such people about the conclaves of the past, such as, for example, one in which Cesare Borgia controlled all the votes but two either by poison or bribery. The response is that these things don't happen anymore, or that one shouldn't talk about such things because that would give comfort to the enemies of the church.

Neither of these responses is pertinent to the unquestioned theological truth: the Holy Spirit works through secondary causes, that is to say, through humans. Sometimes he has a lot more material to work with than others; but nevertheless his intervention is not miraculous. There are no visions, there are no tongues of fire, there are no deep baritone voices saying, "Vote for Wojtyla."

What is the bottom line belief in the Catholic Church?

ONE often hears it said from the left, "I won't be a Catholic until the bishops take the right stand on race, on feminism, or on the Third World." Doubtless it would be gratifying if bishops were among the most far-sighted teachers and prophets in a society.

It does not seem likely, however, that Jesus intended the leaders of his community of followers to have such remarkable abilities. Surely the crowd he began with was something less than impressive.

Why left-wing angelists expect more from church leaders today than was visible in church leaders at the time of Jesus is impossible to understand. Pastors, bishops, popes are human beings like us with all the limitations and failings that come with human nature. They exist not to be perfections of virtue, insight, and vision, but merely to hold the community together, a task at which they sometimes do a good job.

The community has held together more or less for a very long time, so it must have something going for it besides human skills. The promise of Jesus to be with it all days even to the end of the world did not involve a guarantee of leadership that would be enlightened, progressive, and sophisticated.

Just as the right-wing angelists must pretend there is no fault in the church at the cost of ignoring the failings of the past, so the left-wing angelists must demand a church without fault at the same price: "The church may have been weak, mistaken, and badly led before, but now, for our time we demand perfection." Or as someone once remarked, "If you find a perfect church, by all means join it; but the minute you became a member it stops being perfect."

The bottom line is not, do you believe in the pope or papal infallibility or the primacy of Peter? The bottom line, as always, is, do you believe in God? In the case of the church it becomes specifically do you believe in God who is revealed to you, however imperfectly, in the Catholic church that you know? Can you hear his gospel, receive his sacrament, respond to his challenge together with those you love in that church?

It is a modest bottom line indeed, until you stop to think what that gospel is, what those sacraments reveal, and what those love relationships must be like.

How much do you have to believe? Do you have to keep all the "rules?" How many rules can you break and still be a Catholic?

Again, the very wording of the questions betrays a fundamental misunderstanding. Catholicism is viewed as a set of rules and regulations, a lengthy loyalty test to which you must have the right answers as a price for admission. An enormous number of people are convinced that's the way it is, and many rise up and announce that you simply cannot be a Catholic and not keep all the rules, adding that they don't care if 90 percent of the so-called Catholics don't keep the rules because those folks simply are not Catholic.

We have encountered this often in our research when right-wing critics say that we are not sampling "real" Catholics, meaning that the only people who have a legitimate right to claim they are Catholic in response to an interviewer's question are those who have already measured in on extensive loyalty tests of doctrinal and ethical propositions.

If Jesus said, "Let the one who is without sin throw the first stone," some folks are perfectly prepared to start throwing. You've got to accept the church's teaching, they will say, or you're not a Catholic; and if we don't throw the stones, at least we'll draw the line with you on the outside.

But, Jesus came to save sinners, not the saved—a point he made quite vigorously to the Pharisees of his own day and which needs to be repeated to the Pharisees of our day.

Even a bishop can be wrong, like the one who told the young people in his diocese that if they did not accept the church's teaching on premarital sex, they were no longer part of the church—a standard for church membership which goes far beyond that of the code of canon law, which says you are a Catholic if you have been validly baptized and have never formally apostasized from the church. In this respect the code merely systematizes the traditional Catholic approach of drawing the boundaries as widely as possible so as to include as many people as possible, leaving to the heavenly father the final judgment about who is a sinner and who is not.

It has always been difficult to get yourself defined as a notorious and public sinner; these days it would seem that mafia types are the only ones really able to measure in. The church is for people not for saints, not for angels, not for the perfect, and not for Pharisees either.

Did Jesus establish the Church? Why did He establish the church?

THERE is a church simply and solely because of the social aspect of human nature, because humans are gregarious creatures who cannot survive long by themselves. We need other human beings to be born, to be raised, to be loved, protected, educated, fed, clothed.

There are very few things we can do alone, and we certainly cannot effectively respond to the demand of a challenging religion by ourselves. We do not love by ourselves, we do not hope by ourselves, we do not care for others by ourselves; and so we do not worship, pray, nor respond to a God of love by ourselves.

The apostles did not sit around and say, "Should we have a church or not? Should we each do what the master told us without any organization? Should we each respond to the Easter experience of the risen Jesus in our secret hearts and not waste time and energy by setting up a structure?"

Nor did they say, "Let's sit down and make up a bunch of rules which 1900 years from now will be embodied in the code of canon law." They were a group of human beings who had been brought together by Jesus to hear his preaching, share his life, and to extend and continue his work. They continue to be a group of human beings doing their best at these tasks—and oftentimes, as we know, their best was not all that good—because it never would have occurred to them to proceed any other way.

Jesus did not found a church in the sense that he sat

down one day and said, "All right, fellas, now we're going to start a church. Peter, I want you to go to Rome and open a savings account, a deposit of faith, into which you will enter all the things I've told you, and leave word for your successors to set up the College of Cardinals, write up the code or canon law. And I want the rest of you fellas to be bishops, set up diocesan curias and write pastoral letters and meet every once in a while at an ecumenical council to define doctrine. Having done that, you'll be a church. Oh, incidentally, Peter, you're going to be infallible, and the rest of you guys will be infallible, too, when you're with him."

What Jesus did was gather together a group of people, preach to them, teach them, love them, and then send them forth to do his work. In that sense he founded a church. But then, of course, that is precisely the church we know very well in our local parish communities, a church which is in fact very much like the apostolic one—sometimes enthusiastic, sometimes disheartened, sometimes brilliant, sometimes disgraceful, sometimes generous, sometimes narrow, sometimes devout, sometimes missing the point completely, but always human, always straining for something beyond the human, always trying, however ineptly, to respond as best it can to the transhuman message that was revealed in Jesus and preached by him.

Where does authority rest in the church?

I DO not think that papal authority and infallibility should be an object of obsessive concern in any introductory discussion of Catholicism, which survived nicely for 1800 years without having to define it. It was a major issue for certain special reasons in the 19th century; it is not a major issue any more. One can find ample discussion of it in many books and articles, if one thinks it is important to agonize over.

If one is ready to accept the church, then issues like infallibility should not get in the way, because there are explanations of it that are adequate and thoroughly orthodox with which virtually everyone can live. Jesus promised that he would be with his church all days even to the end, not to protect it from every possible mistake, but at least to protect it from making those mistakes that would be disastrous to its goals. For our purposes that ought to be enough by way of a bottom line.

As for the papacy, if one did not have it, one would have to invent it, because Christianity needs a world leader; and the papacy is, as we have seen demonstrated time after time in the last 25 years, the most important religious leadership position in the world. It is not because of any special prerogatives it may claim, but rather because of its historical and institutional position.

As to where authority rests in the church, it obviously rests in the whole church, though in different ways in different parts of the church. In the first thousand years of Catholic Christian tradition no document of major importance was ever issued without an assertion something like, "with the consent of the whole Christian people." It was assumed that the consent of the faithful—their "acceptance" of a doctrine—was absolutely essential to the validity of a doctrine.

The relationship between that authority which rests in the faithful and that authority which rests in the leadership is intricate and complex, beyond the scope of these essays. Is is sufficient to assert the historically orthodox Catholic doctrine that authority indeed rests in the leadership, but it also rests in the faithful.

Finally, in this stage of Christian development, it is no longer necessary to demonstrate how Catholic Christianity is "better than" Protestant Christianity. Such comparisons are pointless—irrelevant and often offensive. It is merely pertinent to assert where Catholic Christianity stands, and let people decide for themselves whether that is where they also wish to stand.

Historically, of course, the basic difference between Catholic and Protestant Christianity is that Catholic Christianity has emphasized far more heavily the social nature of humankind's response to the gospel. It has argued that we respond not as isolated individuals but as part of a human community. However, while there is certainly more of a tendency toward religious "individualism" in contemporary Protestantism, there is a remarkable convergence now between the two Christian heritages on the need for an institutional church and the social nature of Christianity.

What, then, is the bottom line on the church? The bottom line on the church is whether you believe that you encounter Jesus Christ in a community of fellow human beings, the preservation and protection of which Jesus committed himself to. It is where he is preached and where his sacraments are administered today even as they were among the earliest band of brothers and sisters who followed him.

Chapter Six

Mary, the Mother of Jesus

What is the power of the symbol of Mary?

THE durability of Mary, the mother of Jesus, as a key
symbol in the Catholic Christian heritage is astonishing.
In the last fifteen or twenty years explicit emphasis
on Marian devotion has waned inside the church. May
crownings, May processions, rosary devotions have van-
ished in many Catholic parishes. Sermons on Mary are
rarely heard.

Many Catholic thinkers seem willing to give up "Mariology" as a price for church unity. Pope John Paul's
obvious devotion to Mary is offensive to some Catholic
ecumenists and intellectuals. Most of the younger generation of theologians pay little attention to the Mary
symbol, even though such outside observers as Professor Harvey Cox of the Harvard Divinity School and the
New York Times Magazine seem to have discovered her.

For all this decline in Marian emphasis, however, pil-
grimages to the various shrines to Our Lady around the
world have increased, not declined. A study my colleagues and I have done recently among young people
revealed that for Catholics under thirty, the image of
Mary is still powerful. She is viewed as warm, gentle, patient, kind. Indeed, she has a better "image rating" than
Jesus or God.

Furthermore, images of Mary *matter*. Those young
people with warm and positive images of Mary are more
likely to pray, more likely to be hopeful, more likely to
have happy and sexually fulfilling marriages, and more

likely to be committed to the causes of racial and social justice.

Whenever we report these findings there is astonishment and dismay among certain Catholics who don't like to think that Marian devotion has survived and find it impossible to accept that it is precisely the socially and religiously committed Catholic who has the strongest devotion to Mary.

Whence the remarkable durability of the Mary symbol? As I have tried to demonstrate at great length (and perhaps too obscurely) in my book *The Mary Myth,* Mary reflects the femininity of God, the fact that in God masculine and feminine are combined, that God is both a father and a mother.

The power of the Mary myth is ultimately rooted in the revelatory capacity, indeed the extraordinarily powerful capacity, of sexual differentiation. Most religions of the world have a mother goddess, a feminine deity, or at least a feminine component of the deity, precisely because sexual differentiation is such a powerful experience in the human condition. Mary continues to be popular because she reveals to us the tenderness of God, and in our Marian devotion we are really honoring God, whose "femininity" is revealed to us through Mary.

The bottom line for the question of Mary, the mother of Jesus, is whether we are prepared to believe that God's tenderness is revealed to us through the loving tenderness, the life-giving care and affection of a mother.

Incidentally, if anyone is inclined to say that the notion of God's "maternity" is virtually unheard of among contemporary Catholic Christians, I must report that one-quarter of American Catholic young people under thirty think of God as a mother—no difference between young men and young women, just as there is no difference between young men and young women in their imagery of Mary.

Many of the nature religions see creation—the organized cosmos of which we are a part—as the result of sexual love between life-giving chaos and life-ordering cosmos, between two primal principles, maternal and paternal, one providing life and the other providing order and protection. With the exception of Islam, Protestantism, and prophetic Judaism, almost all religions the world has ever known recognize the "androgyny" of God.

Pagan and Christian thinkers, such as Cardinal Nicholas of Cusa, have repeated this fundamental insight, arguing that in God those things which are perceived as opposite in the human condition (including the masculine and the feminine) are somehow combined in the "coincidence of opposites."

Both the primal religious instinct, and the abstract philosophical reflection are based on the fact that we all have experienced, both as children and as adults, maternity and paternity, a relationship to a mother and a relationship to a father. We have also experienced the extraordinarily powerful dynamic of sexual attraction which results in our capability of becoming a mother or a father. Sexual differentiation of humankind into potential mothers and potential fathers is one of the most powerful experiences and one of the most powerful graces in the human condition.

In addition, primitive peoples depended completely on the forces of fertility for their food, their clothing, and the continuation of their tribes. (We do, too, but for us the importance of reproduction is less obvious.)

Something as powerful and as important both in humans and in animals as reproduction through sexual differentiation simply had to be sacred from the ancients' viewpoint. If one defines sacred as "grace-revealing" and "hope-renewing," it also has to be sacred from the modern viewpoint.

As was mentioned earlier, folk Yahwism and pre-Sinai Yahwism knew a shadowy consort of Yahwism in Shekinah, Yahweh's presence or Yahweh's spirit. Even in the rigorous prophetic tradition, the spirit of Yahweh had certain affectionate, tender, and cherishing roles to play, not unlike that which one would expect of a mother goddess.

Did Judaic beliefs and practices, in fact, lead up to the Christian emphasis on Mary?

AS was also noted previously, the concept of the Holy Spirit comes to us with a certain "feminine" resonance. In some of the variant forms of Yahwism that we are rediscovering, the consort played a much more obvious role in both the folk traditions and also in the high religious traditions to be found in the diaspora.

Furthermore, Wisdom, so beloved by the Israelites, particularly in the diaspora, was often pictured and praised as feminine and became, for all practical purposes, a consort of Yahweh in some of the variants within the Israelite tradition—even to the extent of statues of Wisdom as a woman.

Prophetic Yahwism, and its offshoot Rabbinic Yahwism, absolutely and steadfastly refused to consider the possibility of such a mother goddess both because they resisted the abuses of Canaanite fertility cults and because in theory they wanted to place the Lord Yahweh above and beyond fertility and reproduction as the one who dominated all and gave all but was subject to the limitations involved in sexual gratification.

There was no room for a mother goddess in official Yahwism, because she was viewed as a threat to Yahweh. To put the matter precisely, prophetic Judaism did not see how it could deal with femininity in God and still preserve Yahweh's absolute and total uniqueness.

Nevertheless, prophetic Judaism certainly knew the revelatory power of sexual differentiation. Human intimacy as a paradigm of divine love is a theme that runs throughout the Old and the New Testaments. Instead of Yahweh having a goddess spouse, his people became his spouse, and the femininity of God was reflected in his passionate, caring tenderness for his people.

It must not be thought, however, that the rigid monotheism of the prophets excluded completely from popular Israelite beliefs and devotion imagery and practices that vaguely hinted of a maternal deity. One of the reasons Christianity was so quickly able to develop its emphasis on Mary was that the folklore, folk custom, and folk belief of Judaism, particularly in the diaspora, have prepared the way.

Nevertheless, the transformation that occurred from Judaism to Christianity, even from popular and folk Judaism to Christianity, in the space of a century or a century-and-a-half is extraordinary.

How is Mary presented in the New Testament?

IN the New Testament the person of Mary plays a theological role. She stands for Israel and later for the church. Father Raymond Brown, in his masterly analysis of St. John's gospel, tells us that such powerful Marian scenes as the marriage feast of Cana, Mary and

John at the foot of the cross, are theological exercises in which Mary has come to stand for all Christians and for the church.

In other passages of the Scripture where Jesus is conceptualized as the new Adam and there is need to find a comparable new Eve, Mary seems to be playing that role —a construct that results from the early church's "type" catechetics, in which Jesus is explained in terms of the roles of Old Testament "types," whose functions he fulfills in a much more exalted way.

Furthermore, in the first fervor of the Easter experience, early Christianity was for the most part extremely optimistic, indeed, perhaps more optimistic than we can possibly comprehend. Everything that was good and true and beautiful was thereby Christian, and all that which was noble, or at least potentially noble, in the pagan religion would be baptized, that is, adapted for Christian usages.

The patronal goddesses (like the Irish Brigid) were converted almost overnight into patronal saints with scarcely a Christian eye batted. Just as prophetic Judaism could see how a maternal component of the deity could harmonize with the supremacy of Yahweh, so the early Christians could not see why a maternal component of the deity was any threat to the supremacy of Yahweh. A god who brought Jesus back from dead to validate his love was not going to be threatened by anyone.

So we have the optimism of the early church, the residual benign practices of pagan antiquity, and the theological constructs of the New Testament as the explanations for the dramatic apparition very early in the Christian tradition of a fully developed and powerful Mariological devotion.

I must confess that these explanations do not seem to me to be wholly adequate. I am prepared to concede that the scripture scholars who minimize the importance of Mary in the New Testament may be right—though I often wonder how many of them are leaning over backwards not to offend their Protestant counterparts.

But I do not think that once they have virtually explained away the Marian texts in the New Testament they have solved the problem of the flourishing Mariology of the middle of the second century. Father Brown is no doubt correct when he tells us that the Mary of St. John's gospel is a corporate person representing the church, and that the Mariology we know from scriptures at the end of the first century is not personal.

What about the real Mary behind all the titles?

FIFTY or 75 years after St. John's gospel we have evidence of a personal Mariology in which Mary stands for individual—herself—as well as for the corporate people, the church. It seems to me that in addition to the explanations given above, the historical phenomenon of the emergence of a personal Mariology points back into the first century.

Mary was an extraordinary woman who left a powerful mark on the early church even if this mark is not explicitly recorded in the Scriptures. In the absence of a memory of such a person I do not think you can fully account for the flourishing devotion that appeared so quickly despite the hesitancies, reservations, and occasional outright opposition from church leaders.

Doubtless, since that time there have been abuses in the Marian cult; but they are not the ones to which the Reformation objected. If one conceptualizes Mary's function as the one who reveals the tenderness of God (and historically, psychologically, and anthropologically there can be no doubt that this is her function), then it is absurd to suggest that Marian devotion interferes with devotion to God.

Nor is the feminist objection to Mary of much more merit. Even when one discounts the anachronism of expecting Mary to sound like she was a member of the National Organization for Women, the mother of Jesus does not play a secondary or inferior role in the Catholic Christian tradition. On the contrary, the Reformation objection to her was just the opposite. From the point of view of the reformers—themselves surely male chauvinists—Mary's role was altogether too primary.

The abuses of Mariology have gone in another direction, consisting essentially of attempts to dehumanize her, to turn a person who represents the revelatory power of sexual differentiation into someone who isn't sexually very differentiated at all—a negative sex goddess whose stern, cool features remind one of warnings, prohibitions, negatives, and "patent leather shoes."

Under the pretense of glorifying Mary, we have heaped upon her title after title, all of which effectively deny her womanhood. We have made her the object of silly, sentimental, saccharine piety that would make any healthy woman sick.

How is one to understand the role of Mary?

A CERTAIN kind of church leader, not capable of exorcising the feminine sacrament of the deity, set about to defeminize her (though our research would indicate that the staying power of the Mary symbol has been enormous). To really understand the role of Mary in the

Catholic Christian tradition, we must, I fear, go not to papal encyclicals or the doctrinal texts but to the poetry, the art, the music of the Christian tradition. We must go to El Greco, to Chartres, and to the "Ave Maris Stella" to discover the femininity of Mary and her clear and decisive role as the revelation of the tenderness of God.

But if the Holy Spirit represents, at least subliminally, the tenderness of God, why do we need someone else? And isn't there enough tenderness in Jesus and in Yahweh as revealed in the Old Testament for us to be able to dispense with yet another symbol of tenderness?

Such questions are the result of a mistaken tendency of the modern mind to apply logical rules to poetic categories. Religious language is poetic language and only becomes theological upon reflection. The worship of God is not a zero-sum game in which what is given to one symbol of God is taken from another. In the laws of poetic expression symbols reinforce and strengthen one another instead of detracting from one another.

Luther and his contemporaries, products of the declining philosophy of the Middle Ages, could only cope with the laws of logic when they approached religion. They were unable to apply the laws of poetry. Some of their modern followers, like Professor Harvey Cox, who sings the praises of Our Lady of Guadalupe, understand much better.

While it may well be appropriate for Catholics to purify their Marian devotion of the dehumanizing aspects of it, it would be a tremendous mistake to think that we must give up Marian devotion as a price of ecumenism. Rather, our Protestant brothers and sisters must be challenged to understand the actual role that the Mary symbol has played in Catholic Christianity.

One look at Notre Dame de Paris will convince anyone that the Mary symbol is the most powerful religious symbol in 1500 years of Western history. The challenge to our Protestant brothers and sisters is not to abandon it but to understand it. The same challenge exists for us too, of course.

Is Mary the "Mother of God"?

THE answer is yes, of course, provided you understand the philosophy of the "communication of idioms," developed after the first four ecumenical councils in which it becomes theologically legitimate to attribute to the person of Jesus characteristics which apply to one or the other of his natures.

Mary as the mother of the human nature of Jesus can, in this view of things, legitimately be called the "mother of God" or the "theotokos" of the Council of Ephesus. However, having asserted the validity of this traditional Christian mode of expression, one must also quickly add that neither the communication of idioms nor the philosophy on which it is based are readily understood, by contemporary people. There are other descriptions of the role of Mary that might explain her presence in the Catholic Christian heritage more effectively in our world.

When I refer to Mary as revealing the femininity or the tenderness of God, I am striving to convey exactly the same Catholic conviction that was once conveyed by the term "theotokos." Similarly, the various Marian titles and attributes which have piled up through the centuries should also be understood in this context. I pay relatively little attention to them here because the terminology is often simply unintelligible to contemporary humans, even those who are well educated, indeed even those who have many years of Catholic education.

What does psychology tell us about Mary?

IT seems to me much more fruitful to rely first on the categories of the psychology and sociology of religion to derive an understandable approach to Mary the mother of Jesus and then briefly the so-called Marian doctrine in the light of their contribution to our understanding of the femininity of God.

Let me quickly note that I reject categorically the old cliches of the man being "head of the family" and the woman being "the heart of the family," as well as the somewhat more elevated version of the same thing expressed in theories of "the eternal feminine."

There is some evidence in the primatological and psychological literature that men tend to be more aggressive than women and women more skillful than men at certain precise tasks which require adroit hand movements. It would also appear that these differences are biologic and genetic rather than psychological.

It is also the case that in most societies we have known, men have been more likely to take up instrumental or "getting things done" tasks and women the more "socio-emotional" or "keeping the family together" tasks. For our purposes, it is not necessary to decide how much of this differentiation of work may be genetically programmed. Nor is it necessary to determine which set of tasks are superior.

Both the patriarchal society and contemporary feminism, which buys much of the patriarchal worldview, think that socio-emotional tasks are inferior and that the work of hearth, home, and neighborhood is not nearly so valuable as the work of job, profession, and downtown. Having lived my life in both worlds, I dissent from both the patriarchalists and the feminists. There is more dignity, more nobility, and more importance, and also more admirable humanity in the neighborhood than there is downtown. But that question is also beyond the scope of my present intent.

The important point to remember is that there are strong strains of femininity in the most masculine personality and strong strains of masculinity in the most feminine personality. Both men and women are combinations of aggression and tenderness.

What does Mary reveal about God?

MARY reflects the androgyny of God as it is manifested in a tender, loving mother who is also fiercely brave and courageous. The Mary myth in its essential historic tradition revealed that an androgynous God frees women to be strong and vigorous and men to be gentle and tender.

Doubtless the image of the virgin has been used often in history to oppress women. I contend, however, that as one looks at the history of the psychological and anthropological structure of the Marian tradition, this is an abuse of the Mary myth which is not faithful to its basic nature.

Mary reveals to us God working in four different roles which men experience in their relationships to women and women experience in their relationships with men. (1) The warm, life-giving mother; (2) the inspirational, ennobling virgin; (3) the passionately loving spouse; (4) and the tender and compassionate pieta, gently holding us as we slip away from life, back into the earth whence we came.

These experiences of womanhood, experiences of
both men and women, are revelatory of different aspects of the passionate, life-giving, inspiring, all-
embracing tenderness of God. They are locked into both
the structure of the human condition and the structure
of the Mary tradition (as that tradition is revealed
especially in poetry, art, and in music). Notre Dame de
Paris a symbol of woman's inferiority? Don't be silly.

The various Marian titles—Immaculate Conception,
Assumption, etc.—can be understood as emphasizing
one or the other of these fundamental roles of God as
woman. Immaculate Conception and the virgin birth
emphasize the inspiring virgin theme, the Assumption
emphasizes, perhaps, spouse and pieta themes.

It is surely not my intent to deny any of these doctrines nor to minimize them. I am only asserting that if
you wish to explain them to contemporary humans, you
must subsume them under a paradigm that shows
Mary's role as reflecting the womanliness of God.

The bottom line is, do we believe that God loves us
with the tenderness of mother and wife?

Chapter Seven

Resurrection

What is the basic Christian belief concerning resurrection?

TROUBLED Catholics or skeptical nonbelievers often ask, "Do you believe in the *physical* resurrection of Jesus?"

The implication of the question seems to be that the questioner might by some considerable stretch of his intellectual integrity be able to accept a variety of resurrections so long as they weren't *physical*. Maybe Jesus does continue to live in some *spiritual* way; maybe it was a *spiritual* Jesus who appeared to his apostles. That would be all right, tolerable, or at least not totally unbelievable.

However, the notion that Jesus really had his body back again—well, a person has to draw the line someplace, and that's where the questioner draws it.

Similarly, some Christian theologians will say that they accept all the teachings of Christianity except the idea of *personal* resurrection. They will even argue that it is "selfish" or "self-centered" to be concerned about "personal" resurrection.

The implication here seems to be that the theologian can again stretch his faith to accept the notion that some part of the human personality may survive after death. There is a form of "immortality" that is acceptable so long as "I" am not very conscious that I have survived. Indeed, the less conscious "I" am of my survival, the better the resurrection seems to be for these altruistic theologians who pretend that they are above worrying about whether they "personally" are going to be around after the end of things.

I must confess that I can never quite see the qualifying words "physical" and "personal." Either Jesus lives or he doesn't live. If he lives, then his expectation that the heavenly Father would not abandon him is validated, justified; if he does not live, then the heavenly Father has failed in his promise.

Furthermore, either we will live as Jesus lives or the promise of survival uttered by Jesus and repeated by the early church is meaningless. "If Christ be not risen," St. Paul said, "then our faith is in vain."

In both the case of Jesus' resurrection and the case of our own resurrection there must be continuity between that which has died and that which has risen. If Jesus walked the lanes of Galilee with the apostles, he must have been alive; if you exist as a person, you must still be alive, or the obvious sense of the scripture and the universal belief of the Christian tradition is simply wrong. One will not be able to weasel out of it by throwing in qualifying words like "physical" or "personal."

We may not be able to explain the precise how of the resurrection of Jesus, and we may be even less able to describe the quality of our own risen life yet to come. The bottom line is still the top: Jesus lives and so do we, or forget the whole Christianity business, because resurrection is what it's all about.

Why is resurrection central to Christianity?

JESUS preached God's implacably faithful and non-abandoning love, a love that was stronger than death. If the heavenly Father really loved Jesus, then the Jesus that continued to live after Good Friday was not some ethereal spector but the *real* Jesus.

Similarly, that same love is extended to us, and not some vague, amorphous, homogenized mass which has become indistinguishable or barely distinguishable from all others. Lovers love their beloved; they don't love undifferentiated blobs.

The theologians (like John Cobb) who reject "personal" resurrection while pretending to believe in a God of love baffle me. What kind of a love is it that permits the beloved to be destroyed or absorbed into a mass in which she or he no longer exists?

If God is really the lover he claims to be, then why would he let our personhood be dissolved? Why should he permit us to be deceived for a couple thousand years by revelations of himself through Jesus which vigorously and explicitly assert the survival of that which is most uniquely and most specially himself?

If one takes the enormous step of believing in a God who is passionate love, then why does one hesitate to take the much shorter step to believe that this God of passionate love will not abandon his beloved? It seems to me that there are only two reasons why a god of love would permit us to perish. The first reason is that while he is able to bring creatures into the world, he is not able to guarantee their survival. But in that case he would not be God.

The second is that while he loves us, he doesn't love us quite enough to sustain us in existence even though he has permitted us to have structured into the very fiber of our personalities the hunger for survival. Indeed, what kind of a god would it be to send Jesus to reassure us about our basic and fundamental fear of nonexistence and then cheat in the fulfillment of his promise? Christianity without resurrection, in other words, is simply not Christianity at all.

The bottom line, then, for belief in the resurrection is

really the bottom line of the whole of the Christian faith—the non-abandoning love of God. For if God abandons us at death, then he is not a non-abandoning God at all but a faker. If one tries to hedge at the end and say, "Well, yes, we do have a God who does not abandon us, whose love is stronger than death, but it's not quite so strong as to permit us to survive death," or "He really abandons us at least to the extent that 'I' am not conscious that I am still "I" after death," then the Christian revelation of the implacable fidelity of God's commitment to us is finally an empty promise, a waste of time, a cruel joke.

Resurrection is not something added on to the basic story of Christianity. It is at the core of the story precisely because it exists to validate the story. The resurrection of Jesus and our own eventual resurrection is not so much a "proof" that Jesus was God, as it was used in the old catechetics, but rather, and much more importantly, a validation, a confirmation from God of the truth of the love that Jesus claimed to reveal.

And it is important to note that it is not a validation introduced from the outside, a kind of spectacular trick so that Jesus could say, "See I told you so!" It is rather an inevitable consequence of the kind of love that was revealed to us. If God loves us the way Jesus says he loves us, no other finale for human life is possible either for the life of Jesus or for our lives.

What are the origins of resurrection belief?

MOST of the ancient peoples believed in some kind of survival after death. For early Judaism the survival was vague and hazy. *"Sheol"* was a world of shades, of disembodied spirits who had very little, if any, personal existence of distinctiveness. Indeed, it is not unlike the "impersonal" resurrection or immortality preached by some semi-Christian scholars and thinkers.

However, in the Second Temple era, when the relationship of love between God and his people was developed to signify the relationship of love between God and the individual person, then Jewish religious thought rapidly expanded to include a belief in the resurrection of the individual, for the obvious reason that if God so passionately loved the individual, he would hardly permit that individual to perish forever.

The doctrine appeared two centuries before Jesus and was clearly articulated by the Pharisees in the years before Jesus began to preach. The promise of the resurrection, in other words, was not unique or special with Jesus. Indeed, he came not primarily to speak about resurrection but to speak about God's love, a love which inevitably implied for Jesus, as it did for the Pharisees, the survival of the individual whom God loved.

Surprisingly, however, neither the Pharisees nor the early Christians paid much attention to the nature of the resurrected life, and many of the "qualities" of the resurrected body which we were taught in our catechism classes are later medieval reflection on the descriptions of the risen Jesus contained in the New Testament, descriptions which probably represent the popular notions about the resurrection which were prevalent in Second Temple Judaism.

Indeed, one way to describe the Easter event is to say that the followers of Jesus had from their religious heritage, a notion—perhaps better, a "story"—of resurrection. They used that story to describe the Jesus who had died and yet was still alive, the Jesus triumphant over death whom they experienced on Easter morning and subsequently. The experience, then, was of the living Jesus; the story of resurrection was one that was part of their heritage which the followers used to proclaim and explain what had happened to them.

How did the early Christians develop their resurrection tradition?

MOST contemporary exegetes will tell us that the Scripture stories we presently have available in the New Testament of the appearances of Jesus are theological rather than historical in content and ought not to be taken as videotape replays of actual events. The earliest traditions of the resurrection of Jesus, however, according to such analysts, go back to the years immediately after his death, surely to well within the first decade of Christianity.

There were oral traditions at least as early as 37 or 38 A.D. that Jesus, after being buried in the tomb, was seen again as alive by the apostles and many other of his followers. The oldest tradition seems to have set these encounters with the still-living Jesus in Galilee, though one very old tradition also records appearances in Jerusalem.

By the time we get not just to the scriptures but to the relatively fixed oral tradition out of which the New Testament books evolved, there seems to be a tendency to merge these two traditions. It would also appear that the tradition of the empty tomb goes back to the very beginning.

There is some debate as to whether Christians have to believe in the empty tomb. The most obvious response seems to be that they do not; they simply have to believe that Jesus still lives. However, the tradition of the empty

tomb is so ancient and seems so solidly grounded historically that there is not much reason to question it. Some
writers also think that the Pentecost experience recorded
in the Acts of the Apostles was one of the many encounters with the still-living Jesus experienced by his
apostles.

We need not detain ourselves in this series of notes
with arguments to prove what virtually all careful
scholars today admit; namely, that the apostles were not
prepared to believe that Jesus still lived; they did not
want to believe it, but came to believe it despite themselves on the basis of what they perceived to be actual
experiences of him as still alive and triumphing over
death despite his crucifixion. With only a very few
bizarre exceptions (such as the author of *The Passover
Plot*), most scholars today accept the fact that the
apostles honestly reported an exprience they had and
which they did not particularly want to have. There can
be no explanation for the emergence of Christianity
other than such an extraordinary experience.

Were the apostles victims of enormous self-deception or did they experience a living Jesus?

THERE is no way one can prove that the apostles were
not deceiving themselves; likewise, there is no way to
prove that they were deceiving themselves.

Finally the issue becomes God's love. If we believe in
the loving God about whom Jesus preached, then we
should have no trouble believing in the conquest of
death, because God's love is stronger than death. Jesus
still lives as we all will still live, and it is perfectly
reasonable to assume that the heavenly Father would
confirm in a special way the triumph of Jesus over
death.

But the object of faith ought to be placed where it properly is, in God's love as validated and revealed by the resurrection, and not in the physical process of resuscitating a dead body.

Jesus lived, and it is proper to describe the story of his still being alive through the story of a resurrection after death. How was the resurrection accomplished? What was the event like? What was the body of Jesus like after resurrection? The answers to all these questions must be highly speculative because we weren't there.

Since the body is part of the self, however, and it is hard to imagine the self without at least some relationship to the body, one has to be committed to the notion that the Jesus who still lives still has a body or at least a relationship to his body. Therefore one must speak of the bodily resurrection of Jesus just as one must speak of our own bodily resurrection without being able to specify precisely what the term means. Karl Rahner argues that even in the survival of the individual person after his own death and before the general resurrection, there must be some orientation towards our relationship with, if not the precise physical body a person had, at least with the physical world.

The Christian faith is not based on belief in the immortality of the "soul" (a Greek philosophical concept which the Scripture did not know), but on the survival of the human person, body and soul alike. It is enormous fun to speculate about the life of the resurrection and there's nothing wrong with such speculation. Clearly the writers of the New Testament books engaged in it. But we must not confuse the speculation with that fundamental truth to which we are committed by our faith: *Jesus lives and we will, too, because God does not abandon the ones he loves.*

And that is the bottom line of all bottom lines.

Did Jesus have the same body after rising from the dead?

WAS the body that rose from the dead the *same* body that hung on the cross? The answer to this must be yes if one is committed, as Catholics must be, to the notion that the same Jesus who died still lives. But we do not know how it is the same body in the sense that we do not know exactly how the resurrection occurred, and in the sense that we do not understand what the still-living body was and how it was related to the body that existed before death. (We must, it seems to me, believe it is the same body, but then we don't know what "sameness" means in this context).

Two questions are often discussed about this matter. I once heard some very learned theologians wondering whether, if a television camera had been placed in the tomb on Easter morning, one could have seen Jesus emerging from the tomb. One theologian argued that it was a matter of faith to believe that the television camera would have recorded Jesus coming out of the tomb; the other was not so sure whether it was a matter of faith or not.

The question always struck me as being rather ridiculous because there was no television camera there, and the precise events that happened in the tomb on Easter morning are not, it seems to me, questions of faith, however interesting they may be on other grounds. One believes that Jesus still lives. We don't understand much about the process by which he triumphed over death because God hasn't told us.

The second question, raised sometimes in fiction, is whether our faith requires us to believe it is impossible that the earthly remains of Jesus might be found someday in a tomb in Palestine. If such a body were ever uncovered, it is asked hypothetically, would that mean the end of Christianity?

The question is absurd. Christianity is based on an absolute commitment to God's non-abandoning love, to the permanent and implacable fidelity of God to the creatures whom he created and whom he loves. Such a love can neither be confirmed nor refuted by archaelogical excavations.

Furthermore, since we do not understand very much about the link between the risen body and the body which preceded it before death, there does not seem to be any a priori and theoretical reasons for saying that someone could have survived death, could have risen, could have a risen body, and still have left behind in the earth some earthly remains.

Must we believe in the empty tomb and the shroud?

MOST Christians, I think, would be inclined to believe that the empty tomb tradition, neither refuted nor seriously questioned even by the enemies of Christianity at the beginning, means that the link between the risen body and the earthly body is sufficiently close that no earthly remains are left. I would certainly count myself among those who would have such a conviction.

If the question, however, is concerned with whether it is a matter of faith that the tomb was empty and that no earthly remains could ever be found, then I think there would be a difference of opinion among Christian teachers. The majority probably would still say yes; a minority would argue that it is unwise to include under the rubric of religious or divine faith convictions which should more appropriately be considered part of human faith.

The bottom line clearly is that Jesus lives and that we live. That's what counts. To make that conviction dependent upon other phenomena is simply not to do justice to faith and also to miss the point completely in the traditional Christian doctrine of resurrection.

The phenomenon of the Shroud of Turin can be discussed in this context. In an earlier book I expressed considerable skepticism about the Shroud. However, on the basis of the scholarly research that has been published since that book, I am now constrained to admit —not as a matter of religious faith, surely, but as a matter of reflection upon the scholarly evidence—that the best available explanation of the shroud is that it was indeed the burial sheet of Jesus.

The image of a man has been imprinted on that sheet through a process that we simply do not understand. It is not a painting, as we know painting, nor does it appear to be a serious attempt at fraud. The image has been "scorched" on the shroud, perhaps by a sudden, powerful burst of radiation—quite possibly radiation that occurred when a body that was dead comes back to life.

More scholarly research on the shroud is both possible and necessary. The shroud is not an object of faith, nor is it a proof of faith. However, it does add a degree of plausibility to the preliminary rational exploration that might be required before a leap of faith becomes possible. One should not minimize the importance of the shroud as historical evidence. (I plead guilty to having done that in the past.) But neither should one equate it with "proof" of faith, because, finally, faith is a leap of the total person and not an intellectual "proof."

The shroud phenomenon provides a useful occasion

to make the following observation vis-a-vis the subject of the resurrection: our faith requires us to believe in the resurrection of Jesus rather than the resuscitation of a corpse. We do not have to believe that god anticipated the Baron von Frankenstein in instilling life into a body that was dead. We simply have to believe that the Jesus who preached by the shores of the Sea of Galilee and who ate in Peter's house, who talked with his colleagues around the table at the Last Supper, who was scourged and crowned and crucified and buried, is still alive.

The whole Jesus, body and soul, yet lives. This distinction is of enormous importance and must be made resolutely. We know that Jesus lives. We don't know how the heavenly Father specifically accomplished the process of maintaining the life of Jesus. It does not follow, however, that God did not resuscitate a corpse. He may very well have done just that. Indeed, it seems not unlikely that he did just that.

It may very well be that life came into the actual body that was lying in the tomb and that actual body walked out of the tomb. Candidly, I personally am inclined to think that that is what happened. I see no reason to put any constraints on God's ability to accomplish such a phenomenon. But I also see no reason to insist that God had to do it that way.

The point made in the previous paragraphs is that our faith is in the resurrection of Jesus—the fact that Jesus still lives—and not in the particular process by which the heavenly Father accomplished the continued life of Jesus. This emphasis is made not so much to reassure those moderns who have a hard time believing in "miracles," but rather to emphasize the traditional and solid Catholic doctrine that the object of faith is God and not particular processes and mechanisms which we deem it appropriate that God follow.

Did Jesus really die?

WE must believe in the physical resurrection of Jesus in the sense that the Jesus who died is the same Jesus who now lives, and that he possesses the same body that he once possessed. We have no specific clues as a matter of faith as to how God continued—or "brought back"— the life of Jesus; nor do we have to get into the bind of defining for God what is necessary that the risen body be the "same" as the earthly body.

Two points are pertinent in this discussion. First, the words "brought back" used previously are not precise. Jesus was alive before Easter morning; he was alive, indeed, at the moment of his death. He did not stop living when his body was placed in the tomb, even though there was no life in the body. What happened on Easter Sunday was that Jesus' physical body was restored to the living Jesus.

If one accepts Karl Rahner's idea that a disembodied soul without any relationship to the physical world is not admissible to Christian thinking, then we must say that the Jesus who lived between Good Friday and Easter Sunday had at least something "bodily" about him. Thus, to talk about the Father bringing Jesus back from the dead or even about Jesus rising from the dead, is less than precise, although it may well be harmless. Even though his body died on the cross, Jesus wasn't ever dead.

After Easter morning the fact that he wasn't dead was more evident, because the living Jesus with his now restored body was seen by his followers; but Jesus' new life, Jesus' life with the resurrection, did not begin in the tomb in the garden on Easter morning; it began the moment he died on the cross just as our new life with the resurrection begins when we die and not on the final Judgment Day.

Secondly, whenever the final resurrection does occur, the mortal remains of most human beings will have long since corrupted in the grave, and the atoms and molecules which constituted it will have been absorbed by other living forms. Yet the bodies we have in the life of the resurrection will be our bodies even though they will not be, one presumes, constructed out of our earthly remains.

Is it therefore possible to have a resurrection which is not resuscitation of a corpse? Herein is the importance of the distinction which has been adhered to in this chapter. I am fully prepared to believe that in the case of Jesus, the heavenly Father did indeed reunite the living Jesus with the corpse that was in the tomb. There was, so far as one can see, no reason not to do it. But, I am not prepared at this point in the development of the church's understanding to say that those theologians are in doctrinal error who say that God did not have to do it that way, and that it is not an appropriate matter for religious faith to have to believe that he did it that way.

I fear that I have done precisely what I think we should not do: I have spent too much time on the fascinating but ultimately less important issue that surrounds the question of how Jesus rose from the dead to the exclusion of the much more fundamental question of why he rose from the dead. I can only plead that this mistake seems to be historically an inevitable temptation to which Christian teachers succumb.

Chapter Eight

Our Own Resurrection

What is the real challenge to belief in the resurrection?

WHAT is more difficult to believe, the resurrection of one person or the resurrection of all persons? Those Christians, or near-Christians, who are troubled and harassed about the resurrection of Jesus seem to me to miss the point. That's not where the major problem lies.

One could grudgingly concede, perhaps, that God might have performed a spectacular miracle and brought Jesus back to life one way or another by way of exception. An isolated, remarkable event, it doubtless would present certain difficulties; but why swallow the elephant and strain at the gnat?

Or, better, why *ignore* the elephant and strain at the gnat? For the real challenge to Christian faith is not the notion that God's love was so powerful it clung to Jesus despite death but rather the notion—or, I should say, the story—that God's love is so powerful that it clings to all of us despite death. The big problem is not in believing that Jesus survived death, body and soul, but in believing that we too will survive death body and soul just as he did.

If you want to find a good reason for not being a Christian, stop worrying about the resurrection of Jesus and start worrying about your own, because, you see, gentle soul, you cannot heave a sigh of relief and assume your Christian faith is intact when you've said, "Okay, Jesus died but still lives body and soul." You must add, "So, too, will I!" If you want to worry, worry not about the resurrection of the Lord but about your own. To outrageously transform John Donne, "Ask not for whom the bell peals, it peals for thee."

What will the life of the resurrection be like?

MUCH of what was taught in our grammar school and catechism classes seems to make heaven an uninteresting place. One would sit around on clouds strumming a harp, enjoying "beatific visions." However splendid that vision was, it always occurred to one of us that after a while heaven must get dull. If it did not include a chance to watch an occasional Chicago Bear or Notre Dame football game, it might not be much of a place at all.

Similarly, seeing God face-to-face—doubtless an interesting experience for us, if not for God—did not seem to be something that would hold one's attention forever. Knowing and loving God perfectly was again undoubtedly highly desirable, but it might not be all that splendid after you got used to it, especially if there wasn't time left for knowing and loving our families and friends and those who were important to us in this life.

In current Catholic thought there is tremendous emphasis placed on the importance of this world. It has tended to play down the eschatological, to accept the Marxist criticism that Heaven is "pie in the sky when you die," and has not attempted to update the traditional Christian eschatological terminology.

It seems safe to say, however, the life of the resurrection will be a life of action, of fulfillment, of celebration, of delight, of happiness. We human beings were not designed to be satisfied with stagnation, passivity, loneliness, and boredom. The life of the resurrection will not be any of these things.

Any images or pictures we have left over from inadequate religious education which suggest that the resurrected life will be a drag ought to be rejected out of hand. The Lord has told us that eye has not seen nor heard nor has it entered into the hearts of humans the things that God has prepared for us.

One cannot imagine the unimaginable or fathom the unfanthomable. One can surely say, though, that the God who prepared the spectacular vistas of this world will not stint in his preparation of the world to come.

Will there be sexual pleasure in the risen life?

IT is often asked in this Freud-influenced era whether there will be sex in the risen life. The reply of Jesus to the Sadducees, that there would not be marrying and giving in marriage in the life of the resurrection, is cited by some that there will not be. Many people have responded that if there isn't, they don't want to go to heaven. C. S. Lewis in the face of such response, said that if sex were not at all like eating chocolate candy, the child would reply that in that case he would much prefer the candy.

A more plausible interpretation of this scripture passage suggests that Jesus was simply refuting the Sadducees and not making any observations about the activities in which the saint might or might not engage. Some contemporary Catholic thinkers argue that the concrete human person which "I" know as "myself" exists in a sexual modality either male or female, and that if my maleness or femaleness is taken away, then I will not know myself as me in the life of the resurrection. Other thinkers and teachers are somewhat more reluctant to put such limitations on God's freedom.

Perhaps the best response is that we will love one another in the resurrected life even more intensely, even more joyfully than we do in the present life, and that the pleasures of that love will be even greater than the most ecstatic pleasures of love we know in this life. It is utterly unthinkable that there would not be between those who work close to one another on earth an even more powerful and more rewarding intimacy in the life of the resurrection. Of those things we can be sure, though we must say that we honestly have no idea of how God will arrange them.

How will life after death be different?

IT would seem reasonable to assume that the life of the resurrection will be a life of continued growth of the human person, though, again, we don't know how this growth will occur. Humans are only happy when they are meeting challenges, responding to them, and growing in their knowledge and love.

Since we have a capacity for the infinite, it would seem that our potential for growth would never end. How this growth will occur and what it will involve is beyond our imagining, though we must say that all the joys, all the pleasure, all the excitement, all the rewards that we have in this life are not only a preview, they are a down payment on the joys of the resurrection.

It is important to stress, both because it is accurate to the Catholic tradition and it enables us to avoid the pie-in-the-sky-when-you-die trap, that there is a substantial continuity between this life and the life of the resurrection. In the strict sense of the word, we Catholics believe not so much in life after death but simply in life. As G. K. Chesterton once put it, we believe that life is too important ever to be anything but life.

That life which is in us survives the tragic breaking apart that is the death experience. We don't try to cover up the tragedy, we don't pretend that death is not an awesome evil; we just assert that death does not have the final word, and that even on the last days of our lives we who are followers of Jesus of Nazareth can say confidently, tomorrow will be different. How the continuity is sustained and what form it takes is another question to which we simply have no answer yet.

Should we speculate about heaven, hell and purgatory?

THE British Protestant theologian John Hick, one of the few modern writers to take seriously the dating of Christian thought about eschatology, has suggested that the risen life may take place in a different time and a different space. Surely that is possible, even though it does sound a bit like science fiction. It would seem that we must go along with Hick to the extent of saying that the life of the resurrection must involve space, because wherever there are bodies present, there is surely space.

It is less certain, but still rather likely that the risen life will also involve time, particularly if human action and human growth are going to continue. We must note, though, that both time and space may mean something different in our continued life.

Such speculations are inevitable and healthy. Indeed, inattention to them is probably unhealthy. But the speculation can never be very satisfying, because we are not capable of imagining it.

The bottom line, however, must be sharply distinguished from such speculation, for the bottom line is that, like Jesus, we survive. The Father in heaven is faithful to his promises to us just as he was faithful to his promises to Jesus. He will not abandon us any more than he abandoned Jesus.

What about Purgatory, Hell, the "particular" and the "final" judgment? Need one repeat again that compared to the fundamental eschatological issue—human survival—these other questions are derivative and substantially less important. One must at least admit the possibility of a final and definitive "no" to the offer of love that God makes to us. It is possible that humans can turn their backs irrevocably on God. Therefore one must insist on the possibility of "damnation."

Is personal damnation really possible?

IT is difficult to take human freedom seriously if there is no real choice. The doctrine of hell exists not so much to terrify us as to reassert the fact of human freedom, the necessity of human choice, and the urgency of making that choice as quickly as possible in our lives.

Presumably there are few Christians today who would subscribe to the Dante-like visions of Hell in which God sadistically tortures those who didn't quite make that act of perfect contrition in the last brief moment of their lives. God is not vengeful, nor does he take pleasure in suffering. The agony of Hell will not come from fire or from devils with pitchforks but from the worst of all torments, that of the wasted chance, the lost opportunity, or refused love.

To assert, however, the possibility of damnation is not to assert the reality of it for any person. I add this caveat not for liberal humanitarian purposes but simply because traditional Catholic teaching has always insisted that we can be certain of the damnation of no one. The possibilities that God offers to his creatures are simply beyond human imagining and also indubitably beyond human powers to draw limits.

Those whose growth in the power of knowledge and love in this life has been arrested for one reason or another may be given other options, other opportunities about which we know nothing. To say "may be given" is not to say "will be given"; it is rather a warning that if lines are to be drawn, they will be drawn by God and not by us, particularly in our hellfire and brimstone moods.

How does the existence of Purgatory fit into Catholic doctrine?

THE possibility of further growth is nothing more than the traditional Catholic doctrine of Purgatory, which, while it may not be an article of faith, strictly speaking, is a wise and consoling teaching, especially when Purgatory is no longer painted as one of the outer suburbs of Hell with the "poor" souls shrieking in agony and suffering as they occasionally did in some of the more imaginative catechetical classes of the preconciliar church.

If one assumes that a certain level of capabilities of knowing and loving are required to be able to deal intimately and directly with God, and if we further assume that many/most/all of us do not quite develop those capacities during the present phase of our life, then there is no reason to doubt that somehow or other there will follow another phase in which we are given further opportunities for growth and development.

Indeed, theologian John Hick uses the Catholic doctrine of Purgatory to postulate many other reincarnations of the same person that "I" am now, each one of which will be in a different time and a different space.

Hick's Purgatory, sounding a bit like the science fiction writer Philip Jose Farmer's "Fabulous Riverboat," may be finally unacceptable to Catholic teaching (though Hick certainly ought to be praised for taking the lead in an imaginative reformulation of Christian eschatology).

However, Hick's vision does emphasize both the importance and the possibility of the purgatory notion: there is no reason to deny and many reasons to assume continued development and preparation at the end of the present phase of our life. What such preparation will be like and where it will occur is utterly beyond our imagination.

What is Catholic belief about the end of the world and final judgment?

CATHOLIC Christians must also accept the notion of "judgment," of the final successful fulfillment of God's plan that began with the creation of the world, continued with the emergence of humankind, was revealed spectacularly in and through Jesus, and will finally someday be definitively accomplished.

Unlike some other religions, Christianity is linear. It believes that the particular "economy" in which we live has a beginning, a middle, and an ending—and that we live somewhere in the middle. How this definitive fulfillment will occur is beyond our comprehension, though we need not take literally the vivid apocalyptic imagery of the New Testament.

We need not, for example, be terrified in the night if we hear a loud trumpet or if we see a flash of lightning going from the east to the west. Attempts to predict "the end of the world" on the basis of a literalist and fundamentalist interpretation of the New Testament are utterly misguided, however much fun they may be for those who have nothing better to do.

I am reminded of the story that in the year 1000 all the royal courts in Europe, save one, went forth on January 1 outside the towns and cities to await the return of Jesus at the end of the first millenium. None of the people involved knew about the monastic mistake that made them five years too late. The one court that did not go into the hill country to await the end of everything was the Vatican. Naturally.

To put the matter popularly, Jesus will come back when the job is done. Beyond that there's not much else we can expect. Attempts to link this final fulfillment at "the end of the world" accomplished, say, by a collision with a comet, or the sun turning into a supernova, or the universe collapsing back on itself, or the coming of another ice age, or the final application of the second Law of Thermodynamics, are as frivolous as trying to figure out the "name of the beast" or to seek guidance from the rumored reports of what the "Fatima letter really said."

Finally, one may cheerfully concede that both the "Dies Irae" and the *Last Judgment* of Michelangelo are superb artistic creations but neither constitutes the bottom line of our religious beliefs. Indeed, both of them are somewhat distorted versions of the story. God's "final judgment" will be a victory of mercy and love, not a day of wrath, not a day of somber and devastating destruction.

What does the Christian faith say about the existence of angels or other rational creatures?

JUST as there is no reason in the Christian faith to exclude the possibility of other rational creatures in this universe and, indeed, of other incarnations, other apparitions of Jesus (the poet Alice Meynell once wondered, "in what shape he walks the Pleiades?"), so there is no reason to think that there cannot be other "linear plans" or other "economies" by which God is involved in love affairs with other rational creatures about the universe or in other universes or in other manifestations of our own universe. Whether it would be possible to "transfer" from our "economy" to another one is a question which patently goes beyond theology and religion, however fascinating it is for science fiction writers.

It is in this same spirit that one must approach the question of angels. It would appear that in the Scripture and in the Catholic tradition, the symbolism of "angels" represents God's loving and careful protection of his creatures. If we are to accept the word of most competent Scripture scholars, the texts of the sacred books do not "prove" the de facto existence of disembodied, rational beings.

Many theologians would hold today that the existence of angels is not a matter of faith. It doesn't seem very likely that anyone would get tossed out of the church for refusing to believe in their existence. However, it would seem to me too absurd to insist dogmatically that there are no such creatures.

One of the reasons for the popularity of the movie, *Close Encounters of the Third Kind* was precisely its conviction that we are not alone in the universe. Indeed, the "light creatures" that emerged from the flying saucers to antiphonal computer music were, perhaps unconsciously, designed to be quite cherubic. While it may be that angels aren't on the bottom line, I must confess that I, for one, will be terribly disappointed if there aren't any.

What happens at the instant of death?

THERE is no reason not to think that the moment of death is a judgment situation for us, though perhaps by now we Catholics are able to dispense with visions of a legal tribunal in which God is the Judge, Peter the Recording Angel, the Devil the prosecuting attorney and our pathetic guardian angel the embarrassed defense attorney, with the Blessed Mother an enthusiastic, if handicapped, character witness. Indeed, much of the sudden death literature emphasized the "review of life" phenomenon that goes on a split second before human life comes to an end, a review in which we, in effect, judge ourselves.

It seems reasonable to me to expect that in that vision there is a clear, definite, and perhaps overwhelming exercise of God's mercy and love. Indeed, the death research would indicate that the review is followed by resignation, acceptance, peace, and then joy turning into ecstasy. Such a reaction to death may well be a genetically programmed response of the only creature (of whom we know) who is conscious of his own mortality. It does not follow, however, that such genetic programming is not part of God's loving mercy.

In any case, once one puts aside a legalistic approach to the particular judgment, one will perceive that if it is an encounter with the God whom Jesus has revealed to us, then it must be an encounter of mercy and love. What about all the parapsychological phenomena, descriptions of which fill many shelves in paperback bookstores these days? There is nothing in the Catholic tradition which forces us to disbelieve in ESP or related phenomenon. Clairvoyance, deja vu, precognition, extrasensory perception, out-of-body experiences, and other related phenomena are matters for scientific research. (And reputable scholarship seems to demonstrate that phenomena do occur rather frequently.)

The same must be said for reported contacts with the dead (one-quarter of the American people have had such experiences) and similar phenomena. They do not add anything to faith, nor do they detract from it— though they certainly refute a rigid, hyperscientific approach to the universe and make scientifically "probable" the existence of a human spirit distinct from the body and also "more probable than not" the fact of some kind of human survival.

What is the bottom line belief in resurrection?

CHRISTIANITY does not believe in the Greek notion of the "immortality of the soul." It believes, rather, in the "resurrection," that is to say, the survival of the whole human person. While much of the scholarly research in immortality may be useful to refute the a priori scientific argument that it is impossible, such arguments are no substitutes for faith, because the object of faith is rather God's non-abandoning love. That's where the bottom line is in this issue, as in all previous and subsequent issues.

(I do not see how a belief in "reincarnation" is compatible with Catholic doctrine. John Hick thinks it is, but only if the reincarnation occurs in other times and other space.)

The hunger for survival seems to have been part of the human consciousness since consciousness began. (Neanderthal burial sites indicate how ancient the tradition is.) It also seems built into the structure of our personalities. We hope despite ourselves, we hope against hope, we hope even when there is no hope. We apparently end our lives hoping. The most critical religious question we can ask is whether that hope is justified. Jesus came to tell us that it is. The bottom line for Catholic Christians is that the heavenly Father validated Jesus' expectations of survival and someday he will validate ours, too.

Chapter Nine

Marriage

Are human beings biologically and genetically programmed for the marriage bond?

THE comparative biologists tell us that both the family and love had to emerge in the evolutionary process before the proto-hominids could evolve into homo sapiens. The evolutionary process was to select those proto- or pre-hominids who were genetically programmed to "quasi" pair bonds, because those members of the species who were inclined to remain with their mates were those whose offspring were most likely to survive to adulthood.

Since the presence of both a male and female was an overwhelming asset in such survival, the species evolved in the direction of producing highly plastic individuals with little in the way of genetically-provided instincts to direct their behavior, and an enormous capacity for cultural self-direction—a condition which requires a long period of learning and a long period of dependence on parents.

It was the "quasi" pair bond that was the key link in this evolutionary change. I use the word "quasi" because pair-bonding in the strict sense seems to exclude the possibility of union with other mates while the present one is alive. Such pair-bonding is found, for example, in many species of birds. Humankind has a strong proclivity toward permanent relationships; it also has, however, in common with higher primates, a wandering eye.

115

Comparative biologists and comparative primatologists point out that most of what is specifically different from human sexuality compared to that of other primates is oriented not toward reproduction but toward pair-bonding, toward the sustaining of permanent relationships or, if you will, toward the reinforcement of the family. It does not take nearly the elaborate, pervasive, and preoccupying sexuality which we humans possess to produce a small primate. Animals closely related to us do it with a minimum of fuss, inconvenience, and time consumption. They do not fantasize about it; they have sexual relationships only at certain times, and they achieve it quickly, efficiently, and with little display of affection.

The readiness of the human animal (male and female) for sexual relationships at almost any time, indeed, almost all the time, the rather lengthy duration of the human sexual embrace, the affective component of the well-developed male and especially female secondary sexual characteristics, all are utterly unrequired for reproduction. They emerged in the evolutionary process to strengthen and reinforce the link between one male and one female. The propensity for a durable marriage bond, in other words, is built into our genes and antedates the emergence of homo sapiens.

What does our Jewish-Christian heritage say about human sexuality?

I BEGIN with this biological observation because it provides a solid foundation for any discussion of human marriage and because it seems to me that the church, for all its obsessions with the biology of human sexuality, has managed to keep itself remarkably uninformed about the growth of understanding of human biology.

To put the matter even more bluntly, some churchpersons, for all their insistence on "natural law," seem almost criminally negligent in their efforts to keep up to date in their understanding of nature. I presume the reason for this is that they are afraid the growth of scientific knowledge will be a threat to their position.

However, in the case of the sociobiological, primatological, and comparative biological findings I have cited in the previous paragraphs, church leaders would find much to strengthen their convictions and their teachings about marriage and family.

The powerful attraction of the human male and the human female for one another is not merely for transient sexual episodes but toward a durable relationship—an attraction which we call love and which is programmed into our genes. It may be a more powerful proclivity in some of us than in others; it may be one we are able to resist for reasons of selfishness or for reasons of generosity; but it is there. It is an integral part of the nature of human nature, and hence (for those of us who believe that human nature is basically good) it is neither evil nor perverse. The natural law, in other words, tells us that sexual love is good.

So, too, does the Jewish-Christian heritage, although many of those who have propounded that heritage have frequently tried to pretend the opposite. The Christian heritage does more, however, than merely assert the basic goodness of human sexuality. It repeatedly uses the story of human love to reflect, mirror, reveal, to be a sacrament of the story of divine love.

Two humans passionately in love with one another, the tradition tells us, experience an intense effect which is something like—though not nearly so powerful as—God's passion for us. What is God's love like? The response of the Christian heritage is that it is something like—though more powerful than—the attraction one experiences at the height of sexual love.

How do person and sacrament come together in marriage?

THE bottom line for the Catholic theory of marriage is not indissolubility, a prohibition of contraception, rules against premarital or extramarital sex; the bottom line is that marriage reflects the intensity of God's love for us. The more intense the married love, the better a "sacrament" it is, because the better it reveals God's love for us.

From this solidly traditional perspective, the most fundamental and important challenge to a marriage is not to avoid divorce or extramarital affairs or contraception, it is rather to sustain and develop an intense and powerful relationship, because the more intense and the more powerful, the better "sacrament" (in the sense of a revelatory symbol) it really is. The more passionate the relationship the more effective the sacrament.

There can be no doubt that this is the bottom line that many times Catholic teachers seem to forget. They warn people of the need for self-control, and urge them to avoid "unbridled" passion. Yet most married couples would admit that the exact opposite is usually the problem. Self-control is not hard to practice in marriage; self-surrender, self-abandon is.

The worst threat to a marital relation is not unbridled passion but bridled passion, passion which has become monotonous, routine, indifferent, unchallenging, and unrewarding, passion which is scarcely passion at all.

Why has the church traditionally equated sexuality with evil?

MANY Christian leaders and teachers seem terrified of passion, possibly because they are afraid of it in their own lives and possibly because they are appalled at the thought that human passion can reflect divine passion. Without knowing it, perhaps, such churchpersons have a bit of the puritan problem, which has affected the church almost from its beginning.

Whatever may have been the faults of the Old Testament approach to human intimacy, it was not characterized by prudery or puritanism. However, when Christianity ventured into the world of Greek and Roman culture, it encountered human styles of thought, which however libertine people were in practice, were prone to condemn sexuality as evil.

The human spirit was imagined as being imprisoned in the body; the spirit yearned to be free to contemplate. The body, particularly the body's sexual hunger, was a burden that chained the spirit, tied it down, and interfered with its essential activity of contemplation. The more one controlled and dominated one's sexuality, the more one eliminated its effects from one's life (in the case of the great Father of the Church, Origen, through self-mutilation), the better human being and Christian one was.

This Platonic philosophy was totally pervasive in the world of Greek and Roman culture and virtually irresistible. It affected Christian theology for at least a millennium-and-a-half. Even sexual intercourse between married people was viewed by some of the greatest teachers of the church as at least somewhat sinful, even if it were not engaged in for reasons of passion. (How passion was excluded was something that theologians like St. Augustine didn't seem prepared to explain.)

One has to say in retrospect that however understandable this Platonic aberration was in terms of the cultural milieu, it has been a great misfortune for the church, and has obscured tragically the bottom line in the Catholic Christian heritage on marriage.

The tradition was kept alive in marriage ceremonial, devotional handbooks, art, literature, and music, folk custom. The puritan, Platonic tradition of the theology books and the love tradition of popular piety both coexisted in the church from the beginning and still do today. The periodic repetition of the warning against "unbridled passion" indicates that the puritans have yet to be routed.

Why does the church seem to concentrate on negative restrictions?

SOME of the more modern puritans are prepared to concede human sexuality is good, though they are more concerned about the aberrations and the abuses than they are about the goodness. They justify their rigid, narrow, and punitive approach to sexuality on the grounds of the frequency of sexual sin. As one friend put it to me, "We have produced a dirty-minded church, one in which the principal religious concern of the teaching authority seems to be fixated on sex."

Sexuality, in other words, might be good, but human beings abuse it so often that the emphasis has to be on the abuse instead of the goodness. Doubtless, the sexual dimensions of our personalities are extremely powerful, and doubtless, too, they are affected by the fundamental flaw in human nature discussed earlier in these notes.

Nonetheless it is bizarre that a Catholic Christianity which vigorously argues that human nature is deprived and not depraved is willing to act as if it were depraved and not deprived on the subject of sex. In most other areas of human behavior, Catholic Christianity is committed to developing a positive, constructive vision as an antidote to human fraility.

When it comes to sex, however, we seem determined to abandon our ordinary style and concentrate entirely on negative restrictions, with a few vague pieties about "unbridled passion" and "self-control."

Such an approach may have worked in an era when human marital relationships were brief. Until the middle of the last century, the average marriage lasted no longer than 12 years; now the average marriage lasts 48 years. (Also, in the previous era, a woman would need to produce seven children in order to see two survive to adulthood—with perhaps 10-11 pregnancies; now 10 or 11 pregnancies would mean that many children living to adulthood.)

It may also have sufficed in an era before psychology understood and articulated that which poets and lovers always knew, that for all its pain and poignancy, sexual love is one of the most powerful experiences available to us for self-fulfillment and personal growth. The church seems thus far utterly incapable of coping with changes, and of marshalling its resources to shake off the last traces of puritanism and articulate a positive and constructive approach to human intimacy.

When it comes to sex and marriage, church leaders and church teachers seem to have a very hard time getting to their own bottom line: marriage is a sacrament which reveals the passion of God's love.

It is often thought that the fault is to be found in the

celibacy of the Catholic clergy. Not knowing sexual fulfillment themselves, it is contended, they are incapable
of coping with the sexual problems or understanding the
sexual situations of their people. I do not find this argument particularly persuasive. I know of no evidence that
our Protestant brothers and sisters in the married minis-
try have been any more successful at overcoming their
puritanical hang-ups.

And the empirical evidence suggests that it is not the
parish clergy but the higher church leadership which has
isolated and insulated itself from the problems of ordinary human beings. The same observation could be
made of the church's professional theologians. Thus,
the book issued by the Catholic Theological Society of
America on sexuality deals almost entirely with moral
theological questions, and provides virtually nothing for
married Catholic heterosexuals who propose to remain
faithful to one another.

Does the spirituality of marriage need to be updated?

THE empirical research in which my colleagues and I
have been engaged provides confirmation (if any is
needed) of the thesis that marriage is a "sacrament."
The more satisfying a relationship and the more fulfilling the sexuality of the relationship, the more likely both
partners are to have a warm, positive, passionate "story
of God."

If your images of God are passionate, then so, too, is
your marriage and vice-versa. Indeed, the resolution of
the intense crisis which seems to affect so many marriages toward the end of the first decade, also seems to
involve a dramatic increase in the passionate imagery
about God which can be found in married people's religious imaginations.

It is not clear whether passionate stories of God cause

an increase in the passion of a marriage or whether the resurgence of passion in a marriage facilitates a resurgence of passionate "stories of God." It may not matter much which comes first, for they certainly mutually influence one another.

Moreover, it is also true that the religious imaginations of husbands and wives converge through the years of marriage, so that after a time together, their images of God and the understandings of the purpose of life which these images embody become similar. Marriage reveals God's love, and God's love in its turn facilitates the growth of marriage.

Empirical evidence demonstrates these truths incontrovertably, yet a spirituality for marriage based on the bottom line of marriage as a revelation of God simply has not been developed. As noted, Church leaders are still too busy warning people about the risks of "unbridled passion." They seem to have little or no interest about the much more serious marital problem of "bridled" passion.

Is sexual fulfillment essential to the sacramentality of marriage?

OFTENTIMES it was said in our high school marriage classes and in our pre-Cana conferences that the church was strongly committed to both marriage and the family and tolerated sexual pleasure as something which had to be conceded to people because they took on the responsibility of marriage, family life, and child-rearing.

If you were so spiritually and humanly weak that you needed sex, well then it was all right so long as it was in marriage; but the sooner you could get along without it, the more "pure" you would be and the better Catholic you would be.

We have to insist that this is a profoundly mistaken

and unchristian view, no matter how widespread it was. There would not be marriage among humankind unless it had been arranged (by God through the evolutionary process) that humankind would reproduce through sexual differentiation with quasi pair-bonding. It was precisely the intense sexual passion, its almost irresistible demand, as well as its exquisite pleasure, that led to sexual activity.

To parallel the story of human love with the story of divine love is not to say that the less sexuality there is within marital intimacy the better it is, but exactly the opposite. All other things being equal, the more intense the passion between husband and wife, the better the marriage is.

Love between a man and a woman obviously involved more than sex, but it just as obviously involved sex too; and it is unlikely that the love can continue to be powerful if the sexual fulfillment is inadequate. The nature of sexual fulfillment will doubtless vary in different times and places for different people, but it is essential to the sacramentality of marriage precisely because it most powerfully reveals the intensity of God's passion for us.

The Catholic heritage does not approve of inhibition or prudery. On the contrary, it rejects both, although certain Catholic leaders and teachers (for reasons, perhaps, having to do with their own hang-ups) may seem to preach prudery and inhibition. The more playful, the more uninhibited, the more imaginative, the more fantastic, the more surprising, the more "wonder-full" is the sexual relationship between a husband and a wife, the more authentically sacramental it is.

The old prudery is still powerful within the grass-roots teachings of the church and in the imagination of Catholics. In addition there is a new "feminist" prudery, which is offended that people find the bodies of members of the opposite sex attractive. You are not, it would seem, permitted to enjoy such attraction, because that makes other people "sex objects."

To reduce another person to an object is, of course, horrendously evil; but to find another person sexually attractive does not mean that that person is necessarily reduced to an object (though in many cases it does). It rather means that we perceive the other as a "sexed" person. Sexed persons, incidentally, are far more attractive than sex objects—and far more frightening, too.

What is the basic insight of the sacramentality of marriage?

MARRIAGE is inevitably a risky relationship, because a person gives so much of himself/herself in it, both body and spirit. One reveals not only one's body, but, more terrifyingly, one's self. Marital intimacy requires openness to the point of vulnerability. We become so defenseless with the other person that that other person has power to cause us grave pain, indeed to break our homes.

Moreover, not only might we be hurt, but in any ongoing intimacy we most certainly will be hurt, and we will also hurt the other. After a certain number of pain-producing incidents, we tend to reduce our expectations and settle for a minimum level of satisfactory coexistence in which the pleasures and payoffs may not be very great, but then neither are the risks. There won't be much joy; neither will there by much pain. It is to be feared that such "adjustments" are the norm in most modern marriages, Catholic and otherwise.

In such relationships of modest expectation and limited liability, things run smoothly; there are no lows, but there are no highs either. Sexual fulfillment, sexual excitement, sexual joy diminish to a situation that may be adequate—but only just.

Most such marriages survive, though some just barely, and they are certainly ill-equipped to deal with the turning points that come with mid-life crises. They are also much less effective as "sacraments."

It may well be true, from the canonical and moral viewpoint, that a marriage between two Catholics from which most of the joy, the excitement, the adventure, the fun, and the pleasure have evaporated is a better marriage than one which has ended in divorce.

However, we have to say that from the viewpoint of the sacramentality (i.e., the revelatory power of the relationship), there is not much to choose from, for neither marriage reveals to children, to other people, and to the spouses the passionate love of an intense, surprising, wonder-full God.

Without vulnerability, there can be no intimacy, and vulnerability challenges the depths of selfhood. One can risk the repeated breaking of one's heart only if one is confident one lives in a universe in which there is a loving power that will protect one from ultimate heartbreak. Risk in marriage, whether in the explicitly sexual dimension of marriage or in the less explicitly sexual dimensions of the relationship, requires some kind of basic and fundamental faith in the ultimate Goodness of things.

Here we have this reciprocal flow of influence between human and divine love. Human love at its most intense, passionate, and ecstatic moments gives us a hint of God's love, and then, confident of the power and the passion and the protection and the non-abandonment of

God's love, we have the courage and strength to risk ourselves again in human love.

My colleague Teresa Sullivan once pointed out: "marriages last on the average four times as long as they used to; but that means more than four times as many reconciliations."

Skills in the art of seeking and granting forgiveness, of reconciling and being reconciled are essential to the happiness of modern marriage. But reconciliation renews risks, heightens vulnerability, and invites pain; it also means that if one is to be effective, one analyzes one's own mistakes and not those of others.

Furthermore, it means that one also is not afraid of conflict, because reconciliation can only come after conflict. If a marriage has no quarrels, no arguments, no fights, then it will have no reconciliations; it will also, it is to be feared, have little room for communication or for growth and development.

Conflict and reconciliation, the pain and suffering of death and rebirth involved in fighting, forgiving and beginning again is not the only way for human intimacy to grow, but it is one of the best ways—although it risks enormous vulnerability.

Spouses who live within the Catholic Christian heritage know they can take the risk of reconciliation because they have already been reconciled with God through the love of Jesus. It still hurts, however, but the joy that comes after the hurt, the wonderful pleasures of love reborn become, if anything, even more pleasurable because one perceives them as anticipations of the ultimate rebirth of all love when we sit around the table at the eternal wedding banquet with Jesus, the heavenly Father, our family and friends, and all those whom we love.

Chapter Ten

Sex

What is unique about human sexuality?

IN the last chapter I insisted that the bottom line for marriage is its sacramentality, its revelation of the intensity and the passion of God's love for us.

The bottom line for this chapter is that our nature as sexual persons reveals to us a dependence on the love of others and, hence, ultimately on the love that created us. Human beings are caught between selfishness and selflessness, between aggression and altruism, between the genes that program us to seek our own good and those that program us to be good to others.

The power of sexual hunger breaks us out of the hard shell of selfishness and tips the balance of the scales ever so slightly in the direction of selflessness. Our sexuality forces us to live not only for ourselves but to live for others.

This, then, is the other side of the sexual bottom line: sexuality reveals to us, powerfully and poignantly, the need to live for others.

We may convert our sexual passions into selfishness. Most of us do this some of the time, some of us do it all of the time. It is also possible to forego certain kinds of sexual pleasures (though not our sexual nature) for certain kinds of special and generous service.

Not all people who make this sacrifice, it is to be feared, do so unselfishly. Some do it merely to escape from the responsibility for other human beings, to find a way to hide from their fears, or because they want the power to manipulate others more than they want the pleasure of relating to them. The commitment to celibacy, in other words, is a commitment to selflessness that is sometimes honored and sometimes not.

Sexual differentiation and the hungers for union which result from it reveal to us our incompleteness as human beings unless we enter into relationships with others which have at least some measure of self-giving and self-sacrificing.

It will be recalled that in the last chapter, I cited the socio-biological finding that the particular kind of sexuality to which we humans evolved biologically, as a prelude to the emergence of homo sapiens, occurred precisely because it forced the prehominid to be concerned about others.

Our sexuality seems to be one of the sources, if not the principal source, of our cooperative propensities. That which is unique and special about human sexuality, in other words, is that it opens us up to intimate and affectionate relationships with others.

What are the ethical and religious dimensions of sexuality?

IN the era just before Vatican Council II, there was a kind of Christian personalism which heavily emphasized the "vulnerability" which sexuality created in the human personality—usually with quotations from Paul Claudel and Leon Bloy. There was a reaction against the "etherealizing" of sexuality in this approach. More recently, some Catholic writers on marriage and sex have tried to treat it as a "simple biological function."

Both treatments are clearly wrong. The old "personalist" view ignored the biological aspects of sex, but the "new realists" fail to understand that what biologically distinguishes human sexuality from the sexuality of the other primates is precisely its demands for interpersonal selflessness.

Self-giving is not a nice psychological adjunct to human sexuality, it is a biologically programmed essential in human sexuality. Thus, one can say that it is the "natural law" that human sexuality must be selfless.

It does not follow, of course, that we do not also seek our own happiness in our sexual relationships. If we are wise, we discover that our happiness comes precisely from being concerned with others. As Martin D'Arcy remarked in his famous *The Mind and the Heart of Love*, "love means not so much the desire to possess as the desire to be possessed." One might paraphrase, stating love means not so much the desire to have someone else belong to you as the desire to belong to someone else.

Generosity is not the only norm that must be considered in judging the ethical and religious dimensions of human sexual behavior. It is not enough to ask, "Am I generous?" However, it is essential to ask that question for if the answer is not "yes," there is something fundamentally wrong in our sexual behavior.

The basic philosophy of the Playboy philosophy is, "Am I hurting anyone?" This question will not do. When one considers the nature of human nature, to say nothing of religion, one must ask, "Am I helping anyone?"

Sexuality which is not other-oriented, in other words, runs against the nature of human nature. That is not a rule imposed from the outside by puritans, prudes, or spoilsports; it is part of the nature of the beast.

True, because we are such pliable and flexible creatures, we can indeed engage in sexual behavior which is not other-oriented, or at least minimally other-oriented. But it is not likely to be very satisfying or very fulfilling.

Is sex a sacrament?

THE sacramentality—the power of sex to reveal the basic love which is at the center of the cosmos—is not something added on from the outside. It is rather an insight into the nature of sexuality which we might have suspected to be true. (Note how "cosmic" so many love letters and love poems are.)

The role of Christianity is to validate, confirm, elaborate and illustrate this insight. Christian revelation did not discover that love is what makes the world go around, but it confirms beyond all possibility of a doubt our hunch that this is so.

Therefore, those who are committed to the Christian belief system realize that their special vocation and mission is to reveal God's passionate love for us. One of the ways we do that, as we observed in the last issue, is to be passionate in our own relationships. Another way we do it is to witness to God's permanent and public love for us by reserving our most intimate loves for those relationships to which we are permanently and publicly committed. This is the way the followers of Jesus of Nazareth live—for religious and "sacramental" reasons rather than for moral or ethical ones.

Of course, one can make excellent ethical, moral, and psychological arguments against promiscuity; but for Christians the decisive argument should be the religious one, that the love of the followers of Jesus of Nazareth is permanent and publicly committed love.

This may be an ideal we do not always achieve; in practice we often fall short of the ideal. We believe that God forgives us for these failings, but we still strive for the ideal. We are conscious of our role as "sacraments" of God's love.

With this in mind as the bottom line, two observations are pertinent:

1. *It often seems that the faithful are less troubled about sexual questions than are church leaders.* (This is an ecumenical, not just a Catholic problem.)

Perhaps the faithful are more realistic about the human condition, more tolerant of human failings, or have a better insight into what God is really concerned about. They may well confess their failures to live up to the sexual ideal, but they seem instinctively to doubt that God will condemn them to hell forever because of such failures.

Perhaps this attitude might be expressed in the terminology of the old moral theology by saying that the faithful seem to sense instinctively that sufficient reflection and full consent of the will are especially hard to come by in matters of human sexuality.

2. *Continental, especially Italian, moral theology makes a distinction which we Americans find somewhat unpalatable between moral theory and practice.* Thus the man who wrote one of the Holy Office's most stringent documents on homosexuality could quite easily say that in terms of pastoral practice, of course, he would counsel homosexuals to stable rather than transient relationships. Similarly, such an approach to moral theology would be tolerant of the human weaknesses which lead so many married people to fall short of the ideal with artificial contraception.

Can the moral ideal by reconciled with sexual practice?

WE Americans tend to be affronted by distinctions between theoretical ideal and pastoral practice. American couples, for example, resent the implication that their decisions about family planning, arrived at after mature consideration of all the circumstances of their marriage, are in fact a failure to meet an ideal and a manifestation of human weakness. Instead of wanting to accept the compassion of pastoral practice, we Americans tend to want to challenge the ideal.

This stylistic difference is extremely important if we wish to understand the Roman attitude toward church doctrine and the American attempt to interpret such doctrine. Americans tend to be very angry at the utter lack of sensitivity displayed in Roman statements on sex, whereas the people that make these statements, and many other Europeans, are baffled by the strong American reaction. The place for compassion and sensitivity, they would say, is not in the theoretical document but in pastoral practice.

American that I am, I do not like this approach to sexual morality at all, and would want to question whether the ideal might be somewhat distorted if it has to be ignored most of the time in pastoral practice.

However, my purpose in these pages is not to wrestle with that argument, but to make the more modest observation that the Catholic church is not really interested in multiplying the number of "mortal" sins with which people can be charged. In practice, all but the most rigorous Roman theologian would be willing to concede that very often there is neither sufficient reflection nor the full consent of the will that are required even in a traditional theology for grievous sin.

Americans and some American moral theologians want to challenge in some cases whether the "matter" is grave or even sinful at all. The Mediterranean approach is to free people from a multiplication of mortal sins not so much by questioning the gravity of the matter as by doubting the reflection and consent component of a moral action.

In both cases the practical conclusion is the same: many, many sexual offenses do not end up as grave sins. In the American approach it is because they are not the kinds of actions that constitute grave sin (birth control and masturbation, for example); in the Mediterranean (and official Catholic) approach, while the act itself may be gravely sinful, human weakness normally excuses it from grave sin either because of insufficient reflection or lack of full consent of the will.

It is not my intention to discuss these differences of opinion at great length, much less to argue. The church officially teaches that all kinds of sexual offenses are grievously sinful.

But neither the Vatican nor the liberal American theologians are prepared to insist that each and every, or even most, human sexual failings are in fact mortal sins (however much the Vatican may want to insist on the theoretical and objective gravity of the act itself before the failings and weaknesses of human nature are considered).

There are also some historical complexities to take into account:

1. Moral theologians in pre-modern Europe seem to have been less concerned about the sinfulness of fornication and masturbation than we are today. No one argued, of course, that they were not sinful; but the gravity of the sinfulness was not thought to be nearly so great as adultery. And some moral theologians were even willing to argue that masturbation was a venial sin.

Similarly, in the 19th century, when France was solving its population explosion through coitus interruptus (and infanticide), the Vatican consistently refused to take any public stance on contraception. Questions submitted to the Holy Office generally met with responses urging that confessors be very cautious and discreet about the subject.

Leo XIII wrote his encyclical on marriage right in the middle of this era and said not a word about contraception. The official policy of the Vatican in the 19th century was not to trouble the consciences of Catholic married people.

I cite these historical facts not to say that previous Vatican policies and previous moral theological thinking were correct and that contemporary ones are wrong, but to illustrate the point that it is something of an exaggeration to contend that there is no change in moral emphasis if not in moral teaching.

2. Until the decree *Tam et Si* of the Council of Trent, the presence of the pastor and two witnesses was not a requirement for the validity of Catholic marriage. So-called "common-law unions" (or their equivalent) were assumed to be valid and were quite numerous.

The requirement for marriage banns and for the presence of a pastor and two witnesses imposed the demands of the new and emerging middle classes which actually made use of marriage as a means of economic aggrandizement (as had royalty and the nobility in previous eras). The Protestant church's prohibitions against "clandestine" union were much sterner than the Catholic restrictions.

I cite this historical fact not because I'm advocating a return to pre-Trent marriage customs or because I am advocating "premarital" sex, but simply to point out that in the past there was a great deal more leniency about defining when a marriage began than there is now.

3. It is very difficult to sort out religious and moral considerations on the one hand from property considerations on the other when one is trying to understand the development of the norms of marital morality. The "bride price" was paid in part to guarantee the virginity of the bride, so that the husband's family might be certain that its property would truly be handed down to its own off-spring.

Similarly, much of the horror about adultery was also economic. The risk was that off-spring of an adulterous union might claim family inheritance. Since the family has long ceased to be primarily an institution for passing out property, these concerns are no longer valid.

One can, of course, present a powerful case for chastity on religious and ethical grounds quite independent of the contractual and hereditary grounds of the past. The problem, however, is that the case has not yet been developed as effectively as it might, both in the church's teaching and in popular attitudes. The residues of financial/legalistic approaches still survive in marital thinking as well as religious instruction.

All the above observations are by way of creating a context in which I can assert that things are much more complex than they often seemed in our high school instruction classes.

A person who tries to decide what he or she "may" do and how to evaluate what he or she has done, doesn't have an easy time of it, especially from the ethical, or moral/theological viewpoint. Even if one attends primarily to the religious dimension—the selflessness and sacramentality of human sexuality—decisions must still be made in difficult, concrete circumstances in which it is not always clear what either selflessness or sacramentality might mean.

It is true of all human behavior, but especially true of sexual behavior, that we make our existential decisions in fear and trembling, knowing full well how easy it is to be wrong, though confident that God will forgive our mistakes even if they remain with us for the rest of our lives.

Let me emphasize here that I personally believe in chastity, not merely for religious reasons but also for social science reasons. Promiscuity is not only wrong and non-Catholic, it doesn't work. However, it is difficult sometimes in concrete circumstances to know what is chaste and what isn't, and God is on record as demanding effort rather than success and remains willing and eager to forgive failure.

I do not propose to turn these pages into a moral theology discussion, especially since, at present, moral theologians seem to be badly confused on sexual subjects.

Is current moral theology reasonable?

I DO not believe that the approach of moral theology is the most helpful one in our own era. A few points need to be noted in passing, however:

1. The church now subscribes to the perfectly reasonable notion that many people who get married lack the psychological maturity necessary for contracting a *sacramental union,* which does not mean, of course, that the union was not civilly valid. Hence the church is now often ready to declare that such marriages were not in fact sacraments and the parties are free to marry again.

2. While no Catholic teacher will approve of abor-

tion, the issue of when the life of a human person begins is not yet settled. Doubtless there is human life from the first moment of conception, but for at least the first 14 days, one could not argue that there was a human soul or person present, because twinning can take place during these first two weeks of pregnancy, and one can hardly suppose that the person and the soul are divided and can become two persons and two souls.

3. Finally, the church still does not condone homosexuality (and is not likely to do so), but there has been enormous growth in tolerance for, and sympathy toward, homosexuals. Here especially the Vatican theory/practice solution seems to be applicable.

What obligations (rarely noticed) flow from the bottom line Catholic view of sexuality?

WHILE there is a tragic dimension to human life and a tragic dimension to human intimacy which many of the cheerful pop psychologists of our day ignore, sex was still intended to be joyous for humankind. Those who hate, despise, fear, or only grudgingly acknowledge their human sexuality are puritans in the sense of Bruce Marshall's famous old definition: "They think the Almighty made an artistic mistake in ordaining the mechanics of procreation."

The joy of human sexuality has to be personal; that is to say, it must both contribute to and flow from a joyful personality. Such a thorough and joyless approach as *The Joy of Sex* series illustrates that when sexual fulfillment is divorced from the rest of human life, it is inevitably joyless. On the other hand, too many who claim to be Christians seem unwilling to admit that God intended us to enjoy our sexuality and to celebrate it, not to run from it.

Sexuality permeates all human relationships, because all human relationships involve our bodies and our bodies are sexual in every cell. The sexual dimension of most of our relationships is not genital. We do not sleep with our friends or most of those we love, but the capacity for openness and the ability to develop friendships is a consequence of our specifically human sexuality and not something that existed before it or independently of it.

Despite all the nonsense that has been spoken about the "third way" and other such immaturities in the last 15 years, one must finally acknowledge that there are powerful sexual attractions in the world. These attractions are both enjoyable and potentially dangerous, and they are not necessarily limited to the attractions between marriage partners.

The mature and Christian way to respond to this fact is to recognize that it is part of the complexity, adventure, romance, and danger of the world in which we live. We cannot circumscribe our relationships by a few simple rules. In the lives of all of us there will be a number of intense and powerful relationships in varying degrees of appropriateness, importance, and security. The wise person neither runs from these relationships nor heedlessly and thoughtlessly indulges in them.

There is little to choose from between prudery and promiscuity, between infidelity and frigidity, between bland sexual optimism and grim sexual pessimism.

A woman who is faithful to her husband or the man who is faithful to his wife but fails to bring celebration, joy, openness, and sensitivity to their marriage bed may be only marginally better than the faithless spouse.

The person who is caught in a prudish, neurotic shame is at most marginally better than the person with no modesty at all.

Much of our Catholic sexual morality as it has been practically taught has been one-sided. It has warned us, oftentimes quite properly, of the risks of promiscuity, but it has also been willing to accept prudery as a perhaps necessary price to pay for quelling promiscuity.

In the future it is to be hoped that we will turn to the bottom line and realize that our sexuality is for others and that it is sacramental. Perhaps then we can stress the positive obligation to grow in the skills of sexual self-giving as well as avoiding the sins to which our passions sometimes lead us.

Chapter Eleven

Prayer

Why do we feel compelled to pray?

MORE Americans pray than are certain God exists; more Americans pray every week than believe in life after death; more Americans pray every day than go to church on Sunday.

Americans pray more often than they have sexual intercourse, and frequent prayer correlates with mental health (while frequent sexual intercourse does not). Half the nation prays every day, one-quarter prays more than once a day, four-fifths prays every week, and 95 percent pray at least once a year.

The church need not impose on its membership any particular obligation to pray. The challenge for it, rather, is to explain to people why they want to pray, why they like to pray, why they cannot escape praying.

One of my social science colleagues remarked that he had prayed more when his infant son was sick than he had the other "42 misspent years" of his life, and he had prayed for his son even though he was rather sure there was no God listening. Why had he prayed? Because it has seemed the natural thing to do, the only thing to do.

Prayer, then, is not so much an obligation to be imposed as a mystery to be understood.

Frequent prayer correlates with psychological well-being, with marital satisfaction, and even with sexual fulfillment in marriage. As a matter of fact, among young Catholic couples under thirty in which both spouses pray every day, the likelihood of each person in the marriage saying the sexual fulfillment in their marriage is "excellent" is twice as high as it is among other couples (44 percent versus 22 percent). Interestingly enough, the kind of prayer that correlates with psychological well-being and marital fulfillment is a prayer of gratitude. Those who respond to God's love also respond to their human lover, it would seem.

Prayer is a result of our contingency, the fact that we are beings who exist but did not always exist and who will, at least as far as earthly life goes, one day cease to exist. We *are,* but we didn't have to be, and at almost any time we may cease to be. We are beings standing precariously on the edge of nonbeing.

Prayer is the acknowledgment of our existence on the edge and the plea, however confused, that we not be permitted to slip off the edge. Contingency, however, is not by itself a sufficient explanation of prayer. There would be no point in praying unless we did not intuit, somehow, some way, that there was goodness to which to pray.

Are hope and prayer linked together?

WE pray because we hope, and just as hope is practically inevitable, indeed perhaps even a biological given, so prayer is an almost irresistible reaction to hopefulness. Because we are contingent, we will someday cease to be, for our hope tells us that our being is not purposeless, so we respond by praying.

We live in a world of absurdity, but occasionally in the midst of that absurdity there is goodness which regenerates our hope, and so we pray—sometimes almost despite ourselves when we think there is no one listening to our prayers, sometimes, like my social science friend, despite the explicit conviction that no one is listening. Of course, there is still a possibility that the goodness we intuit and which reinforces and strengthens our hope may actually be responsive.

Minimally, praying does no harm and may possibly do some good. Nothing can be lost by praying. The inclination to pray is powerful. As one of my agnostic friends said, "I address my prayers 'to whom it may concern' because occasionally I think it's possible there might be someone who is concerned."

Only when we completely eradicate our hope can we completely eliminate from our lives the propensity to pray. My colleague praying for his son had powerfully experienced hope in his marriage and his fatherhood. Joy, peace, contentment, happiness were surprising and unexpected gifts after a life which was not misspent but certainly not very happy.

Then it appeared that he would lose part of that happiness. The mixture of goodness with contingence, the contingency which revealed goodness, was too much for him. He prayed, perhaps "to whom it may concern," perhaps to no one at all, perhaps simply to the goodness from which his wife and son had come.

I did not push the issue with him. The fact that I call the goodness to which he prayed "God" and that he was unable to use the name will finally, I think, be less important than that neither of us, indeed none of us in the world, can escape the fact that goodness keeps intruding in our lives and demanding some kind of response.

Why is prayer essential?

IN the rush of excitement after the end of the Second Vatican Council, as some Catholic teachers and thinkers rediscovered the "secular world," there was a tendency to minimize the importance of prayer. One could hear it said that prayer was social action, or prayer was conversation with one's friends, or prayer was doing one's daily work, or prayer was loving one's family.

While all those things are doubtless admirable Christian activities, they are not quite the same as prayer. If prayer means everything, then prayer means nothing. As in the case of so many other fashions and fads which swept through the church after the Council, some Catholics were busy abandoning prayer (some even announced in public they "got nothing out of it"), while a considerable number of secularists and agnostics were rediscovering prayer.

Zen, Yoga, Transcendental Meditation swept the country just at the time some Catholics were loudly proclaiming they didn't have to pray anymore, or that they got nothing out of prayer, or that conversing with friends was prayer. Their mistake was to view prayer as an optional exercise or even as an obligation that may or may not be honored. They failed to comprehend that for humankind prayer is virtually a necessity. As Henri de Lubac once put it, humankind is most fully human when the light of the divinity is reflected in a face upturned in prayer.

There are two reasons why this is so. The praying person acknowledges his or her own dependence, his or her own finitude, his or her own limitations, his or her own mortality. We don't want to admit that we are mortal and finite, yet it is good for us to do so. Any other attitude is unrealistic and, indeed, sinful in the strict sense of the meaning of original sin that we discussed in an earlier chapter.

The proud, aloof, defiant person who denies or rages against his or her own mortality may think that he or she is strong, but it is the strength of one who whistles in the dark while walking past a graveyard. It is a spurious strength rooted in fear. On our knees, physically or psychologically, we accept the realities of the universe and try to work out our salvation, whatever it may be, within the constraints reality imposes.

There is much more dignity in being a realist than an escapist, much more honor in accepting our limitations than in defying them, much more grace in acknowledging our weakness than in trying to cover it up with hollow defiance.

But there is more to be said than the acknowledgment and acceptance of our finitude. The praying person also realizes, if he permits himself to do so, his own lovability. To pray is to concede finitude but also to assume that the one to whom we pray cares. A minor bit of cosmic dust we may be, but when we pray we assume that whatever power is responsible cares enough about us to listen to what we say.

What is the most perfect prayer?

WE pray because we have received a faint hint that we are lovable and like a man who cannot believe a beautiful woman loves him (and vice versa), we respond eagerly to that hint, hoping against hope that it is true. In our response we discover a second hint that we may be even more lovable than we had thought. Given half a chance it becomes a self-fulfilling prophecy.

The Catholic Christian tradition has always believed that the most important kind of prayer is the prayer of gratitude. Thus, the official Catholic worship is called the "Eucharist," which is the Greek word for thanksgiving. Jesus deliberately chose the "grace after meal" during the Last Supper to offer himself through bread and wine as food and drink for all Christians, because it is most appropriate that the official public prayer of his followers be a prayer of gratitude.

The empirical research my colleagues and I have done confirms the age-old Christian tradition that prayers of gratitude are the most important, for the relationship between prayer and mental health and marital satisfaction seems to be true only for those whose frequent prayers are prayers of thanksgiving. Prayer brings psychological peace and personal happiness precisely insofar as it becomes a grateful response to a gift of love that is perceived as having already been given.

If we were to pray only one kind of prayer, it ought to be one of gratitude. When our prayer life has little gratitude in it, then there is something profoundly wrong with it. That the mass is called "Eucharist" is not accidental or extrinsic. Public worship in the church is gratitude precisely because gratitude is prayer par excellence.

The best kind of prayer, the most perfect prayer, the essential prayer is, in some sense, the only prayer. Here the empirical evidence once again sustains the age-old tradition: the most effective kind of prayer is a prayer of gratitude.

Prayers of adoration—or of worship—are closely akin to prayers of thanksgiving. The distinction made in some of our catechism classes between prayers of adoration and prayers of thanksgiving is largely verbal. "Adoration," come to think of it, is a poor word, for adoration is really nothing more than love addressed to God. If one views the prayer of adoration as a prayer of love, then it is a prayer in response to love and hence quite indistinguishable from gratitude.

Similarly, a prayer of contrition, or of sorrow for sin, is nothing more than love seeking reconciliation, love apologizing for its weakness, love healing wounds, love transcending guilt. Indeed in a prayer of contrition we are in effect expressing gratitude for the fact that reconciliation is possible and asserting that attempts at reconciliation will be accepted.

Adoration and contrition are merely different forms of gratitude, different ways of acknowledging our hopeless dependence, but also realizing that it is a dependence that throws us trustingly into the arms of enormously powerful love.

Are prayers of petition appropriate?

THERE is nothing wrong with prayers of petition, which are probably the most frequent of all human prayers. In petition, of course, there is a strain of gratitude, because we are implicitly acknowledging the goodness of being in a situation where there is a superior power who cares enough about us to listen to our petition.

Some people think there is something second-rate or inferior about prayers of petition, that they represent a kind of inappropriate selfishness, that those who are truly brave, truly believing Christians would not engage in asking things of God who knows what we need already and does not need to be reminded. Praying for others might be appropriate, but, according to these folks, there is something disgraceful about praying for ourselves. It is tolerable, perhaps, but a sign of weakness.

Yet the prayer of petition springs spontaneously to our lips. Anyone who prays at all can't help asking for help. While one might have reason for being uneasy about a prayer life that is entirely made up of petitions, it is still true that such a prayer acknowledges the two fundamental realities upon which prayer is based, dependence and lovability.

One should not feel guilty about asking for things. No lover is ever offended by hearing the requests of his/her beloved. Surely God, above all lovers, can hardly be hurt when we pray, "this day, for our daily bread."

Does God need our prayers?

DOES he need to be told what we need? Does he need to listen to our sorrow? Does he need to hear about our puny, paltry, hesitant human love?

Our first impulse in answering these questions is to say, "Of course, God doesn't need human prayer." We may need to pray; it is a good thing for us to express that need, to experience in the act of praying both our dependency and our lovability. It is psychologically healthy for us to pray.

The existential obligation to pray, which is rooted in our personalities, comes not from anything that God wants or needs but rather from something we have to have. We pray, such an argument would contend, because of our own need to pray, not because God needs to hear our prayers.

There is something a bit suspicious about this position, though it does sound theologically unassailable. What kind of love is it that doesn't need to hear expressions of love in return? And what is the point in our expressing our love if it is finally a matter of indifference to a divine listener whether he hears such expressions or not.

If our lover is so perfect that he or she is really quite unaffected by our expressions of love, are we not going through an empty act which may be psychologically useful but doesn't make much difference in terms of its impact on the Other?

God's love, admittedly, is different from human love, but it is not totally different. It is rather both different and similar. One is permitted to wonder whether it can be different in such an important dimension and still have any parallel or similarity with human love.

Maybe our Aristotelian philosophy—useful to Christianity in so many ways—has gotten us into a rather intolerable bind on the subject of prayer. Do we really want to accept that all our expressoins of affection and gratitude to God are due for his "extrinsic honor and glory?" Is there not something more that can be said?

To reconcile Scripture and our philosophical tradition, it seems to me that we absolutely have to say that if perhaps God doesn't need our love, he at least wants it, and he wants it passionately. Presumably, being God, he can do without it, but since he is also a lover, like any lover he wants a response. Of course, we cannot even begin to guess what "wanting" means for God.

I must confess that I am not altogether satisfied with such a solution. I cannot understand why it doesn't bother more people than it seems to. If we take seriously the parallel between human love and divine love, if we believe that our human loves are sacraments, that is to say, revelations of God's love, can we really be content with an answer that God's passion for response is relatively bland compared to human passion for a response?

I feel that I would be irresponsible to the purpose of this book if I didn't raise these questions. I am sure that most modern human beings, once they begin to think seriously about God's love and our love, are bound to raise them.

By way of answer to the question, I want to suggest that perhaps we ought to shift the location of the mystery—though let it be clear that I am here engaging in highly speculative personal opinion (something I do not ordinarily do in this book). I do not want to place the inexplicability in the seeming contradiction between God's immutability and the demand for a response from us. I would rather place the mystery in God's perfection combined with God's need and say that the inexplicability—for the present, at any rate—is how God's need for a response from us is compatible with his perfection. To put the matter another way, how are God's needs different from our needs?

I think we have a hint of an answer if we analyze the dynamics of human love. A husband may be absolutely and totally convinced of his capacities as a lover and of his wife's responsiveness to these capacities. Yet it remains necessary for her to demonstrate a responsiveness not because he doubts it but because he enjoys it.

Similarly, a woman who is serenely confident of her husband's obsession with her beauty and has very little question about her own attractiveness does not need to be told she is beautiful to believe it, but she certainly enjoys being complimented on her loveliness.

Might it not be possible to cope with the seeming conflict between God's perfection and his demand for our love by saying that God *enjoys* our love? There is certainly nothing selfish or self-centered or imperfect about the enjoyment of love. A husband delighting in his wife's responsiveness, a wife delighting in her husband's compliments are not indulging in insecurity or selfishness; they are rather luxuriating in a perfectly delightful experience of being loved.

Maybe God made us because he or she likes to luxuriate in the perfectly enjoyable experience of being loved. And it is not because he or she needs to so luxuriate but because it is *fun* to do so.

To express personal opinion again, it seems to me that while we can only dimly imagine what it means for God to enjoy, nevertheless when we phrase the question this way, the answer becomes a rather obvious yes. Maybe this is why God created us—because, like any lovable person, he or she enjoys being loved not because he or she needs it but because he or she revels in it.

I acknowledge the awesome inexplicability of it, I still find very attractive the image of a God who revels in the experience of being loved. That image—that "story," to use theologian John Shea's term—makes creation quite understandable.

Would God intervene in human events as a direct response to prayers?

A RELATED question, which I suspect will baffle many Christians who reflect on God's love and our response through prayer, is whether prayer changes the outcome of anything. God knows our needs, he knows what's going to happen, he knows what we are going to do. Granted that it may be good for us to pray, that he might even delight in and revel in our prayer, does prayer make any difference in the outcome of human events?

When I was working with teen-agers it was customary with some of the young women in our parish to start going to communion three months before the junior prom, beseeching the gates of heaven (as we used to say) that they would find someone to take them to the prom. This was a prayer which was almost always heard, if one were to judge by the outcome.

It would be very easy for a purist, a theologian, or a secularist to ridicule such a petition. What does it matter if a sixteen year-old girl can find a prom date? If she does, she will get over the fun of the prom in a rather short period; and if she doesn't, she will get over the pain in a rather short period. There are lots more important things to pray for. Doesn't God have better things to do than to hunt up dates for addled adolescents?

An even more basic issue that is implicit in the question is the issue of Divine Providence. One can be completely committed as a Christian to the notion that God protects us even as he watches over the lillies of the field and the birds of the air. But in what does that protection consist?

Can we expect that God's protection includes his willingness to intervene in the ordinary course of human events, to heal a sick person, to find us a parking place, to get us a job, to help us win a basketball game, to overcome our fears before an examination or a job interview, or even to persuade the boy of our choice to accept a prom invitation.

Again, I must say candidly that while I believe in providence, I am not satisfied with the answers that our contemporary theologians provide to such questions, and I am even less satisfied with the refusal of most of them even to consider it a serious question. Karl Rahner has tried to wrestle with it, and while I have enormous respect for Father Rahner's genius, I must admit that I have no notion of what he is talking about when he tries to explain divine providence.

I cannot quite accept the conviction of some Catholic charismatics that one can at random flip open a page of the Scriptures and find a message that is especially designed by God for the circumstances in which the page-flipper may find himself or herself. On the other hand, I am not prepared to say that a God who loves teen-age girls as much as he or she loves anyone else (and being a person of taste, perhaps a little bit more) would not pay attention to an adolescent girl's attempt to grow in self-possession and self-confidence in her own womanhood.

To put the issue differently, I am not prepared to assert that God intervened in some extraordinary, dramatic, and quasi-miraculous fashion in the election of the two Pope John Pauls, but neither can I believe that the spectacular outcome of the Year of the Three Popes was pure chance.

I am committed, against the charismatics and against the cardinals who thought they heard the Holy Spirit whispering in their ears, to a conviction that God works through secondary causes. I am also committed, however, that God is involved in everything that happens, that our prayers do matter; that a teen-age girl's prayers are heard, that they do have an effect on her life, that they do enhance God's delight in her womanliness.

What is the Bottom Line on prayer?

I THINK everybody who is a Catholic Christian believes that God does care, does protect us, does hear our prayers, and that they do matter. I think they also believe that in the normal course of events God does not work miracles but works through other human beings in the ordinary events of the world.

Might not one say, at least as a beginning, that our prayers matter because in the act of praying we understand ourselves and God better, the persons around us and the world better? More concretely, might not the teen-ager who has prayed for a date know a little bit more about herself and a little bit more about the young man who wouldn't mind being invited to the prom at all? And might not such an insight be a manifestation of both God's caring for his or her beloved and of the ordinary working out of human events?

The bottom line on prayer is that prayer is our response to God's love as we experience it, a response which seems almost to be structured into our personalities, and a response that, however we may cope with its theological difficulties, is utterly convinced that our prayers matter and that God not only wants but even delights in our responding to his or her love.

Chapter Twelve

The Prayer of the Church

What aspect of the mass is most important?

THE bottom line on the mass (and the sacramental system that clusters it) is that the church prays because it is the community of those who endeavor to respond to God's love. The mass is a collective response of love.

The proper, bottom-line question for us, then, is do we believe the mass is more than just a sacrament of sacrifice and memorialization; do we, in the end, believe that it is also a wedding banquet, a love feast, a celebration? I am not denying the importance of the sacrificial and memorial aspects of the Eucharist; I am stating that to fixate so intensely on those aspects—which tend to be residual controversies that are less pertinent in our day than they were in earlier times—and to ignore the wedding banquet, love feast, and celebratory aspects of the church's public liturgy, is to miss the point completely.

The church's public prayer, the mass, is a celebration of love. That is definitively and irrevocably the bottom line.

We eat with those we love, and we love those with whom we eat. These two truths are psychological givens of the human condition. The meal is a time of vulnerability.

Our enjoyment of the taste of the food and drink and our necessity of focusing our attention away from daily concerns make us especially vulnerable at mealtime. We tend to relax partly because the food and drink make us relax, but also partly because the sheer mechanics and dynamics of eating require some relaxation from holding the gun, pounding the typewriter, or grabbing a telephone.

Therefore, whenever possible, we choose to share these interludes of vulnerability with those we love and who love us. In such moments we have both greater capacity for love and greater need to receive love. Eating alone is no fun, and while eating with our family can result in chaos, and sometimes angry chaos, we still believe that family-meals ought to be times of love and affection. Sometimes, in fact, they are just that.

Why is the meal a natural means of celebrating God's presence?

WE celebrate the great events of our lives with dinners. We court those whom we hope to influence over meals, be they client, patron, or possibly lover. The relaxed, casual, vulnerable ambiance of the common meal seems to be the ideal place to influence another.

It is also true that there is a tendency for us to become open and friendly with those with whom we eat. The people who sit at the table with us in strange circumstances (the high school cafeteria, the new job, the service, college) are those who are most likely, in such novel situations, to be our friends.

By the very fact that we are destined to sit across the table from one another for a while, both we and the other persons have fairly strong motivation for breaking through the barriers of formality, rigidity, defensiveness and resentment to establish some sort of tranquility and even intimacy over our meal. This becomes especially easy because there seems to be something in the physiological and psychological reaction to a meal which opens up the human personality and makes it more prone to sharing, to friendliness, to vulnerability.

We may end up not liking those who sit at the same table with us, but there still seems to be a powerful propensity in human social situations to at least attempt to have good relations with those who, for one reason or another, are sharing a meal with us, even though we have not chosen them freely. We tend, though not irrevocably and not irresistibly, to establish close relationships with those we eat with, and we tend to eat with those we have established close relationships with.

The sacred meal, then, is surely not a Christian innovation and is a common phenomenon, if not a given, in human religions. Equally common is the conviction that whenever the devotees of a deity assemble around the table to eat a sacred meal in honor of the deity, that deity, somehow or other, becomes present at the table with them. The human conviction seems to be that in such interludes of affection and vulnerability the deity ought to be present and might even want to be present.

The Eucharist as Real Presence is rooted solidly both in human psychology and in the great historical tradition of human religions.

It would appear that much of the teaching of Jesus was "table talk," relaxed, affectionate conversation with his apostles and other followers as they reclined about the table at dinner. The Last Supper was but one of many such sessions, and when the early Christians began once more to eat the Lord's Supper, they were retaining a tradition that was not begun on Holy Thursday but was already thoroughly established by then (though no claim, obviously, can be made that these previous fellowship meals were "Eucharists").

The earliest Christian assemblies, then, were fellowship meals with Jesus, the same Jesus who had once visibly participated in such meals and who would return to participate in them again. As time went on, other purposes and legitimate meanings would be found for the Eucharist assembly: it was a sacrifice in which the Calvary victim was again offered to the heavenly Father, and it was the sacrament in which Jesus really and truly was present under the appearances of bread and wine.

Both the sacramental and sacrificial dimensions of the Eucharist are important, though the religious and theological controversies which have been fought through the centuries over these dimensions should not obscure the bottom line on the Eucharist: the Eucharist assembly is a fellowship meal, a love banquet, of the followers of Jesus in which they celebrate their union and love with him and, through him, with the heavenly Father, and also their union and love one with the other. If we do not have this most fundamental and most basic truth about the Eucharist assembly clearly in our minds, then we are not fully able to understand the meaning of the Eucharist as Sacrifice and Sacrament, because we have not been able to place it in its proper context.

What do we mean when we speak of the Eucharist as sacrament and sacrifice?

UNFORTUNATELY, in much of our teaching over the years the "memorial" and "love feast" context of the Eucharist gets lost. We worry about age-old controversies on sacrament and sacrifice, controversies which have less meaning now than they once did. These controversies, argued over in arid theology books, seem to overlook completely the most obvious aspect of the Eucharist as sign. It is, after all, a meal in which food and drink are consumed—a sacrificial meal, a sacramental meal indeed, but primarily a meal.

When we speak of the Eucharist as Sacrifice, we must keep in mind all the things that were said in the chapter on salvation.

In the Eucharist as Sacrifice we are not "paying off" God with the blood of Jesus, nor are we atoning, with the broken body of Jesus, for our own sins, as though God were a banker trying to balance our sins in one column against the suffering of Jesus in the other. We are offering again the life and death of the servant of Yahweh who responded to God's love with totally committed and utterly dedicated love of his own, a love that did not falter in its confidence and hope even in the face of death, a love which death could not smother.

We offer to the heavenly Father the loving response of Jesus and our own faltering, loving response along with his, precisely to show that we believe he has made us an offer of love, and that it is possible for us to overcome our fears, our weaknesses, our sinfulness and respond with dedication and commitment by walking the same path that Jesus walked by imitating, however poorly, the dedication and commitment of his response.

Similarly, when we say that Jesus is really and truly present at mass and under the appearance of bread and wine after mass is over, we are asserting that Jesus is present as the crucified and risen one indeed, but also as the one who showed the way in love and who invited us to come down the way after him. It is Jesus' presence as sacrament of God's love, both renewing the invitation to love and demonstrating how one responds to the invitation.

Both sacrifice and sacrament themes of the Eucharist, in other words, are most usefully understood within the context of the Eucharist as a memorial banquet and a love feast, an assembly of those who are, with the help of Jesus, trying to respond to the love that the heavenly Father has offered us.

Is the fact of Jesus' presence in the Eucharist more important than the how?

THIS is not the appropriate place for a description of the long controversy over the Real Presence. From the very beginning, Christians believed that Jesus was present in the bread and wine, though many different explanations for the nature of his presence have been offered through the course of history as philosophical and theological tools have changed.

Catholic Christians believed, for instance, that the word "transubstantiation" adequately conveyed the nature of the presence of Jesus under the appearances of bread and wine. However, this word does not limit us to the Aristotelian philosophical framework which produced it. The question of how Jesus is present is not an unimportant one, though it remains doubtful that we will ever have a philosophical explanation of the Real Presence that is completely satisfying.

However, we utterly miss the point of the Eucharist by becoming so obsessed with the philosophical and theological arguments about the "how" of the Real Presence that we pay little attention to the fact of it, much less to the fact of the Eucharist's proper context as a love banquet. One may advance brilliant arguments about the precise mode of transubstantiation and yet profit very little if, in the process, one doesn't pay much attention to the fact that Jesus is present in the Eucharist as a lover who wants to be with us in love, who renews the heavenly Father's offer of love, and who demonstrates it by his life, death, and resurrection. How Jesus responded to that love has transformed human consciousness and the whole objective reality of the human condition.

The Eucharist, then, is a love feast precisely because it reenacts the drama of our salvation, a drama in which we are free of the bonds which imprison us and reconcile us to God and to our fellow humans. It is, additionally, the principal channel by which God's grace—God's love —is revealed to us and communicated to us.

In the Eucharist we are freed and we are reconciled because we gather together around the table with our fellow followers of Jesus, and together publicly commit ourselves to receiving God's love and responding to it. We offer the life and death of Jesus and our own lives and deaths, and then receive back in Holy Communion the risen savior as a pledge and a promise of our own resurrection. The Eucharist summarizes, enacts, and applies the salvation that Jesus reveals to us and earns for us.

All of this, mind you, is accomplished in what is essentially, fundamentally a warm and affectionate family dinner. If we accept the bottom line that the Eucharist is a dinner with Jesus, then all the other truths about the Eucharist follow naturally enough. It is worth observing that to believe that the church's public worship is indeed the Lord's Supper, a love feast with Jesus and his friends, a marriage banquet celebrating the love of God for his people is a much more challenging belief than the doctrine of the Real Presence.

One misses the point entirely if one gets hung up on the theological explanation of the Real Presence (an important enough issue by itself, surely) and overlooks the challenge to our fears, our timidities, our anxieties, our defensiveness that the picture of the Eucharist as a love feast with Jesus represents. To put the matter somewhat differently, it is much harder to believe that a fellowship dinner with God is possible than to believe that Jesus is present under the appearances of bread and wine.

If God really loves us so much that he wishes to share a meal with us, then the Real Presence becomes something of a "pushover" task for him. The real challenge of the Eucharist is its challenge as a ritual reenactment and representation of God's saving love. To miss that point, to fixate on lesser issues, is to fail to understand the Eucharist and to avoid the bottom line for intermediate lines.

What do we (or should we) experience in the liturgy?

IN the early church the Lord's Supper was merged with a scripture service which was the ordinary worship ceremony of the Jewish synagogue. The first part of the combined liturgies is now known as the "liturgy of the Word" (in the old days it was called the mass of the Catechumens, because those who were under instruction had to leave at its end). In the second part, the festival meal is called "the liturgy of the Eucharist."

In both parts of the mass we experience the loving salvation of Jesus. In the first three (or two) scripture readings and the homily, and through the reenactment of the Lord's Supper, we respond to our reexperiencing salvation with the Prayer of the church after the homily and the Lord's Prayer and the reception of Communion after the liturgy of the Eucharist. Both liturgies, then, have a descending and ascending movement; they are both dialogues, colloquies, loving exchanges of gifts and affectionate intimacy between God and his people, with Jesus, as it were, an intermediary.

In the old pre-Vatican II mass the love feast dimension of the Eucharist was not particularly clear. Indeed, nothing was particularly clear unless one knew a lot of Latin and a lot of theology.

In the new liturgy, however, at least when it is done properly, the love feast context of the liturgy is clear (though I have often thought that we should give consideration to taking out the pews and putting dining room tables in the church instead). Home liturgies done around the family dining room table are often much more effective signs of the Eucharist as a love feast than the big Sunday morning masses, which seem poorly designed to reflect the wedding banquet nature of the Eucharist.

On any Sunday morning the congregration has to exercise more than a little imagination to recall the symbolism of what is occurring—the brothers and the sisters of the community of the followers of Jesus have come together to eat a meal with him and so, together with him, respond to God's love and attain the nourishment they need to go forth from the church into their separate lives and witness by what they say, what they do, and who they are to the liberation and reconciliation they have experienced as renewed once again in the Eucharistic community.

The act of the imagination doesn't have to be quite as spectacular as it used to be before the Vatican II liturgical reform, but we must still strive to remind ourselves that the human event which is the closest to what goes on in church on Sunday is the family dinner in which those who love one another come together to enjoy each other's company and to renew their love.

As with so many other church symbols, there is a two-way influence. Human love dinners reveal to us that the Eucharist strengthens us so that our family, friendship, and love meals may be deeper, richer, and more powerful.

It is something of an understatement to say that the Eucharist is the church's public worship. It is surely that, of course; but it is more than that: it is the church's reason for being, a synopsis of what the church is for and what it is supposed to do. It is the essence of the church; it reveals the church in action, serving its essential mission of supporting our response in love to a gift of love God has given us in Jesus.

Many of the Catholic laity seems to have grasped this point: they insist on good liturgy almost as much as they desire good sermons, and are skeptical of a parish where the liturgy is not done which care, elegance, reverence, and power. Perhaps one of the greatest successes of the Second Vatican Council was its impact on the liturgical sensitivities of the laity. Indeed, it may be that the liturgical reformers prepared the way for the Second Vatican Council, underestimating what would happen. For not only have the laity been won over to participation in the liturgy, many of them also seem to clearly understand what the liturgy is and why it is important for it to be done well.

But neither understanding nor excellence of liturgical action is enough. That which is enacted in the liturgy must be lived in life. Those of us who, through liberation and reconciliation, are renewed at mass must go forth to live lives in which our sense of freedom and community is revealed to others.

The mass is an experience of religious renewal not merely because it is a beautiful ceremony and not merely because it is a spiritual oasis at the start of the week, but rather because it is a public experience of grace, a public event in which we are reminded once again that we have been saved, we have been freed, we have been reconciled, and it is all right to risk ourselves in love because God loves us. If participation in the church's public worship does not have that impact on us, then it has not been a successful experience.

We come to the liturgy with our failure of the previous week; we renew our faith in God's love and try to improve our life in the week ahead, simply because in the liturgy we experience once again the fact that God loves us.

Are we "obliged" to attend mass?

FOR almost a thousand years there was no strict requirement for church attendance. The Council of Lateran imposed the obligation because at that time it seemed to be the only way to educate the barbarian converts the church had made who had never experienced the mass as a normal and natural part of their lives. Obviously, a millenium later, the obligation has been more successful in some countries than in others.

Many historians of moral theology are now prepared to assert that the Lateran Council obligation was not intended to be under pain of serious sin. Quite apart from the sinfulness of missing mass, a sinfulness which seems to disturb Catholics less today than it once did, there is a religious obligation which is more fundamental and critical than any obligation of church law.

If one is a serious believing Christian, one simply should not deprive oneself of the renewing experience of a love feast that re-enacts the fact of our salvation. If the remnants of the legal obligation were removed, it would still be a profound religious obligation to orient ourselves toward God's love and to renew our experience of salvation. The Swiss theologian Hans Küng, who can scarcely be described as reactionary in most things, put it beautifully when he insisted that Sunday worship was a natural and normal part of the Christian life. One participates in it not because it is an obligation but because it is a privilege and a joy.

If the Sunday liturgy in a given parish does not seem to be a joyous privilege, then it is up to the laity of the parish to demand that the priest make it such. The clergy ought to be reminded that they have an obligation in strict justice to their people to enact the liturgy well and to preach effectively during the liturgy of the Word.

How do the other sacraments relate to the Eucharist?

THE other six sacraments are best understood in their relationship to the mass. *Baptism* ordains us to the common priesthood of Jesus and gives us the right to celebrate the liturgy together with the ordained priest, who in the sacrament of *orders* receives, as one chosen from the community, the privilege and the obligation of presiding over the Eucharistic assembly.

The sacrament of *reconciliation* or *penance* re-unites us with the church so as to deepen and intensify our experience of the Eucharist. *Confirmation* provides us with the strength, the inspiration of the Holy Spirit both so that we can understand the events of our salvation more fully and live them more joyously as we go forth from the Eucharistic assembly.

Matrimony commits husband and wife to be sacraments of God's love for one another, for their children, and for all those who come into contact with them during their lives together. The family comes to liturgical assembly to strengthen its own bond and goes forth with faith and hope renewed, so the love between husband and wife, parents and children, may be intensified by what has happened at mass.

Finally, in the sacrament of the *sick,* the Eucharistic community comes together to intercede for its ailing members. Water, fire, oil, bread and wine, sexual love, reconciliation, death-bed support, the selection of community leadership—all are normal, natural, commonplace human events. When they are oriented around the Eucharist, however, they take on added meaning.

Each of these commonplace events, in its own way, reveals to us the life-giving love of the heavenly Father which we experience in the life, death, and resurrection of Jesus, and respond to with our brothers and sisters in Jesus who constitute the church.

The rhythms of the church's year, at Christmas, Epiphany, Lent, Easter, and Pentecost, are also sacramental in that these rhythms are natural, normal, inevitable parts of life. They are used by the church as yet another means to reveal God's saving love. Unfortunately, when they were a part of the daily life of the ordinary citizen in the Middle Ages there was not available the understanding we now have of their implications.

Now that we have a much deeper, richer understanding of the Eucharist and of the Eucharistic year, there is often a discontinuity between its rhythms and those of ordinary life. The Eucharistic year and the secular year are "out of sync," and the Christian must once again exercise his or her imagination—and his or her self-discipline—if he or she is to profit from the symbolism of the Eucharistic year.

What is the bottom line on the Eucharist?

THE bottom line for the Eucharist is the same bottom line that runs through the whole of the Catholic faith. Is one willing to believe in God's love, a love which is revealed and whose saving events are reenacted in a memorial dinner which is also a love feast, a wedding banquet celebrating God's passionate love for his people?

Chapter Thirteen

Faith

How does Christianity differ from any other moral philosophy?

WITH this chapter we turn to a consideration of the Christian life. In the first twelve chapters we have examined some of the basic dimensions of Christian belief, studying, so to speak, various facets of the single jewel of God's love which was revealed to us in Jesus. God's love is an invitation and a challenge.

As I have said repeatedly, Jesus reveals the passion of the heavenly Father's love for us, and by so doing, creates the demand that passionate love always creates, a passionate response. Christian life is basically and fundamentally a loving response to love that has been offered.

I have chosen to organize my description of the Christian life around virtues rather than commandments (as is usually done in catechisms and similar instructional manuals). I have done this for a number of reasons. While a discussion of the virtues will certainly cover the same issues as a discussion of the commandments, the virtues of faith, hope, charity, justice, temperance, fortitude, and prudence describe the Christian life in a positive rather than a negative format.

A loving response is far more than a matter of keeping rules. When two persons love one another, they do not set down rules, but rather challenge each other to growth in the skills and talents of love. The so-called ethical teachings of Jesus were not ethical at all in the sense of the moral philosophies of others like Aristotle and Plato.

Jesus was neither an ethical theorist nor a moral philosopher but a witness to God's love. The life he described in the Sermon of the Mount was not one imposed as a moral obligation, but rather a life of possibility revealed in the dazzling illumination of God's love.

The Catholic church is in the business of highlighting the possibilities of a life of loving response and not, primarily at least, in the business of moral or ethical philosophy. Religion, obviously, cannot be separated from ethics, and the ethical system adopted by Christian teachers during New Testament times is quite similar to the best of the ethical systems of the era.

Yet Christianity goes beyond ethics, beyond obligation, to offer a vision of the possibilities of a joyous and loving life. Ethics do not cease to be important, of course, but Christianity is something more than ethics.

What is faith?

MANY Catholics grew up believing that their faith was little more than a series of rules. Many, even today, become upset when someone tells them that this is not the case. (They manage somehow to miss the fact that St. Paul said it in his epistles.)

There are ethical and moral rules, of course, which the Christian must keep, as must any other human being. Christianity, however, is essentially a revelation of the possibilities of human life, and this goes far beyond rules. If one must choose, in a limited space, a brief series of instructions as to whether to describe the Christian life in a context of negative rules or positive virtues, it is obvious from the examples of Jesus and St. Paul and the other New Testament writers that one must choose virtue.

The first of the traditional virtues, faith, suffers from a problem parallel to the "rule mentality" in that many Catholics were raised to think that "The Faith" was a lengthy series of doctrinal propositions, all of which has to be believed under pain of mortal sin.

Faith in this respect was rather like an admissions test to college—College Boards or a Graduate Record Exam —a series of questions to which you had to give the right answer if you were to be admitted. There was little distinction of what was important among these lists of doctrinal assertions. Obviously, some were more important than others, but if you rejected even the least important (like, say, the existence of angels), you failed the test and could no longer consider yourself a Catholic.

This approach to faith was purely cognitive and intellectual, indeed, hyperintellectual. It was the assent of the mind to certain "revealed truths," many of which were purported to be hard to believe, some which seemed virtually impossible to believe, and all of which had to be believed because they were "mysteries."

It is not my intention to eliminate the cognitive and the intellectual from faith. Faith does involve intellectual assent; but faith is not constituted or defined by intellectual assent. Rather, faith involves the entire human personality. It is not enough as a person of faith to subscribe to certain propositional tenets.

One can be a person of faith and still have difficulties of understanding, and even accepting as they are normally explained, some of the propositional assertions of Catholic Christianity. It is extremely important that one understand the point that faith does not exclude the cognitive or the intellectual; it includes the cognitive, the doctrinal proposition, if you will, but it transcends it.

The faith that we have in God, as revealed in Jesus, is much like the faith of a man and a woman who are in love which each other. It is a faith which both causes and results in implacable, irrevocable commitment. When a man and a woman are united by such commitment, misunderstandings, uncertainties, hesitancies, even anger and conflict can enter into their relationship, but the mutual commitment remains. It may be disturbed, perhaps, on the periphery, but remain unshakable at its core. Faith, like the other six virtues we will discuss, is one facet of the fundamental response of love to Love.

What is the basic New Testament notion of faith?

IN the Old Testament, faith was essentially a religious experience, not merely an adhesion to interesting truths. Faith was an intense reaction to the Word of God, a reaction of obedience, confidence, certainty, and hope.

In the New Testament these notions were taken over and focused on Jesus. To believe was to hear the Word of God, the Word of his gracious and saving love from Jesus Christ, a Word summarized not merely in the teaching of Jesus but especially in his death and resurrection. To believe in him was not to accept speculative propositions but rather to become converted to Jesus, to commit oneself to follow him, to cling to him as the center and basis of all Truth.

Faith in the New Testament, in other words, involved a personal relationship with God in and through Jesus. So it must be for us today. The notion of faith as relational, interpersonal, is not a development "tacked on" to the Christian heritage by existential philosophy or modern psychology. It is at the core of the tradition, based fundamentally as confidence in the power of God.

Remember the story of the fig tree? The day after Jesus cursed it, he and his apostles walked by it again, and Peter said, "Look, Rabbi, the fig free you cursed has withered away." Jesus answered, "Have faith in God. I will tell you that if anyone says to this mountain, 'Get up and throw yourself into the sea,' with no hesitation in his heart, but believing that what he says will happen, it will be done for him. I tell you that for everything you ask and pray for, believe that you have it already and it will be yours."

Jesus was not literally suggesting that one can dispense with excavation, machinery, and hard work when one is trying to build a road through a mountain. He is telling us that God's love is so powerful that the mere moving of a mountain is a minor feat in comparison.

Faith is not so much God's willingness to forgive us or to cover over our sins, as Martin Luther thought (though confidence in forgiveness is certainly part of faith). Faith is, rather, confidence in the enormous, overwhelming, shattering power of God's love, for which no obstacle in the universe, not even death itself, is too great.

This confidence in God's power is based on the revelation of that power in Jesus. As Paul concludes in his epistle to the Romans, his followers now have "the strength to live according to the Good News I preach, in which I proclaim Jesus Christ, the revelation of a mystery kept secret for endless ages. I now proclaim that it must be broadcast everywhere."

Later, in his letter to the Corinthians, Paul said that

he did not come with any show of oratory or philosophy "but simply to tell you what God guaranteed. During my stay with you, the only knowledge I claim to have is about Jesus, and only about him as the crucified Christ. . . . Still we have a wisdom to offer those who have reached maturity. . . . The hidden wisdom of God which we teach in our mysteries is the wisdom that God vested you in glory before the ages began. . . ."

The content of Paul's teaching, then, is not specific doctrines (though he did teach specific doctrines). The great secret, the great wisdom hidden through the ages, is the power, the perseverence, the implacability of God's love.

John, in his account of the Bread of Life sermon of Jesus in the 6th chapter of the gospel, presents Jesus as being as blunt as possible about the meaning of faith. "I am the bread of life. He who comes to me will never be hungry. He who believes in me will never thirst. . . . I tell you . . . everyone who believes has eternal life. I am the bread of life. Your fathers ate the manna in the desert and they are dead. I am the living bread which has come down from heaven. Anyone who eats this bread will live forever, for the bread that I give is my flesh for the life of the world."

While there are Eucharistic overtones in this passage, the scripture commentators agree that at least up to this point in the Bread of Life sermon Jesus is talking not so much of the bread of the Eucharist but rather about the bread of the revelation of God contained in his person.

In effect, Jesus is saying, "I am the bread of life, because I can tell you who God is. Believe in me and you will believe in God." It was a startling, outrageous statement which angered many of those who had walked with Jesus. But note carefully that there are no doctrinal propositions involved. Jesus is demanding a personal relationship of commitment to him because he reveals the Father in heaven.

Jesus is even blunter in the words which St. John attributes to him at the time of the resurrection of Lazarus. We have heard the words many times, and we have taken them for granted, perhaps. Yet we have not comprehended that they are the revelation of the essence of the Christian faith. "I am the resurrection. Anyone who believes in me, though he die, he shall live; and whoever lives and believes in me will never die."

In the Johannine epistle, the tradition of the followers of the beloved disciple continues to be emphatic. "Whoever believes that Jesus is the Christ has been begotten by God (John 1:5-10). Then, later on in the fifth chapter: "We may accept the testimony given as evidence for his son. Anyone who believes in the son of God has this testimony inside him; anyone who will not believe God is making God out to be a liar. . . . This is the testimony: God has given us eternal life, and this life is in his son. Anyone who has the son has life; anyone who does not have the son, does not have life."

How does faith resemble the commitment of man and wife?

ONE may look in vain in the New Testament for doctrinal propositions, much less for "revealed truths" which one must believe "under pain of mortal sin" to be a Catholic. Faith is not, for the New Testament authors, the acceptance of doctrinal propositions; it is rather the commitment of one's life to the person of Jesus precisely because revealed in the person of Jesus is the power and the love and the determination of the Father in heaven.

Obviously one can—indeed one must—deduce certain doctrinal truths from this demanding, total, and implacable commitment of love to another human being. Just as in the love commitment between a man and a woman there are certain intellectual propositions which follow from that commitment. (For example, she is fun to be with, or he is loyal and good, or she understands me like no one ever has before, or he wants out of life what I want out of life.)

However, while no human lover would seriously challenge such cognitive assertions deduced from the experience of love, it would simply not occur to a human lover that such cognitive propositions constituted the commitment or expressed the love or was essential at all times to it.

It may very well be that in a marriage relationship, there are times when the other is not fun to be with, doesn't understand at all. But the commitment still stands, as does the love which it embodies. A woman may say of a man, "Right now the so-and-so is driving me up the wall, because he is so compulsive about his career. It's a pain in the neck to have him around the house. But, of course, I still love him."

A man may say, "Right now the kids drive her so crazy that she doesn't even want to talk to me when I come home at night. But it will pass in time, and I love her as much as I always did."

Similarly, in our love affair with God through Jesus, there may be times in our lives when some of the cognitive propositions that reveal the primal and overwhelming truth that God loves us may be difficult for us to accept. There may be other times when the sufferings, heartaches, and tragedies which God permits in our life make us wonder how he can possibly love us. Neither the uncertainty about some of the propositional deductions nor dissatisfaction with the sufferings that he permits have to be considered a violation of the commitment, a denial of the love, or a loss of faith.

To put the matter somewhat differently, faith that binds a man and woman together is never untroubled (unless it is about to come to an end). There are strains, stresses, conflicts, misunderstandings, and disappointments which coexist with the faith/love which bind a man and woman together. There will be no time in the marriage relationship when the doubts and the troubles are completely gone.

And yet faith/love persists. Indeed, its hard, inner core can be utterly unshaken by the troubles and difficulties.

The research my colleagues and I have done on young Catholics indicates that there is a vigorous rebound of marital happiness somewhere between the eighth and the tenth year of the relationship, a rebound which seems to be the result of the raw, fundamental power of the personal commitment of faith and love building up sufficient strength to turn the tide of difficulties, friction, quarrels, disagreements, and frustrations.

So it is in our love affair with God. The uncertainties, the troubles, yes, even the doubts never go away; but they do not eliminate the loving commitment which is faith. Indeed, with the passage of time faith grows stronger, driving the doubts to the periphery where it holds them at bay.

Just as love affairs go through periods of crisis and decline, ebb and flow, growth and celebration, triumph and tragedy, so does our love affair with God. Faith has its rhythms, its cycles, its ups and downs, its depressions and inflations.

Married lovers, at least after a while, take these cycles in their mutual faith/love for granted (which is not to say that they take each other for granted). They do not dismiss as unimportant the "down" periods, but neither do they think they mean the end of their relationship. Nor do they panic or despair in a self-fulfilling prophecy.

Similarly, we who are involved in a love relationship with Jesus and through him with the heavenly Father could assume that there will be cycles. We should assume that there will be times when it will be easier to believe than at other times, and that there will be periods in our life when the problems and the doubts will be terrible and terrifying.

Yet, when one takes human faith/love as our model for our loving faith in God and in Jesus, one can at least avoid the ludicrousness of saying, "I don't know whether I believe in angels or not, so I guess I've 'lost the faith.'" Or, "I'm not sure I can accept papal infallibility, so I guess I'm no longer a Catholic," or "I don't believe in the divinity of Jesus, so I've clearly lost the faith."

If one is troubled with such doctrinal doubts, the proper response is not to say, "I've lost faith," but to say, "I still have the faith, and I want to figure out what these doctrinal propositions mean so that this particular trouble in my faith/love relationship with Jesus and God will be minimized."

The sensible thing to do is to investigate the meaning of the doctrinal proposition. What does the doctrine of angels reveal to us? What is the precise meaning and context of papal authority? What is the nature of the divinity of Jesus? What explanations and answers and qualifications are possible which, while they may not make my problem go away, will at least enable me to live with it until such time as the present crisis in my faith/ love relationship with God is transcended?

Is it possible to "lose the faith"?

THIS question is similar to asking whether it is possible to fall out of love. There are certain kinds of so-called love which are shallow, transient, superficial. They can end easily, though they may leave their mark upon us.

But once a man and a woman, understanding the full implications, the multitudinous difficulties, the inevitability of friction and tension of the relationship, nevertheless make a definitive commitment to one another (and it may take many years of marriage for such a commitment to emerge), they simply do not fall out of love. There may be crises, times of stress, times of unbearably painful conflict. There may be times when they wish they could fall out of love. But they can no more renounce their relationship than they can stop breathing.

Our faith/love relationship with God is similar. It is very easy for young people who have inherited a set of ceremonies and a series of propositions to réject those ceremonies, and propositions (and ethical demands) as a part of their adolescent and young adult stage of revolt and alienation. If their family conflicts are especially intense, then they may never be able to go beyond alienation and never be able to examine their religious heritage with the maturity and objectivity and the sophistication it and they deserve.

This does not mean they have lost the faith; it means they never really had the faith to begin with, for while they were born into the community of the believers, they never made the commitment of that community their own. It is just as though someone went through a public ceremony of loving commitment to a spouse without ever internalizing that commitment so it is built into the structure of his/her personality.

The faith is lost—at least emotionally—only by those who never found it in the first place. They are to be criticized not so much for infidelity as for the immaturity which thinks it is clever and sophisticated to reject one's religious heritage without bothering to understand it.

But even such immaturity cannot fully escape the impact of faith. To be part of the Christian community as one grows up means that one's imaginative life is affected by the symbols and stories and pictures which will simply not go away. Midnight mass, Easter water, May crownings, first communion will persist in one's creative imagination even when one rejects the community and the doctrine and the love relationship of which these pictures are a manifestation and incarnation. The pictures will continue to haunt the person, just as an inexcusably neglected first love will continue to haunt the lover.

The issue, even for one who has never fully embraced the faith, is not that he/she can stop believing but whether he/she can effectively erase the images which childhood experiences have imprinted on the imagination. Even the alienated young adult must come to terms with the stories and the pictures that lurk in her/his creative imagination. To expect those images can be ignored, suppressed, or minimized forever is merely self-deception and, quite possibly, dangerous self-deception.

Does the commitment of faith involve risk?

MAKE no mistake about it. Faith is a leap in the dark. For a man or a woman to choose to believe in one another despite all the reasons that indicate such a belief is risky and problematic requires an act of will power, courage, and strength. No mathematical models, no computer programs, no strict formula will guarantee that the faith/love commitment is not a horrendous mistake.

One can carefully and rationally examine all the possibilities; one can decide that it is not unreasonable to commit one's body and mind to this other person for the rest of one's life. Yet there is a big difference between such a decision and the commiting words, "I love you, and I will love you always."

The evidence is reasonable, plausible, persuasive, *almost* incontrovertible; yet the man and the woman know how much mystery, how much uncertainty, how much obscurity, and how much risk are involved in their commitment. It is reasonable to commit themselves one to the other, yet the commitment will never have the compelling certitude of the assertion that the square root of 4 is 2.

Similarly, there are lots of excellent reasons to believe that God loves us, and that the love revealed to us in Jesus is the way things really are. Nonetheless, the data are never totally and absolutely incontrovertible. God's love is not a mathematical certainty. Life might be a sham, hope might be a deception, faith might be a trap. There might not, after all, be any love in the universe. We think there is, but there just might not be.

And so, hopeful but not totally convinced, not absolutely certain, we are willing to take the chance. We make our leap to express commitment. We say, "I love you, and I will love you always." Then, only in the act of commitment, are our eyes opened. We see the other person as he/she is with "the eyes of faith," and realize that the act of commiting faith is the only sensible thing to do.

The "eyes of faith," which, of course, are the eyes of love, acquired in our act of leaping in faith, dispel the darkness and enable us to see with brilliant clarity that, yes, our choice is the right one. One can only see all the lovable attributes of a man and a woman after one has begun to love that person.

Love gives insight, understanding, perception, a depth of knowledge that is not possible before there is love. Shallow love may be self-deceptive; mature love is revelatory, because it enables us to catch the nuances, the subtle attributes, the marvelous, barely visible characteristics of our beloved. Faith is not only a response to revelation, it is also an act of revelation itself, because in the act of faith, with the eyes of faith, we see the other with more clarity and depth and certainty than we ever had before.

Faith, then, is not an intellectual assent, although it includes that. It is a leap in the dark, an act of love which in itself turns darkness into light, and like every act of love, it also must be sustained, cultivated, developed, tended, and never taken for granted.

Chapter Fourteen

Hope

Is hopefulness a natural human condition?

HOPE is a given of the human condition. Lionel Tiger, the anthropologist, argues that we may be genetically programmed to hope, biologically doomed to hope. He says that it is precisely those prehominids and proto-hominids with hopeful genes that were most likely to bear children and to live to raise them to adulthood so that their children could have children of their own.

The evolutionary process, he suggests, may have selected on the basis of hope-producing genes. Interestingly enough, while admitting that we must hope, admitting that he himself does hope, Tiger is still convinced that there are no grounds for hope, that our hope is self-deception, an evolutionary trick. His position is that we cannot escape hope, but it is a trick.

Trick or not, it sticks with us. My colleague, William McCready, has shown in his book, *The Ultimate Values of Americans,* that more than 80 percent of Americans respond to tragic situations with optimistic or hopeful answers. Freud said that the unconconscious was utterly convinced of its own immortality. Dream analysts tell us that our dreams are irremediably hopeful.

Death researchers tell us that the final phase of dying is a burst of hope, that people who have had sudden death experiences and lived, report that in the last moment, despair and resignation turn into hope. (G. K. Chesterton once described an incident like this in his own life—long before research in this area began—as ending with the conviction that "life is too important ever to be anything else but life."

Resuscitation research indicates that those who are revived after having apparently died often have had experiences of enormous hope, and are never again afraid of dying. Intense, mystical, ecstatic experiences seem to be essentially enormous outbursts of hope; and the ecstatic, describing the experience, says, "I know that everything will be *all right*."

Few would deny the apparently incurable human propensity to hope, even when the situation seems utterly hopeless. The critical religious question—maybe the only religious question—is whether hope is to be trusted, or whether Lionel Tiger is right, that hope is a trick from which we cannot escape. The religious question is whether hope is sacrament, revelation, explanation.

Frequently there does not seem to be any specific object of our hopefulness. A person dying of cancer still seems to hope even when he or she rejects explicitly the possibility of life after death. Those who do not believe in resurrection or survival still hope, although they are unable to specify what they are hoping for.

However, the same thing may also be true of the rest of us. We may say we believe in life after death or resurrection, but those words are, if anything, weaker than the enormous driving power of hopefulness.

Does Jesus validate our hope?

THE mystic, who is inarticulate after an ecstatic experience, says that things are "all right," describes the raw, undifferentiated but enormous human energy that is hope. It is a description of the unshatterable human conviction that "tomorrow will be different" no matter what today was like, even if it were to be the last day of our life.

So, humankind did not need Jesus of Nazareth to tell it of hope. Jesus did not reveal to us for the first time a human emotion we had hitherto been unfamiliar with. Rather he confirmed and validated our hope. He gave us solid, explicit reasons to reinforce our hope. He said there were grounds for hope because the heavenly Father loved us and because he, the one most intimate with the Father, was a message, a symbol, an incarnation of the love which brings hope.

Jesus promised us far more than resurrection or life after death, though these were part of the promise, of course. He promised us the reason why we would survive death, the reason why there would be resurrection, the reason why everything would be "all right," the reason why tomorrow would be different.

Jesus revealed to us God's love, the ground of all our hope, the reality in the world beyond our personality which corresponds to and is both the cause and the object of our unforfeitable hope. The parables of Jesus, the epistles of Paul, are essentially messages of hope. As theologian John Shea says, they are "stories" of hope.

The wedding banquet, which is an eschatological banquet, is a story of hope; the Parousia, of which Paul speaks, when the Lord Jesus returns and makes all "right", is a story of hope. Those stories should not be taken in rigid, literal terms. They are stories which articulate, resonate, re-present, and revalidate our hopefulness.

The work which God the Father began in Jesus will be brought to its fulfillment. We will sit at the messianic feast. How and when this will be is utterly beyond our understanding. The purpose of the stories of hope in the New Testament is not to provide the details of how God will accomplish all, but rather the guarantee that he will, to assure us that the hope which we can't extricate from the depths of our being is indeed valid.

Should our hope be placed only in the hereafter?

INTERMITTANTLY in the course of Christianity, people have announced the advent of the end of the world or the beginning of "the millennium," the thousand years which they anticipate will constitute a rule of God and Jesus and the saints here on earth. Invariably these predictions have been wrong because the predictor misunderstood the stories, confusing literary details with substance.

Still, the predictions continue. The year 1,000 was marked by an enormous outburst of such stories. It seems safe to predict that the year 2,000 will see them too. We all know people today who claim to be able to read the signs that the end of the world is at hand. It cannot be said too often that these predictors utterly and completely miss the point of the stories. For all the Parousia stories in the scriptures have but one point: to guarantee the validity of our hope.

It would also be a mistake to confuse our hopefulness completely with eschatology, as though both the grounds for our hope and the object of our hope could be found in some world to come. The grounds for our hope is God's love revealed to us here and now. While the complete fulfillment of our hope will be in the world of the Parousia, the world of the resurrection—both the raw, human emotion of hope and the Christian story of hope—is by no means limited to the hereafter.

We hope for here and now, we hope for what will happen later today, we hope for tomorrow. Hope is far too powerful to be contained or specified by one time, one place, one goal. We hope that tomorrow will be different, in some way better; and because we hope that, we are able to live for today.

Those who deal with terminally ill patients assure us that the secret of aiding them is to help them live for each day, to enjoy whatever goodness that day will bring and to expect more goodness tomorrow, leaving the evils yet to come for when they do come. While the ultimate goal of Christian hope is resurrection, it is precisely because we believe in resurrection that we can also hope for tomorrow, the day after tomorrow, and even this afternoon.

The love which brings the resurrection also brings tomorrow and the day after and all the good things those times may contain, good things which reveal a goodness far more powerful than the evil which may also lurk this afternoon, tomorrow or the day after. Quite simply, hope means that we think good is a little bit stronger than evil, perhaps a lot stronger.

How is Christian hope fulfilled?

GOODNESS is revealed in Jesus, goodness will take care of us forever; everything will be all right. It is therefore safe to hope. Hope, indeed, we must; but, contrary to Professor Tiger, hope is not a trick, it is a hint of an explanation. It is safe to hope.

Precisely because Christian hopefulness, while grounded in the resurrection, is not limited to it, the Christian is not someone who runs away from the problems of this world. He or she is not a complete eschatologue. The Christian hopes for better in this world if not for perfection. Therefore this hope, which is rooted in the resurrection, also points toward efforts to promote the triumph of good over evil in this world, to make the world a more human, a more just, a more civilized, a more harmonious place.

Christians know that earthly paradise will never satisfy human longings, but they also know that human hope drives them, if not toward an earthly paradise, at least toward an improvement of the human condition. The Parousia is something that is not of this world, but it is also a vision of the possibility of love and trust, peace and harmony, toward which people of unbounded hope must strive in this world, too.

Christians know that they will not achieve the perfection of their hopefulness, but they also know that the effort is a response to hope, indeed, an inevitable consequence of taking hopefulness seriously.

Some Christians are willing to settle for a hope that is entirely focused on the next life; and some secular humanists, socialists, and Marxists are ready to settle for a hope that is to be fulfilled entirely in this life in a secular paradise to be achieved, unfortunately, after their deaths, in some unspecified future that somehow slips away from each succeeding generation. In between the two, the Catholic Christian insists that hope is everywhere. They naturally focus on both this world and the world to come.

Christians expect the totality of this hope will be fulfilled in the world to come, but they also expect that some of their hope will be fulfilled in this world, even before the sun goes down today. Therefore, they look for the Parousia and work in the world. It is not two hopes, one natural and one supernatural, they focus on; it is one hope, a seamless web, part of which hopes the rain will stop before the parade tomorrow and part of which eagerly looks forward to the heavenly banquet table at the end of time, wondering what the menu will be.

What is required to maintain hope?

HOPE is both inevitable and difficult. We are genetically programmed to hope (perhaps), yet always tempted to despair. We have great expectations and easy disillusionment, fantastic dreams and quick frustration. We are subject to strong temptations to quit but also a strong drive to try again.

We bounce back and forth between hope and despair, between giving up and beginning anew, between hanging up our shoes and coming out of retirement for one last race. We think a relationship is washed up, finished, dead, and yet we want to try again. We are convinced that our efforts are a waste of time, yet we are eager to try something new. Despair may be the unforgiveable sin; it is also the most difficult sin, for try as we might, hope is still there saying, "Well maybe it's worth one more try, maybe there's one more chance."

I don't say that no one commits the sin of despair. About that I don't know. I do say, though, that despair is very difficult psychologically. If one believes Professor Tiger, who himself tries to despair and cannot, we may have a genetic inhibition to despair.

The question for our life is not whether we will hope; indeed we will. The question is rather how much we will enjoy our hope, how much we will give in to hope, how much we will permit our hope to dominate our lives. We cannot extirpate hope, but we can restrain it, inhibit it, fence it in, so that it has a minimal impact on us.

We can become sour, cynical, bitter, disillusioned; we

can build up a hard shell of negation around our personalities to protect ourselves from the vulnerability that hope automatically creates. We can cheat ourselves of joy, rob ourselves of happiness, deprive ourselves of the risk-taking propensity that comes with hope, cheat ourselves of the new adventure of reconciliation, fresh beginnings, the excitement of expectation toward which hope impels us.

Most of us inhibit our hope somewhat; a lot of us inhibit it greatly. Hope may well be a basic human energy, but the virtue of hope requires persistence and practice both to focus and discipline the energy of hopefulness (and to protect it from occasional bursts of reckless naivete), and also so that we acquire the skills necessary to draw on the raw energies of hope in times of trouble, difficulty, frustration, or disillusionment.

Is it ever too late to hope?

THE virtue of hope as opposed to the hope energy is the skilled and disciplined conviction that, as T. S. Eliot has put it, "disillusionment if persisted in is the ultimate illusion."

It would appear that there are also psychological and cultural factors—and perhaps, if Professor Tiger is right, biological factors—which may facilitate hope. Some early childhood experiences seem to increase the strength of our hopefulness, while others may impede it. Some ethnic cultures also seem to predispose their members more to hope than do other ethnic cultures. (Research indicates that the Irish tend to have high scores on hope but also high scores on fatalism, a contradiction for others, perhaps, but for the Irish only a paradox.)

Members of certain religious denominations seem to be more hopeful than others. (Catholics are substantially higher on measures of hope than are Jews.) The experience one has in one's lifetime can reinforce or diminish hope. Clearly the acquisition of the virtue of hope or a habitual hopeful response to the world's problems is a disciplined and focused ability to unleash the raw power of hope. It is more difficult for some people than for others.

The virtue of hope, however, is possible for all, even though it may require a lifetime of effort. The most hardened, crusty, embittered, disillusioned cynic can be rescued from or can break out of his or her prison of despair and begin to hope again. Habits of unhopefulness, of course, build up through repeated exercise, as do habits of hopefulness.

But we are never too old to begin to hope, never too old to begin to live anew, never too old to rejoice in the fact that God does love us, that Jesus has revealed that love, and that in our confidence in the power, strength, and passion of that love, it is safe to live, to love, to rejoice, and to celebrate, to begin again even if there is only a small amount of time left.

Note well that hope is not quite the same as optimism. The optimist is so bemused by the good in the world that he/she does not see the evil, just as the pessimist is so bemused by evil that he/she does not see the good.

Hope is clear-eyed. It does not shrink from evil. The optimist sees the world as a mixture of good and evil. He/she does not understand the reason for the mixture, and he/she realizes that evil is always threatening to obliterate good; but he/she also perceives and believes that evil finally does not win, and that good is somewhat stronger than evil—perhaps only a little bit stronger, but that is enough for good to triumph.

Historically, how has religious hope been expressed?

OUR personalities are apparently shaped so that there is a raw instinct in us pointing us in the direction of the conviction that good is ever so slightly (at least) stronger than evil. For us, the question is whether we make that conviction our own and live accordingly, not in the naive pretenses that there are no problems and also not in the equally naive, cynical conviction that there is no goodness.

Religion rises from our experience of hopefulness and is grounded in that experience. Our religious stories are stories of hope, at times very little hope, at times a very naive hope, and at times an enormous hope. Paul Ricoeur in his book, *The Symbolism of Evil,* divides religions into four kinds, Egyptian, Babylonian, Greek, and Jewish.

In the Egyptian religion the world is viewed with relative optimism. The Nile rises and falls, bathing the fields so that crops will grow to maturity and the people will be fed.

Occasionally, however, the Nile rises too soon, too late, or not at all. So the evil in the Egyptian world is explained by divine forgetfulness. Religion, then, is primarily focused on reminding the gods (who live somewhere near the headwaters of the Nile) of their promises to protect their loyal and faithful people. (Some of this prodding of the gods in the Egyptian religion is echoed in the Hebrew psalms.)

In the Babylonian religion it is just the opposite. The devil—the southwest wind—can sweep in off the desert without warning to destroy crops and produce famine.

The gods permit the devil such power because they are contentious, difficult, touchy, and unreliable personages. They are quick to wrath, easy to offend, and absolutely implacable in their vengeance.

In this pessimistic worldview the principal role of humans is to placate the gods, to confess their sins, admit their faults, and to shout their contrition and sorrow, to plead with the gods to forget their anger, control their violence and to give the people another chance. (Again we can find the Babylonian influence in some of the Hebrew psalms.)

In Greece, according to Ricoeur, there was grace, elegance, and beauty; but underneath it all there was grim pessimism, verging on despair. Greek religion was essentially resigned. The gods on Olympus were relentless, impulsive, passionate personages with whom it was best not to get too deeply involved. The ordinary events of human life were in control of the Fates—blind, unreasoning forces with no concern for what happened to human beings.

Religion in Greece was fatalistic. One went through the sacrificial rituals to the gods, knowing that one was at the mercy of irrational forces. One escaped through the brave courage of Stoicism or the philosophical consolation of contemplation, or the blind orgies of Dionysius.

It was possible, however, even likely, that eventually Kronos (Saturn) would wake from the poisoned sleep induced by his children, blind the Fates, punish the gods, his children, and restore order on Olympus, and grant freedom and happiness to humankind. But no one knew when or if it would happen.

The gods, said the Greeks, were not accessible; as for the gods of the Egyptians and Babylonians—one set had to be awakened, another set had to be placated. The God of the Israelites, however, caused the opposite problem. Not only was their god accessible, he was often, it seemed, too accessible—pushing and elbowing his way into the human condition, proclaiming he was their God even when they would just as soon not have had him.

For the Egyptians, the triumph of good over evil seemed relatively easy; for the Babylonians good was precarious; for the Greeks, evil seemed to have won, with only a sliver of hope for goodness. For the Jews, goodness did not eliminate evil but pushed its way lovingly into human existence to protect its creatures from evil and to guarantee that despite suffering and tragedy, goodness would eventually triumph.

The Greeks were fatalists, the Babylonians pessimists, the Egyptians optimists; the Jews were hopers, caught up in a love affair with a God who used hope precisely as the wound in the human condition through which he could enter.

Despite the enormous power of evil, the strength of Yahweh's love was even stronger. It was guaranteed not by minimizing evil—the Hebrews had no illusions about the power of evil—but rather by emphasizing the power and the passion of God's love. The Israelites ran scared because evil was after them, but they ran confident because God was with them.

Jesus was the ultimate revelation of God's living goodness as a confirmation of our hope. Jesus was God presented to us in human form as the final adequate and comprehensive revelation of just exactly how much God loves us, and therefore how safe it is to trust our propensity to hope. The life, death, and resurrection of Jesus was the most God could do to reveal to us that there are indeed grounds for hope, that good is stronger than evil, life stronger than death, love stronger than hate.

What is the Bottom Line on hope?

THE heavenly Father guarantees our hope, Jesus reveals to us this guarantee, and we respond by focusing, channeling, and developing our hope. In the strength of that disciplined hope lies joy, generosity, and loving concern for others. We do not quit, we do not give up, we do not yield to cynicism, disillusionment.

We may be battered, bowed, and broken, but we are not beaten. We bounce back, we keep trying, we never give up, we never quit. We live for the joys of the day, work for the goodness that will come tomorrow, trying to minimize the impact of suffering on those around us. We try to seize the good in every situation no matter how bad it may be.

We behave this way because such is the thrust of the bravest, most noble, most outgoing dimensions of our personalities; but we also do so because we know it is safe to hope. Evil can make us suffer; it will certainly cause us to die. We will be sick, we will grow old, we will be disappointed; but when evil has done everything it can to us—destroyed our youthfulness, wiped out our attractiveness, sapped our strength, drained our vitality, and finally consumed our life—the last chapter of our story has not been told, the last age has not been filled out, the final sentence has not been uttered.

When it comes to the end of every day in our lives or the last day in our lives, the final word will be spoken not by evil but by goodness, the goodness of the heavenly Father revealed to us in Jesus, the goodness of a loving God elbowing his way into our life, taking us into his arms, breathing life into our bent and battered frames even as he breathed life back into the broken body of Jesus.

In the end we know we will win. That is why we hope. And we win because good is stronger than evil.

And that is the bottom line of hope. It is not much to believe at all, not much but everything.

Chapter Fifteen

Love

Can we speak of God in terms of sexual love?

THE first thing we must realize about the virtue of love is that the paradigm for human love is sexual. (And "love" is the proper translation, since the word "charity" has been so distorted.) The human image, picture, story, idea of love is primordially shaped by the fact that we are creatures who are more or less permanently affected by sexual attraction and are capable of reflecting upon that attraction. The sexuality of animals, it would appear, is both intermittent and unreflective, and the affection among angels is rooted in experiences that are quite literally beyond our imagination.

Our raw, primal, and fundamental experience of affection for other people is based on and shaped by our pervasive experience of recurring themes of sexual union.

Many of us may have learned a different view of things in our religious instruction classes. First of all, there is God's love for us, then our love for God, then our nonphysical love for one another, and finally, as an inferior and derivative form of love, comes sex, a love which, to tell the truth, we would be better off without.

However true this paradigm may be metaphysically, it is not true psychologically or existentially. We humans experience the power of affection rooted in our sexuality. We are given joy by its intense pleasurability. Other kinds of experience may be more intense, but they are not so pleasurable (hunger for food, for example); like-

197

wise, some experiences may be as pleasurable but not nearly so intense (the intellectual joy of solving a problem).

Precisely because sexual attraction combines both intensity and pleasurability, we project this emotion onto God and then say that God is Love (a relatively recent, quite advanced, and somewhat daring development in the history of human religions) and that God loves us (an even more daring development).

Actually, we are saying that God is like this pleasurable and powerful energy which disturbs and disquiets, but which enlivens our life. God's passion for us is something like the passion we feel for one another.

I am not suggesting that this dramatic and heroic religious "storytelling" is invalid. On the contrary, I think it is valid. I am pointing out that however things have been set up in the objective and metaphysical order of the universe, we experience sexual love and we experience God. Sexual love is one of the best measures available to us to describe what God is like.

Such a paradigm might offend some Catholics, especially those who are still persuaded that sex is somehow "dirty." Nonetheless it is clearly the way things are.

The Song of Songs, for example, is secular, erotic poetry (perhaps written by a woman) that found its way into the Bible not because the author had God in mind when she wrote it, but because the readers came to see that her love for her spouse was a mirror reflecting our response to God.

Sexual love is not the only way of describing God, of course, but however rarified we want to make our interpretations of the notion that "God is Love," we should still be clear in our own minds that basically we would not even make such an assertion unless we had the experience of the enormous power and pleasurability of human passion.

Is sexual attraction a basic factor in human evolution?

THE pre- and photohominids developed a "quasi" pair-bonding because it was an evolutionary prerequisite for further development toward homo sapiens. The elaborate, complex, pervasive, and persistent sexiness of the human primate is the principal and primary basis for pair-bonding between humans.

Unlike the simple and almost automatic link between Mr. and Mrs. Quail, humans are themselves bound together in an exceedingly pleasurable, confused, chancy, and unpredictable mechanism of passion and affection, a mechanism which, like most other human adaptations, strongly inclines us in one direction but does not absolutely determine our behavior.

In this perspective, which I think is reasonably well established and has important religious implications, humans had to learn to engage in passionate love before they could become human. The family existed before homo sapiens; likewise, the biological, physical, cultural, and psychological underpinnings of human love preceded the emergence of humankind as we know it. Love is not a consequence of humanity but an antecedent to it.

There may well be other mechanisms and propensities in us that also incline us to intense affection for others. Some anthropologists and comparative primatologists and evolutionary biologists suggest that we also had to learn to cooperate with one another, principally in the collecting of food, before evolution could move ahead in the direction of homo sapiens. There may also be a propensity (resistible) to have affection for our children.

But if these propensities are distinct from sexual attraction, they are certainly enormously affected by it. The human ability—indeed, it is virtually an irresistible urge—to enter into a wide variety of intense, intimate relationships is primarily, if not entirely, shaped by our ability to sustain long-term, passionate relationships with a member of our species of the opposite sex.

Biologically and historically, as well as psychologically and existentially, friendship does not precede passion but follows it. We are able to form intense friendships from which genital sexuality is often absent precisely because we have the basic capacity of entering into long-term, intense relationships with a member of the opposite sex.

I do not wish to be interpreted as saying that sexual love is the only kind of human love, the most noble kind of human love, or the principal form of human love. I do not think any of those things are true. Love is a raw, intense, undifferentiated human energy which can emerge in many different shapes and forms, some noble, some degrading, some spiritual, some abysmally perverse.

I am merely suggesting that the human capacity to love and the intensity of human love is ultimately based on our nature as sexual—extremely sexual—beings. If we understand this fact, we have an excellent perspective from which to examine the phenomenon of the Two Loves in our lives—the love of other humans and the love of God.

How did human sexual attactiveness come to be a model and paradigm for the love of God?

THE idea seems to have emerged in different ways in a number of different cultures at about the same time— that era in the millennium before the coming of Jesus

which Karl Jaspers has called the "axial age." It was
then that humans developed their intellectual and imaginative tools as well as having the leisure to reflect explicitly and self-consciously about their relationships as
individuals to the Ultimate Source of life and of the universe.

In the Middle East, India, and China, the great thinkers, prophets, visionaries, poets, and dreamers realized
that earthly power, possessions, and pleasure were not
enough; that one could have eminently satisfying human
lovers and still yearn for more, perhaps for Someone
More. They disovered also that this longing is remarkably like sexual longing, both in its intensity and in its
conviction that the Other was a Thou, someone like us
who was capable of responding with passion like ours.

As humans, we are able to reflect more self-consciously on the intensity, the complexity, the ambigui-
ties, the successes and the failures of our relationships
with earthly lovers; we can transfer more and more of
these insights and experiences to our relationships with
this other Lover of whose existence we are increasingly
conscious.

Those who believed that God is Love were not those
whose human relationships were unfulfilled, one suspects, but rather those who had extremely satisfying and
intense human relationships and were able to use them as
a model and a metaphor to understand the other Lover.
So it was that the story of humankind's relationship
with God came to be described as a love affair whose
passionate intensity, complexity, uncertainty, ambig-
uity, and frustration paralleled human love affairs.

Thus, the author of the book of Exodus has Yahweh
saying, "I am Yahweh your God," implying an intense
interpersonal relationship of decision and choice. Then

Yahweh adds that he is a "passionate" (a word which was translated badly in the old days as "envious") God, a God who literally, according to the Word, "breathed heavily" after his people. He is described a few chapters later in Exodus as a God who does not want a "frigid" people, a people who fail to respond to his amorous advances.

In the books of Ezekiel, Jeremiah, and Osee this notion is developed further and gradually transferred from the whole people to the individual person. By the time of Jesus the so-called "verities of love" had completed the development. God was not only love, God was a passionate lover, deeply involved emotionally with the individual human person.

What is the dramatic message of love revealed in Jesus?

THE nuptial imagery of Jesus in St. Paul, then, was not by any means original with him, but was part of a Pharisee tradition which shaped much of his religious imagery. Jesus and Paul pushed the imagery further, but it was nonetheless an imagery that had been developing for several centuries before them. Especially in the parables of Jesus, the intensely passionate Yahweh, who pays workers a day's wage for an hour's labor and who has a celebration for the return of a shiftless prodigal son, is clearly depicted as a God caught up in the frivolous absurdity that characterizes not merely sexual passion but romantic love.

The notion that God loves us or, more strongly, is in love with us, is so much a part of our own religious ambiance that we do not consider it to be very daring or intimately linked with our own human romances. This is not surprising, since religious institution-builders have always tried to mitigate and trivialize religious insights that seem scandalous or disruptive.

Nevertheless, it would be perfectly true to say that the fundamental Good News that Jesus came to validate is not merely that God is love, not even that God loves us, but more recklessly, more absurdly, more spectacularly, more improbably, that God has fallen in love with us. This is a notion so shattering, so disconcerting, even so scandalous, that much of the history of Christianity can be seen as an attempt to downplay its importance.

The bottom line, however, for the first of the Two Loves is not that we should love God but, far more important, that God has fallen in love with us. God is not about to fall out of love simply because we are not faithful or persistent in our response to his love.

No passionately committed human being falls out of love simply because of the unresponsiveness of his beloved. Certainly God will not fall out of love with us. The language may seem reckless even today. Yet the insight is one toward which human thinking and human responsibility has been drifting for two-and-a-half millennia. It is one for Christians, at least, which was absolutely and irrevocably and dramatically validated by the birth, death, and resurrection of Jesus.

The whole thrust of the parables states the matter quite simply: God is so hopelessly in love with us that his indulgence, his forgiveness, his eagerness for us would be, if judged by human standards, considered a form of madness. God is madly in love with us.

And that is the bottom line about the First Love and, in a way, the bottom line of the whole of Christianity.

The other Love, human love, not only reflects God's love but gives us the initial idea that God might be Love.

What does Christianity, at least in its best and most authentic moments, have to say about our human loves?

How do vulnerability and risk fit into the Christian view of love?

THE bottom line on human love, Christianity says, is that it is safe to give ourselves in love. We don't have much choice, of course, because we cannot live without others and we cannot survive long without some kind of love relationship (which is bound to have a sexual dimension because we are sexual creatures in every cell of our bodies, although many may not have any overt or explicit genital implications).

If we must give ourselves over to the demands of love, and most of us give ourselves over to the demands of sexual love, it does not follow that our gifts must be generous. Precisely because we are the kind of creatures for whom pair-bonding is a sort of evolutionary afterthought, we are afraid of the demands of intense love. We are enormously attracted to it, indeed, but terrified by the vulnerability it demands of us. Egotistic and self-centered creatures that we are, we are wary of putting our lives and happiness in the hands of others; yet love requires that we do so.

But even the most intense sexual passion will quickly cool unless both partners are able to be vulnerable to one another. There is a payoff in love affairs, genital and non-genital, which is directly proportionate to our willingness to give ourselves without defense and without pretense to the other. Vulnerability means the risk of being hurt, indeed the inevitability of being hurt. Once one has been hurt often enough, one is tempted to withdraw into a shell of defensiveness and lead a cool, detached life, marked by occasional discharges of passion but minimal amounts of affection and fulfillment.

Within this Christian view that God is recklessly in love with us, the bottom line is that it is safe for us to be recklessly in love with others and to periodically renew our love relationships so that we once more recover the vulnerability and excitement that we call romantic love. In our human love affairs the bottom line in the Christian tradition is essentially that romantic love can always be renewed because it is always safe to take chances (though obviously they must be taken with discretion and prudence) in a cosmos animated by and presided over by a recklessly loving God.

Jesus taught us that love means the generous and unselfish giving of ourselves in service to others not because it's fun to be a doormat but rather because we win others by serving them. We come to possess (in a non-pejorative meaning of this word) someone else by allowing ourselves to be possessed by that other. We gain the love of another person by giving ourselves in sensitive, tender, affectionate service.

We give ourselves to others neither because we expect something back nor because we do not expect something back; we give ourselves to others because we love them, because we know that love is the surest way to generate love in return. There is a periodicity in human love affairs rooted in the biological and constitutional ambivalences that are inevitable for a creature that is both a higher primate and possesses a powerful but not absolutely determining pair-bond mechanism.

Our love follows predictable cycles of ups and downs, and the downs lead to disappointment, frustration, and then, perhaps, forgiveness and reconciliation. It is pre-

cisely because we have learned as a species how absolutely important reconciliation is to human love affairs
that we have made God's willingness to forgive us and to
be reconciled to us the quintessential characteristic of
our divine love affair.

To put the matter the other way around, God, knowing how critically important, how intensely poignant,
and how wonderfully satisfying reconciliations are in
our love life, chose to reveal himself as a reconciling
God precisely because he/she realizes that this would
make her/him appear irresistible to us. (Presumably I
need not pause here to establish that both of the last two
sentences are true and that they simply look at the same
reality from different perspectives.)

God is revealed to us and perceived by us as a reconciling God precisely because reconciliation is so essential
in human love affairs and because the periodicity which
affects our love for other human beings inevitably also
affects our love for God.

Both of the Two Loves, in other words, have their ups
and downs, their periods of intense affection, boredom
and disillusionment, anger and splendid reconciliation.

What are the four phases in a love relationship?

IN human love relationships there seems to be a four-
phase cycle: falling in love, settling down, bottoming
out, and beginning again.

a) *Falling in love.* In the first phase we recognize in
the other not only someone who is attractive but also
someone who amazingly enough finds us attractive.
Overwhelmed by the attractiveness of ourself as perceived by the other we "fall in love," that is to say, we
are captivated, bemused, entranced, disconcerted, dis-

organized, exalted, preoccupied, and transformed by the other.

This love may be shallow and superficial, as in the teen-age "crush" (though it seems far from superficial for the person involved), or it may be profound and devastating emotions in the life of a mature adult. No one is immune from the temptation of romantic love. Everybody does fall in love; indeed every intense human relationship has at its beginning a certain element of romantic interlude.

b) *Settling down.* The second phase is a time of stabilization, of routinizing the relationship, establishing order and harmony, of combining friendship or love with the other responsibilites of life. You come to know the other person better and discover her/his faults and failings as well as further attractions.

This harmonizing and stabilizing is absolutely essential to the development of the relationship. It also carries within it a tendency toward deterioration. Routine is necessary but it tends toward routinization; harmony is necessary but it tends toward monotony; stability is necessary but it tends toward boredom; ritual is necessary but it tends toward ritualization.

Much of American fiction in recent years has been devoted to just this phenomenon, the turning of exciting routine into boring routinization in human romances. Two lovers, once entranced by one another, once almost pathetically eager to engage in generous service to each other, now become bored, impatient, angry, dissatisfied with each other.

While this phase is most obvious in marital love, it characterizes all close relationships. There is no permanent stability, no continuous plateau in human intimacy. One cannot avoid the ups and downs, the cycles of good and bad in relationships, although one can make disruptions less painful.

c) *Bottoming out.* The third phase in the love cycle is the breaking down, falling apart, or bottoming out, in which love seems to cross the edge of the razor line that separates it from hate. The beloved becomes the enemy. The one who once enthralled us now infuriates us; the one whom we once adored we now despise.

A long agenda of bitterness and anger has built up, and the whole problem of a deteriorating relationship is blamed on the other. "I am faultless; the other person is totally responsible." The interaction is acrimonious, nasty, and often devoted more to attributing blame than anything else.

The intense and angry outbursts which are often characteristic of this phase may be aborted or, as lovers become more skillful at handling their conflict, may be quickly channeled into constructive directions. Often the anger and the dissatisfaction are suppressed and the two people settle down to quiet, only occasionally nasty, coexistence in which the anger is hidden but the passion has ebbed, and what was once love turns into a permanent and chronic state of suppressed conflict. As long as the animosity and conflict are suppressed, it becomes impossible to go on to the fourth stage.

d) *Beginning again.* One scholar I know refers to intense human intimacy as having a "rubber band dimension." The two lovers drift apart, indeed are often driven apart by one another; but the residual power of their affection (pair-bonding) is often, indeed usually, sufficiently strong to impel them back toward one another.

Awkwardly, clumsily, blunderingly they stumble into

one another's arms, forgive each other, and begin again in a new burst of romantic love, which is often more rewarding because it involves a familiar, trusted lover instead of a new one. It is important to note that human nature is such that we will have our romantic loves, and the only question is whether we will renew romantic love within a permanent commitment or turn to someone else for the absolutely indispensable excitement of a love which is just beginning.

The rubber band effect, I postulate, also operates with God. We may drift away from him, but then we are inevitably drawn back to passionate reconciliation with him, and the Divine Romance begins again. The bottom line for love in the Christian tradition, it seems to me, is that not only is romantic love inevitable, it is also possible; and that the renewal of romantic love is not only possible but far more rewarding, exciting and pleasurable than beginning all over again.

We who are Christians know that this is true because we are involved with a God who is a romantic lover, a God who enjoys reconciliations as much as we do, and who draws near to us and draws us nearer to himself/herself with each successive reconciliation.

What is the secret of love?

IN the Catholic Christian tradition we must be careful not to push too far the classic distinction regarding *eros* (self or erotic love), *agape* (unselfish or spiritual love), and *philia* (benevolence, the love of friendship). For Christians, *caritas* subsumes all three of the other terms.

Indeed, most human love relationships are a subtle blend of "spiritual," "erotic," and "friendship" love. No marriage, for example, will amount to anything unless all three are blended without the presupposition that one might be superior to the other two. The Catholic Christian tradition is skeptical of the totally disinterested, totally unself-concerned kind of love. Such love is often neurotic or even demonic (like the love of the French philosophers who would even will their own damnation as long as it served the honor and glory of God).

One cannot assume that one's unselfish "well-wishing" for someone else is going to rebound to one's own benefit. We serve the other because the other is lovely and because we want the other to be happy, but we also know that in the other's happiness our own happiness is to be found.

Such love is not impure, not imperfect, not inferior, not even "mixed." It is simply human. We want both to be possessed and to possess the one we love, which, if one is to believe the language of the Scripture, is the way God feels too.

In fact, however, the secret of love is generous service of the beloved. It is not the service which comes from being a doormat, not the service which denies our own personhood, our own right to be treated like a human, and not the service which refuses to confront the beloved and challenge him/her to all that is the best in himself/herself.

The tragic young people in Eric Segal's *Love Story* were simply wrong. Love *does* mean having to say you're sorry—time after time after time. Sometimes the love of the other and the generous service of the other require confrontation, anger, conflict.

How is Christian love equated with service?

SERVICE is not abject surrender, much less obliteration of self. Service does not mean we put the other's welfare before our own, or that we prefer the other's happiness to our own happiness. It means something much more complicated, much more intricate, much more challenging and, in truth, much more fun.

Service means that the other's happiness finally becomes indistinguishable from our own. The beloved also perceives that his/her happiness is inseparable from our own.

The principal theological contribution of Mark's gospel is the insight—undoubtedly rooted in the actual preaching of Jesus—that the eschatological Son of Man, expected since the prophet Daniel, and the Suffering Servant of Isaiah are to be one and the same person.

The Messiah who was to introduce the new age of human history was not to be a mighty king or ruler or a temple prince with great armies, but the loyal, dedicated, faithful, compliant servant of Yahweh depicted in the servant song of the middle section of Isaiah's prophecies.

The combination of Mark's theological identification of Jesus with the Suffering Servant and Matthew's description of the final judgment provides a solid base for a gospel theory of the practice of love. Like the servant in Isaiah's poetry and like Jesus himself, the Christian loves by generous self-sacrifice and service to others, realizing even at those times when the beloved doesn't seem lovable, that the service and the love relationship is caught up in the higher romance of God's love for us.

The Christian also serves, especially serves, the least of the brothers and the sisters, the hungry, the thirsty, the homeless, the confused, the sick, the disturbed, the lonely. Loving service is extended to include all humankind as a continuation of our service to those who are closest to us.

What is demanded by Christian love?

THE Christian vision sees our happiness as inextricably linked to the happiness of all humans. Whatever we do to the least of the brothers and sisters, we do to Jesus, the heavenly Father's representative among us.

Neither of these two dazzling gospel insights is totally original. Both build upon nature, both confirm the noblest instincts and intuition of the human condition. We dimly perceive without the gospel that no man is an island and that the happiness of any one of us is the happiness of all of us. We also dimly perceive that without generous service love is impossible.

These laws of love are written on our hearts, written often so faintly that we can hardly read them. Jesus came to confirm, to validate, to reinforce, and to make the center of his ethic the law of love, the law of the Suffering Servant, the law of his presence in the very least of the brothers and sisters. It is not a new obligation, an 11th or 12th commandment; it is not a proper subject for casuistic distinction. It is rather a vision of the possibility of human life, of human love; a goal to be striven for, though never to be perfectly achieved.

One does not respond properly to this law of love by asking questions such as, "Isn't my first obligation to my wife or my husband, my children, my parents, my neighbor? Don't they have a prior claim on me before, let us say, the Cambodians? What can I do about the Cambodians anyway?" These questions utterly miss the point of the law of love that Jesus taught.

Obviously there is a gradation of responsibility and a gradation of our power to respond. Obviously, too, there are complex and intricate decisions that we must make about how to allocate our time, resources, energies to our commitments. These decisions are difficult and usually tentative, subject to frequent review.

But the questions that must be answered first in order to make such decisions are not questions which are pertinent to the law of love. It would be less than accurate to say that the law of love is concerned more with the style of our love than with the substance, for the style which Jesus demands of his followers has enormous substantive implications, just as the quality of Christian love has enormous quantitative implications.

Nonetheless, it could very well be that at a given time in a person's life, the spouse makes such an overwhelming demand (legitimately) for loving service that it is impossible to allocate much of one's resources or energies to anyone else. Generosity, at times, may point to extensive service and at other times to more intensive service; it may on some occasions indicate only one or two persons, on other occasions many more.

It is demanded of the Christian that he/she serve and that he/she serve generously, that he/she be passionately concerned about the happiness of other people, and that this concern be the primary focus of his/her life. Who those people are and how exactly they are to be served, are questions for which the gospel does not provide an answer.

What does Jesus' vision of love teach us?

THE vision of Jesus does not purport to offer explicit direction. Jesus wants us to love, love passionately, love generously, love completely. He wants us to do all in our power to see that other human beings are happy. He leaves to us the mature, responsible decision-making

about how that passionate, generous, happiness-pro-
ducing love is to be focused and exercised at different
times in our life.

No decent ethical system permits adults to escape
from the responsibility of personal decision and personal moral choice. One must always judge the circumstances in which one's ethical principles are being applied.

The law of charity is not an ethical system in the strict
sense of the word but a religious vision with enormous
ethical implications. However, as a religious vision, it is
even less able to dictate specific responses than is an
ethical system. Rather, it describes for us the goal of
human living, the secret of human happiness, the purpose of human life, and the nature and the possibilities
of human generosity.

In effect, Jesus says to us, "I will shine the searchlight
of my example on your life to reveal the possibilities of
generous human love. Now that you see what is possible, what are you going to do about it?" We have clearly
come a long, long way from moralistic or legalistic answers, but no one who has had any experience with love
thinks that it is the sort of human behavior which can be
dictated by principles and precepts neatly written in a
textbook.

A man and woman who are deeply in love with one
another know that finally their generous and loving service is something which they learn from one another and
for which no rules, principles, norms, or guidelines can
substitute.

One has the example of the life of Jesus, the revelation of God's passionate love for us. One then must decide from the love of Jesus how one is going to love, and
one generally learns through the example of others who

are close to us, who share the same vision of the possibility of love (without always necessarily seeing it as explicitly Christian).

Most of us learn how to love through an intimate, loving relationship with a parent, a spouse, a child, a friend. If we cannot be generous, unselfish, committed, and passionately dedicated to the happiness of another, it is not likely we will be able to do very much for the brothers and sisters scattered from the next block to the ends of the earth.

What does scripture tell us about the true nature of love?

OUR intimate relationships are the laboratories of love. They make the heaviest demands on us and offer us the greatest pleasures and consolations. They are the boot camps of love, the basic training centers, as well as the rest and rehabilitation centers to which we return when our love grows stale, when we need reinforcement, when our vision must be renewed, and when we ourselves need to receive love as well as give it.

Christian love does not end with our intimate relationships, but it most certainly begins there. It is not because they are our primary responsibilities, although they are surely that, but rather and especially because they are the situations in which we learn how to love and have our love renewed.

Mark's vision of the Messiah as Suffering Servant, and Matthew's account of the follower of Jesus serving the least of the brothers and sisters, and Luke's story of the Good Samaritan, of the enemy turned brother, constitute the gospel theology of love. The person of Jesus incarnates that theology in practice.

The theory and the example are simple; applying the

theory to our lives is complicated and difficult. St. Paul tries to help us in this application by his "phenomenological" description of the man or woman of love in his epistle to the Corinthians. The so-called "Hymn of Love" is a rather unusual pericope of Paul's writing. It is somewhat different from Paul's usual style in that there is no mention of Jesus in it, and it also contains a touch of the "Wisdom" literature of the Old Testament, sounding a bit like practical moral advice.

However, this "Hymn to Love" goes far, far beyond the vision of the Wisdom literature and could easily be a poetic description of the way Jesus lived. Some Scripture commentators think it is a fragment of a poem or a song written by an early Christian who was heavily influenced by the Wisdom tradition and was in fact describing the love of Jesus. It may even have been a poem familiar to Paul's Corinthian audience which he cites (perhaps from memory) because he knows the associations and connotations it will have for his readers.

In any event, we who read this hymn to love today should take it as an examination of conscience about our most intense, our most powerful, and our most intimate relationship—not, indeed, to provide a check list of wrongdoing or to make us guilty, but rather as a series of signposts by which we can judge the path we are traveling, a set of signals which should help us to evaluate the direction of our love.

"Love is patient and kind."

Of course it is. How could you be in love with someone and not be patient and kind? Yet if you go to parties or ride in elevators or tourist buses with people who are presumably in love with one another, you know how much impatience and petty unkindness mars even the most intense of love relationships.

The beloved other is different from us with different perspectives, goals, values, habits, and life experiences. Even if, after a while, the story of the other's life begins to converge with mine into one story, the two of us still would tell that story in different words. The other offends, annoys, infuriates, upsets, disconcerts, and causes us pain. We become angry and store up the memory of that anger, letting it ferment inside until an occasion arises for us to get even.

The punishment might be slight, but punishment it is. The other has learned a lesson, we hope, and will never offend us again. We may even understand that if a little bit of love slips away in such incidents of anger and impatience, we are willing to pay the price; for we have been hurt, and like a hurt little child, we find it necessary to get even.

"Love is not envious."

Some students of human behavior, such as the German sociologist Helmut Schoeck, argue that envy, after self-preservation and reproduction, is the third most powerful emotion of which we humans are capable. Schoeck is upset with American sociologists who completely ignore the importance of envy in human behavior. He suggests that in an egalitarian society like the American one, envy is too powerful and too important a motivation for human behavior to be studied objectively or even to be studied at all.

Whatever one may think of Schoeck's theory, it is certainly true that envy—resentment over another's success and the desire to take that success away—is one of the most deadly and powerful emotions of which humans are capable. It leads to assassinations, revolutions, destruction of other people's character, ostracism, bitterness, and the betrayal of friendships and love. It is especially powerful (God forgive us) in the church. The clergy (again, God forgive us) are especially likely to be the victims of it.

Envy is a completely irresistible energy once it has been unleashed. It destroys its target because it lies, distorts, demeans, denies, dismisses, and hurts. It has an unerring, uncanny ability to seek out the weak link in the armor of its target and inflict terrible pain.

Envy is absolutely without pity, and the envious person is immune to counterattacks or even to pricks of conscience because it is part of the self-righteousness of envy to resolutely deny its own existence. The envious person will insist that he or she is only interested in truth, only interested in protecting reputations of family and community, only interested in protecting the moral law, only interested in exposing sham and hypocrisy. In fact envy is interested in none of these things. It is interested only in imposing pain and suffering. The hated person who dares to show us up by being more successful than we are deserves nothing better.

Envy flourishes among little children and among adults, among those who have nothing and among those who have everything. It is one of the first lessons we learn in life, a lesson that is never forgotten. For some reason or another, some people are relatively immune to its attraction. They do not seem to be threatened by the excellence of others but in fact, rather enjoy it. Those people are, of course, the most likely victims of envy and the ones who suffer the most from it, because they do not understand why people are attacking them and lying about them.

Envy is especially powerful in its devastation of marital intimacy. A wife becomes envious of her husband's success and advancement in the world or in his career; a husband becomes envious because his wife excels in something. (Remember in the movie the look on Mr. Kramer's face when his ex-wife revealed she was making more money than he was).

One would think that husbands and wives would be proud of each other's successes. Indeed they ought to be, yet in the highly competitive human condition (reinforced by our competitive society), we are always evaluating and comparing ourselves, one against the other, and rarely do we take pride in the success of others. Often we attempt to ridicule, demean, and destroy that success.

There is a technical distinction between envy and jealousy. Envy resents another's success and wishes to take it away; jealousy is afraid of losing the beloved other and is willing to destroy that other to prevent that loss (like Othello). However, the root of envy and jealousy is the same: resentment over the success of another person and the need to destroy that success because it seems to be a judgment on and an affront to us.

When one human intimacy has degenerated to a relationship marked by suspicion, nastiness, conflict, and petty punishment, and there seems no obvious explanation for such deterioration, in almost every case envy is the cause. The problem, of course, is that envy not only destroys love but also honesty, and the envious person cannot admit to his/her destructive feelings.

"Love is never rude or selfish. It does not take offense; it is not resentful."

Love, in other words, is not contentious, not defensive, not easily threatened. It is understandable that we are defensive in our intimate relationships. They demand enormous vulnerability. While we are willing to make the commitment of vulnerability, we nevertheless hedge our bets and maintain the right to be angry or upset or resentful, an option which enables us to slip away from vulnerability by trying to protect us from being hurt.

Resentment, anger, bitterness in the love relationship are sure signs of protectiveness and defensiveness. There are times when both are justified, but in a profound love relationship anger is at best a temporary state which should lead to clarification, reconciliation, and a renewal of love. Resentments are brought into the open and dealt with, not stored up as an excuse to punish the other. To rephrase St. Paul in clear but less poetic language, "Love does not store up anger or resentment; it deals with it so that the relationship may continue and grow."

"Love is always ready to excuse, to trust, to hope, and to endure whatever comes."

Love is ready to *excuse* not because it is simple-minded or unperceptive, and surely not because it delights in being abused. On the contrary, love is fierce and passionate and demands response just as Yahweh did on Sinai when he described himself as a passionate God.

Love excuses because love understands. Love perceives reality not only from its own perspective but also from the perspective of the beloved. And precisely because it sees things the way the beloved does, it understands the beloved's needs, problems, motivations, and fears. The excuses that love perceives are not phony.

Love excuses because love understands, because love delights in understanding, because love always seeks greater understanding.

With understanding comes trust—now not just a blind leap in the dark but a reasonable, sensible, posture. The beloved is trusted because the beloved is understood as trustworthy despite differences, despite conflict, despite strains and stresses. The basic trustworthiness of the beloved is not in doubt. There is still the joyful anxiety of reconciliation, there is still respect for the other's radical freedom to be himself/herself, and there is still lots to excuse, because the beloved, like oneself, possesses strains of instability and unpredictability.

Yet the lover is known, understood, comprehended, and trusted. Thus, love is always ready to hope because it believes that the relationship will continue to grow and expand, and that love will perdure no matter what happens. The two lovers are ready to endure together whatever comes because they have forged a common hope that is stronger than individual hopes.

One cannot read Paul's hymn to love without being impressed with the beauty of the love which is being praised and overwhelmed by the difficulty of trying to love that way (the terror of permitting oneself to be loved that way). Love is the toughest challenge in human life, the most difficult task we can set for ourselves, as well as the greatest pleasure in which we engage.

The bottom line on love for the Catholic Christian is that it is possible to love, with the help of and captured by God's love, and to keep loving all the days of our lives.

Chapter Sixteen

Justice

What is the Christian vision of the just person?

IN the Old Testament, the root of the word justice referred to "abundance." It came to mean the use people made of the goods they had over and above that which was necessary for survival.

First of all, and primarily, justice was a characteristic of God, who benevolently dispensed the goods of the universe for the benefit of all its people. With the passage of time, God's justice was expanded to mean generous and benevolent dealing with the people of Israel, his people to whom he would keep his promise of justice. In return, his people were also expected to be just and to observe God's law.

It is well to note that in its origins, the concept of justice did not lie primarily in legalistic or economic implications but rather in the notion of generosity and fidelity to generous promises. In the New Testament, justice continued to mean conformity to God's law but demanded an unselfish response to God's generosity.

Jesus did indeed denounce the unjust, the oppressors, the hypocrites, those who placed unfair burdens on the people. But the perspective of Jesus' condemnation was an ideal of the "holiness" (perhaps a good translation of the word "justice") demanded of God's people, particularly those who had received the revelation of God's great love that was manifested in himself.

We are proclaimed just, or "justified," not by our ability to live up to the demand of responding to God's generosity but rather by the generosity itself; and our response to such "justification" is an effect of God's initial loving justice and not a cause of it.

Down through the centuries, this biblical concept of our generosity in response to God's generosity has been combined with Aristotelian and Roman legal/ethical notions that have created a formidable body of principles and casuistic applications. Justice, which began as a covenant between God and his people, becomes a matter of contractual relationships among individuals and groups.

This development is not an illegitimate one. The precise, fair, Roman notions of legal justice are important contributions to human wisdom. Those who are followers of Jesus of Nazareth are certainly obliged to carefully respect the goods and services of others. Nevertheless there is a risk that we may forget that our vision of the "just person" contains something above and beyond the notions of legal justice which the courts of our country try to enforce.

The just person is one who is generous in response to God's generosity, generous in his/her relationship to God, generous in his/her relationships to fellow human beings. A just person does not, for example, feel that his/her obligations have been properly discharged because he/she keeps all the laws and pays all the bills. Furthermore, the Catholic Christian must be wary of the sharp distinction between justice and charity or justice and love of which the old moral theology made a great deal.

The generosity of the just person is in fact quite indistinguishable from love; it is a generosity which is less a matter of ethical obligation than it is a matter of enthusiastic response to a religious vision of the possibility of human life once our existence has been illumined by Jesus' revelation of how much God loves us.

Here I will deal especially with some of the problems of justice which affect humans living in the contemporary world mostly from the accumulated wisdom of the moral theological tradition. I must confess, however, that I am dismayed at the inability of the moral theologians to deal with the real problems that humans encounter in the marketplace. I want to emphasize, though, that, while it may be necessary to wrestle with these problems, even the most ethically refined solutions to them fall far short of the generosity that is the decisive characteristic of Christian justice. If I am dismayed by the inability of the moral theologians to comprehend the problems of the modern marketplace, I am even more astonished by the utter inability of contemporary spiritual writers to offer to the ordinary Catholic lay person any illumination on what Christian justice (the justice of generosity in response to God's generosity) implies in the complex and intricate problems of life.

To illustrate this problem, let me cite three issues that affect many people in their lives. I also will point out that both the moral and spiritual wisdom currently available to us are unsatisfying and then make some suggestions as to what illumination the Christian notion of justice might provide for some of these problems. The problems are (1) taxes, (2) government regulations, (3) corruption.

I will then turn to some other equally complex issues which ought to involve a response in Christian justice: (1) use of the environment, (2) equity for minority groups, (3) sharing the goods of the earth with all humans.

Is it a sin to break a law — to cheat on taxes?

CATHOLIC moral theology has argued vigorously with itself about the existence of "purely penal" laws. Are there laws made by the government, and perhaps even by the church, which do not bind "under pain of sin" but only under the obligation to pay the penalty if one is caught? If one drives 37 mph at night in a 35 mph zone and there is no other traffic in sight, has one committed a sin?

Whatever the theoretical debates, in practice the conclusion has been that such violations are not sinful. It is therefore the conclusion of most specialists in the area that a considerable number of laws do not bind under the pain of sin, including tax laws. It is not a sin, in other words, not to pay all of one's taxes, although one must run the risk of getting caught and paying the penalty which the government exacts from those who violate the tax laws.

Occasionally, some Catholics have argued even more than this. Thus, a number of the "activists" during the Vietnam war took as their legal defense for burning or pouring blood on draft records the proposition that their moral and ethical opposition to the war immunized them from the law under which they were charged with violation. Not only were they morally guiltless (indeed superior), they were also legally guiltless. And, at least in some instances, juries agreed with this argument.

Systematic "cheating" on taxes requires some sort of falsification of one's tax return—if not outright lying to the government, then not telling the government the *whole* truth. Some economists argue that between 15 percent and 25 percent of the American economy is composed of "underground" transactions, that is to say, transactions in which only cash is exchanged, no records are kept, and nothing is given to the government.

Even if one takes the lower estimate about this underground economy, there is an enormous amount of deception involved here. It is often justified on the grounds that the government is wasteful, oppressive, corrupt, and that the Internal Revenue Service's "adversary" relationship with the taxpayer encourages such behavior. Furthermore, it is said that the wealthy are able to escape paying taxes (as did the President on his peanut warehouse) by various legal loopholes. Why shouldn't ordinary citizens benefit from a few loopholes?

Both moral theology and spirituality, it seems to me, collapse in the face of such practice and arguments. The moral theologians will talk about the need of the citizen to contribute to the support of his/her government. But contribute a fifth, a quarter, a third of one's salary?

The spiritual theologian will talk about the need to be generous in support of the various works that the government performs for the poor and the less fortunate. But support the present inefficient and counterproductive welfare system?

It often seems to me that theologians have been too busy ranting about "liberation" to deal with these enormously practical questions of justice which occur in the lives of everyone. My own personal feeling is that in a society where everyone feels it is legitimate to cheat the government because the government is the enemy, the social order is close to breaking down. Cynicism, dishonesty, opportunism, selfishness become the rule. The result: the edges of the jungle slip inside the walls of the city, and the vines creep around the buildings and begin to tangle and obstruct the streets.

I suspect—but I certainly don't impose obligations on anyone—that the just person takes all the deductions to which he/she is reasonably entitled and does not try to cheat the government, the insurance companies, public utilities, or any other large corporate institutions. Just persons do not do so because they refuse to accept as Christians the validity of the two arguments that support such behavior, that is, it doesn't hurt anyone and everyone is doing it.

The first argument doesn't hold up because someone is hurt every time a large corporate body is cheated, and the second argument doesn't hold up because if everyone does cheat, the social order collapses. The just Christian is committed to maintaining, indeed improving, the social order.

Is corruption or self-deception a necessary part of life?

I WOULD be inclined to apply the same principles, or spiritual guidelines, to the questions of bribery and corruption. Oftentimes a bribe is given as a means to a good end. Give the sanitation worker $5 to take away a special load of trash, an exercise which probably falls within his obligations. You make a contribution to a personal fund of some foreign potentate so that he will buy your jet airline, which is the best airplane he could buy anyhow.

In both cases, one could argue that the expenses are part of the cost of doing business and also that everyone else is doing it. The American businessman who doesn't pay off potential foreign purchasers will lose out every time. A certain "informal" exchange of presents and gifts is part of the human condition, and the stern, puritanical corruption laws on the book are utterly irrelevant to the way business is and always has been done in the world.

Similarly, many of the "codes" passed with reckless enthusiasm by state legislators, it is said, are impossible to abide by and still stay in business. There is no choice but to duck the codes and make an occasional gift to the "flexible" inspector who realizes that in practice administration of the law must be tempered by wisdom and common sense.

The issues involved here, it seems to me, are extremely murky. The argument would appear to be that society has become so regulated as to become unjust, and it will only function when there are systematic "dispensations" (granted to the individual by himself/herself) from the regulations and rules.

The position is arguable, though the generous and just Christian would see the dangers of self-deception that would destroy the social order were everyone to engage in such behavior. I know too many businessmen who have been indicted for doing things which they argue, perhaps not unreasonably, were absolutely essential to stay in business.

I am inclined (again, without wishing to impose moral obligations which I have no right to impose) that one should either strive to remedy the particular marketplace situation in which such behavior becomes a necessity or find another marketplace. The impact on the human personality of working in a situation where corruption is required most of the time is bound to be devastating.

There are, perhaps, circumstances which permit someone to stay in such a situation, but it represents such a twisting of the order of "generosity" that reflects God's justice, that it seems to me the good Christian would be very ill at ease in it. The just Christian who for one reason or another is constrained to remain in such a situation will be powerfully committed to do all that he or she can to change it.

Minorities: discrimination or equity?

WHAT of the requirements of justice that are demanded by some spokesmen of "minority" groups (including women) that past injustices demand reverse discrimination in the present. If women, blacks, or Hispanics were discriminated against in the job or educational marketplaces in previous years, then, the argument requires, they should be the object of reverse discrimination and be treated more favorably than others now.

I confess that I find such argumentation morally repulsive; for it is not the past victims who are being compensated but present individuals, many of whom have never been victimized. Furthermore, I have seen too many "token" jobholders or students and faculty who suffer enormously because they have been placed in positions for which they are not ready, while, on the other hand, some highly qualified people have been dismissed in order to make room for "minority" employees. When that happens, the whole business of reverse discrimination is nothing but a white liberal guilt trip.

Nevertheless, an equitable society, a society in which there is generosity, would be uncomfortable if certain groups are systematically absent from its important activities. I find discrimination against white males in the present on the grounds that other white males in the past have discriminated to be a morally abhorrent practice. (This is perhaps because I have been a victim of it. No-

body sets up quotas for Irish Catholics despite past discrimination against us.)

There ought to be ways to create an equitable and
generous society in which no one is forced to pay the
debts for past injustices. It is disappointing to realize
that Catholic Christians have no vision to contribute to
discussions of how it ought to be achieved.

There has been an enormous outpouring of statements, and exhortations on the just society from Catholic sources; but when it comes to the kind of applied
wisdom at which our tradition was once very good, we
do not seem to have much to say other than an occasional endorsement of busing, a refusal to accept in our
schools children who are escapees from busing (which is,
in my personal opinion, an unjust refusal; but that's another matter).

All I can do here is to point out some of the problems
and outline my own personal ways of thinking about the
problem. I simply have to acknowledge the inadequacy
of the presentation (while insisting that no one else I
know of has made an adequate presentation).

When one speaks of justice today, of a loving generosity toward other human beings which reflects God's
loving generosity to us, it seems the best one can do is to
present the challenging question and exhort the person
to do the kind of moral and intellectual work that is necessary for the church to begin to understand the complexities of justice in the modern world. Even then, I
must say that I hope the church (in the form of its scholars and leaders) can listen when the laity clearly articulate their dilemmas.

Sometimes, I fear, the church, particularly the clergy,
won't listen because they are so eager to impose the answers they have already figured out.

The goods of the world: for the welfare of all or just for the few?

WE can make a more decisive contribution from the Catholic tradition to justice when we speak about the necessity for the goods of the world to be distributed equitably among humankind. Here the original notion of justice as God's generosity speaks powerfully and simply.

The fruits of the earth are intended for the welfare of all humans and not just for the welfare of the privileged few. While the ideal is clear and within the Catholic commitment the struggle for the ideal must be tenacious, the ways the ideal can be achieved in the present world are more difficult to specify.

It is fashionable in certain circles to argue that because Americans are rich, other nations are poor. Indeed, Pope John Paul himself came quite close to taking such a position in his UN talk during his American visit. However, it is not a position for which there is a solid economic base.

American affluence is only to some minor extent dependent on resources gathered from outside the United States—most notably oil, chromium, a few other such things, and for these we pay very heavily indeed. Americans do drink coffee that is grown in Latin America, but if they should stop drinking that coffee, they would destroy the economies of the coffee-producing countries. If we should stop importing oil and chromium, our agricultural production might slip drastically, and we would no longer be able to feed, as we do, half the world.

If Americans consume a considerable amount of the world's goods, they also feed a considerable amount of the world's people; and if they stopped consuming the goods, the result would be the end of international trade and worldwide economic disaster. This is a fact which seems to elude many of the religious leaders who complain about the world's natural resources flowing into America, forgetting that America is also one of the world's prime exporters of raw materials, especially food grains.

The complexity of the problem and the falsity of the "they're poor because we're rich" argument can be neatly illustrated by the oil-producing countries which currently have enormous revenues and still very great poverty. In some cases the revenues are skimmed off by a political elite, but in other more democratic countries like Venezuela, for example, it is because the economic and institutional structures of the society are simply unable to equitably distribute their wealth.

Many Mexican economists, realistically accepting the structural limitations of their own income distribution system, have argued against massive increases of Mexican oil production on the grounds that there is no way the revenues of such production could equitably be distributed within the society. In effect, then, OPEC oil prices are a form of world income redistribution.

It is, however, an income redistribution, which causes minor difficulty to the United States, enormous problems to the poor, petroleum-dependent countries of the world (like India and Pakistan), and yet has relatively little impact on most of the truly poor people of the world. Sophisticated economists argue that worldwide redistribution of wealth across a north-south line will only be effective when there is a commitment within the receiving countries to internal distribution of wealth, a commitment which most of the authoritarian Third World leadership does not want to make, in part because they do not know how to accomplish it.

Justice clearly demands that we help the impoverished countries; it also demands that we help them intelligently, so that transfers of wealth do affect the lives of ordinary people. With the best will and the most generosity and the greatest justice in the world, this latter goal is a tough one to achieve.

So, distributing the "fruits of the earth" with justice—so easy to describe in theory and so richly supported by the Catholic tradition—is an extraordinarily difficult and complex task in practice. Minimally, the just Catholic cannot throw up his/her hands in abhorrence at the complexity, taking refuge in the simplest terms of either the radical right or the radical left. The wise Catholic is terribly skeptical of the pronouncements on complex matters heard from both sides.

Does justice demand that the environment be protected?

THE Catholic tradition, far more than many others, reinforces respect for the physical environment. The material world for us is not a thing to be used and then discarded as though it were a dirty paper napkin. It is a sacrament which reveals God's goodness and is taken up in his redemptive plan, just as we are.

The material world, as well as the spirit world, is ordained for salvation, and we bridge the gap between the two, responsible for the salvation of the material world. Hence, we must reverence and respect it.

But once one states that principle and insists that Catholics cannot be indifferent to the abuses of the environment, one encounters enormous complexity in attempting to apply the principle in practice. What does respect for the sacramentality of the environment, for example, indicate in the way of a wise energy policy? Some enthusiastic Catholic spokespersons would insist that it means we must develop solar energy; others would insist that we must give up our automobiles. These are policy decisions which go far beyond the dictates of the principles.

The economics of energy are extremely complicated, and the facts about the availability of energy are so obscure, oftentimes impenetrable, that men and women of intelligence and good faith may disagree about both the nature of the problem (will we run out of petroleum before the century is over?) and about the appropriate responses to the problem. Nor is one's confidence in the "experts" enhanced by the thought that both the Yom Kippur war and the Iranian gas lines were the results not of actual shortages but of administrative decisions made by government "experts."

Even more concretely, is there a Catholic stand on strip mining? Such a mining technique (in which the top layer of soil is removed and the coal mined as though in a quarry) does indeed do tremendous harm to the physical environment. But can this harm be justified by economic necessity? And are there ways in which strip mining can be done with minimal environmental harm?

The technologies, the economics, and the facts that are necessary to have at one's fingertips in order to understand and answer these questions are simply beyond the grasp of most Americans. One should surely take a stand on these issues as a matter of personal political conviction, but one should be wary about insisting that any particular decision is the only possible conclusion of Christian justice.

If there are no clear-cut answers, what does justice demand?

MY own inclination is to be exceedingly skeptical about the ability of the government to deal intelligently with these problems. I prefer as much of a marketplace solution as possible, since the marketplace seems less likely to create shortages and inequities than government bureaucracy. An increasing number of economists, even liberal economists, share this position. But I am not sure, and I don't think anyone else is sure either. I am not about to equate my economic proclivities with Christian justice. Neither should anyone else.

Environment, equitable distribution of wealth, corruption, minority rights, taxation are all issues of enormous practical importance which affect decisions many of us have to make every day of our lives. Unfortunately, there appear to be no clear "Christian" answers (though in some cases there is a reasonably clear Christian wisdom and in other cases there are tendencies which seem to be reasonable from the perspective of Christian justice).

One might devoutly hope that Christian moralists, ethicians, and spiritual writers might be able to provide more wisdom for us in their suggestions in the years ahead. It is unlikely that there ever will be uniquely and specifically Christian answers to those problems. So, justice, like charity, becomes a virtue which requires a fundamental orientation and then imposes upon us the necessity of working out our own practical answers.

It is not surprising that justice and charity demand almost the same orientation: loving generosity. They both offer us the same motivation: God's loving generosity with us.

The bottom line, then, for Christian justice is more than just "to every one his/her due" insisted on by the old moral theologians; it is rather "to every one we must be generous."

This is a tough bottom line. The obscurities of how we should apply it in practice ought not to deceive us for a minute. It is not easy to live a generous life.

Chapter Seventeen

Catholic Social Teaching

Whatever happened to Catholic social teaching?

IN the previous chapter, we talked about Christian justice as generosity. It seems to be appropriate, before we go on to the other virtues of the Christian life, to continue our discussion of justice.

This time we speak about the just society, the just social order as Catholic Christianity has come to understand it. This theory of Catholic social teaching is something less than revelation but something more than just unofficial opinion in the church; rather, it is the result of many centuries of Catholic reflection on the nature of human society as that reflection has been illuminated by Catholic conviction about the nature of human nature and the purpose of human life.

A year or so ago, after a lecture, one woman religious in the audience rose to assure everyone that she was a "Catholic Marxist." It turned out that she meant that she believed in the Marxist theory of class conflict. In particular, she identified with the "oppressed class" in its battle with the "oppressor class." She had not, in fact, read Marx, nor had she ever lived in a socialist society. (A few weeks of actually living in a socialist society is guaranteed to cure most Catholic Marxists. Try Poland, for example, the most benign, perhaps, of the socialist societies, to see how good capitalism looks.)

The nun was concerned about social injustice. She was unaware that the Marxist response, once it becomes institutionalized in government, becomes more oppressive than the oppression it replaced in every instance the world has known. Nor was she aware, apparently, that there are other responses to social oppression, at least as old as the Marxist one, which do not turn oppressive.

There was a time when all of us who grew up Catholic and went to Catholic schools were exposed to the rudiments of Catholic social teaching. But in recent years, with the enthusiasm of Catholic social activists of various varieties of Marxism and "liberation," Catholic social teaching has become dormant, and now many people have never heard of it.

This is a great loss, not merely for Catholics but for other people in the world.

What is Catholic social theory?

THE Catholic view of the Good Society is profoundly different from both Marxism and capitalism, insisting more vigorously than either on the freedom of the individual. Marxist "liberation" does not mean personal freedom, it means that power is taken away from one class and given to another; and capitalist freedom, certainly more real than Marxist "liberation," often does not mean practical freedom for the many people who are too poor or too powerless to enjoy the freedom to which they technically have a right.

The Catholic social theory is precapitalist (and Marxism is, in fact, a heresy of capitalism). In some sense it is also preindustrial. It might even be called "archaic," because it represents a wisdom about human relationships that precedes the emergence of the nation-state, large governmental bureaucracies, corporate ownership of production, and the vast formal structures which now mediate between government and the rest of society.

For it is the neighborhood, the local community, the direct links to the peasant village which represent in the modern world the best examples of how Catholic social theory recommends humans ought to organize themselves. The anarchists, the syndicalists, and the authors of the Declaration of Independence would doubtless agree.

Catholic social teaching, while a minority viewpoint, is by no means alone in insisting that much of the old tribal wisdom and much of the old informal local communalism can and does survive the industrial state. Nor is it alone in insisting that the organic local community ought to be the fundamental basis of social order, and that the industrial state can be reorganized to recognize such values.

One of the great tragedies of our time is that in their eagerness to become fashionable and tough-minded many Catholics have bought the Marxist world-view, which is merely a variant of the capitalist view, and have ignored the fact that in their own tradition there is a far more profound criticism of contemporary society than the Marxists teach.

There are four basic principles in the Catholic social theory: (a) personalism, (b) pluralism, (c) organicity, and (d) subsidiarity. Each of them requires some extended discussion.

Personalism: Me or Society?

IN direct and systematic disagreement with the explicit theory of the Marxists and the implicit practice of the capitalists, Catholic social theory proclaims that society exists to serve the welfare of the individual member and not the other way around. We do not get our rights, our value, our worth from being members of society. We do not exist for society; society exists for us.

Society has power, it has authority over us, only insofar as it uses that power to facilitate the growth and development of the individual person. When society and its tool, government, so dominate human life that society's leaders assume that the individual members exist only to serve the good of society (which means the will of those who have the political and military power), oppression automatically and inevitably enters the picture.

The vigorous, forthright, and outspoken stand of John Paul II in his UN speech, and in virtually every other speech he has given about international problems, supports the dignity, the value, and the independence of the individual person. He articulates this fundamental Catholic social principle of personalism, a principle which, in John Paul's case, is at the core of an elaborate and highly professional philosophical system.

Both socially and philosophically, John Paul is a personalist with an intense commitment to the dignity of the human person. His tendency is to respond with appalled anger whenever the dignity, the freedom, and the value of the individual person is violated, no matter what the system is that is committing the violation.

The principle of personalism seems so self-evident that some people may wonder why one would dignify it as a crucial social principle. But consider how often the principle is violated: those corporations which pollute the environment to maximize profit, risking the lives of the workers; those companies which make automobiles that explode on impact; those military leaders who consider that a draft will provide a "pool" of personnel rather than a group of individuals whose lives and freedom are unspeakably precious; those educators who are willing to view their institutions as mass baby-sitting factories to keep children off the streets; those governments which deny freedom of speech and criticism or freedom of worship to their citizens; those political leaders who endorse discrimination against presently living persons to expiate discrimination against persons who lived in the past—all such people are violating the principle of personalism. They are using individual persons for political, social, or economic purposes.

Personalism demands that the person is always the end, never the means. Any social order which does not acknowledge this truth is unjust and oppressive. Indeed, whatever its claim, it in fact is treating its citizens as though they were slaves.

The vast administrative bureaucracy which has grown up in the federal government in the last 30 years is little different from the administrative bureaucracy in more formally authoritarian states. The bureaucrats view themselves not as servants of the people but as masters. (Consider the Department of Energy bureaucrats, for example, who cause fuel shortages deliberately so that long lines and high prices will force people to "conserve." Such bureaucrats have turned persons into things. They are not really indistinguishable in their basic premises from Stalinist bureaucrats in Russia.)

Personalism is the primary principle of Catholic social teaching. The other three principles flow from it both as inevitable conclusions and as essential prerequisites so that personalism may function and flourish.

It has been a terrible tragedy that the church's profound commitment to political freedom has not been understood by Catholics in the last four decades. Indeed many Catholics, far from preaching that freedom, permitted themselves to be seduced in the name of justice into supporting regimes which deny and eliminate freedoms. Some such Catholics have even argued that freedom must be sacrificed in the "Third World" countries in the name of the pursuit of economic justice.

It is not clear to me who appointed these Catholic writers as decision-makers for the people in the Third

World. Nor is it clear to me that sacrificing political and personal freedom is a prerequisite for economic progress. The free country of Costa Rica has made as much economic progress as the slave state of Cuba, for example. But more importantly, the bottom line for Catholic social theory is the dignity and the freedom of the individual person. No one, not even self-anointed Catholic "liberationists," has any right to sacrifice that principle for any cause.

Pluralism: variety or assimilation?

BOTH Marxist and capitalist social theory see society as made up of the individual on the one hand and the total society (of which the state is the organ) on the other. Without necessarily denying that there may be intermediary groups between the individual and the state, these social theories pay little attention to and do not take into account either the functioning or the importance of these intermediary groups.

Catholic social theory, however, exalts the importance of the intervening groups precisely because it sees them as necessary to protect the freedom of the individual and to give the individual the fullest and richest chance of developing talent and potential.

The slave state cannot tolerate the independence of the local community (the neighborhood), the church, the trade union or work association, the fraternal benevolent group, the political party, or any of the voluntary or quasi-voluntary organizations which humans join on their own initiative and not because the state constrains them to do so.

Nor can the capitalist social economic order freely accept the idea that any of these intermediary groups are more important than the large corporation. If, for example, the family life of the corporate executive gets in the way of his or her functioning within the corporation, it is the family that must yield. The Catholic social theory assumes and exalts a "messy" social order in which all kinds of overlapping, cross-cutting, independent, voluntary groups flourish without the permission of the state, for humans join such organizations and exercise a fundamental human right that the state has no authority to permit or deny.

The family, the trade union, the political party, the neighborhood community, the church exist as a free exercise of human right, and not as a concession of the state. The state exists to facilitate the welfare of the individual person. Since the individual person needs these intervening groups for his/her welfare, growth, and happiness, the state should facilitate in appropriate ways the functioning of such groups (mostly, one suspects, by leaving them alone, by protecting them from those enemies who would destroy them).

Similarly, the principle of pluralism assumes the right of various cultural groups to maintain their cultural heritage and independence within the larger society. The Catholic social theory believes in variety and heterogeneity rather than in homogenization and assimilation. It believes that unity is created not through the imposition of uniformity but rather through the integration of diversity.

Moreover, Catholic social theory believes that the variegated splendors of God are reflected not by a bland and homogeneous society but by a rich and diversified one, and it is convinced that diversity only becomes a threat to unity when a state or society oppresses one or the other of the diverse groups. It is one of the black marks on the history of the American church that in the

1920s and 1930s its leadership yielded so readily to the "Americanization" of immigrants. "Americanization" meant that the immigrant groups had to give up their own heritages, their own customs, to become "American" like everyone else.

Of course, the genius of American political and social pluralism has always been to respect the integrity of the diversified subcultures within it. During the Americanization phase, the fundamental principles of the republic and the fundamental principles of the Catholic social theory were violated mostly because of the conviction in the "best circles" of our society that certain immigrant groups, mostly Catholic, were culturally inferior, if not racially inferior, and could only be integrated into American society if their cultures were stamped out.

It took a long time for this policy to be formally abandoned. One must say honestly that many church leaders still seem to subscribe to it. A recent statement of the American hierarchy on cultural pluralism is a formal break with the old Americanization emphasis, one that is long overdue.

Catholic social theory believes in pluralism of subcultures, pluralism of organizations, pluralism of institutions because pluralism makes for a richer, more interesting society (one that reflects God's splendors more effectively) and also, especially, because pluralistic societies provide greater opportunities for the freedom and the development of the individual human person.

Organicity: networks within networks?

THE words "organicity" and "subsidiarity" (which we will discuss under the next point) are, I must concede, terrible words. They convey absolutely nothing unless they are explained. By "organicity" I mean that society is not made up of a large number of atomized individuals but rather of dense relational networks. Society is a network of networks.

In a way, the principle of organicity is simply the other side of the coin of the principle of pluralism. Some social theorists believe that with the decline of the feudal lord and the coming of the urban industrial state, the old intimate, informal, casual, traditional relationship of family, local community, church, and region would disappear from the human condition. (Some social theorists added to this "would" the additional connotation of "should.")

Actually, contemporary social research shows that the old "primary" groups survived and flourished in industrial society and are indeed essential to the functioning of the educational and military establishments and even the mass media (whose influences are not on the mass but on key individuals within the mass). Catholic social theory believes that humans form these informal networks as naturally as they breathe and that such networks are the warp and woof of society.

The healthy development of human society and the full perfection of human freedom depend on such networks. Not only are they not eliminated by urban industrialism, they are essential for the large corporation to flourish. Social policy which ignores the organic networks of human relationships runs serious risk of failure, and social policy which attempts to destroy such networks (like so much city planning has tried to destroy city communities) will inevitably be counterproductive.

If you want to work effectively with human beings, you do not destroy their organic networks of relationships, the way Marxism tries to do, or pretend, as capitalism does, that they do not exist. The solution, rather, is to work with human beings in the web relationships in which they live and try to facilitate the reinforcing, con-

structive dynamics that are at work in such relationships.

High school education, for example, in the United
States generally pretends that there is no such thing as a
peer group as the most important influence in the life of
young people. It tries to instruct the teen-agers as
though there were no peer groups.

In fact, as anyone who has worked with teen-agers
ought to be well aware, the peer group either cooperates
with the educational institution, which makes it effective, or it fights the institution, which means failure. The
education of teen-agers absolutely requires that the peer
group be persuaded to involve itself in the educational
process.

There would have been a time in human history when
the above insight would be taken for granted. That it is
not now taken for granted and is not a cornerstone of
educational policy, is proof of how much the atomistic
view of human society dominates our ways of thinking
and our ways of elaborating social policy.

Similarly, in the church one hears an enormous
amount these days about "evangelization." Almost always the "evangelizers" speak and act as though an individual person is the target for their activity. One does
not need the research my colleagues and I have done,
however, to know that to be effective, evangelization
must aim mainly at the family unit and, wherever there
are larger networks of close relationships within such
networks.

You do not preach the gospel as a social structural
gospel. Those who think that the atomistic society exists
or ought to exist or is an evolutionary necessity simply
cannot comprehend it.

Subsidiarity: Small is Beautiful? Live and let live?

THE principle of subsidiarity is the crown of Catholic social theory. It integrates the other three principles and indicates the direction of wise social policy.

Stated quite simply, as it was in the encyclical letter *Quadragesimo Anno* by Pius XI, it is that nothing should be done by a larger or higher organization that can be done equally well by a smaller or lower organization: nothing done in the UN that can be done in the individual country, nothing by the federal government that can be done by the state government, nothing by the state government that can be done by the local government, nothing by the city government that can be done by the neighborhood, nothing by the neighborhood that can be done by the block, and nothing by the block that can be done by the family.

Such a principle maximizes the opportunity for individual growth and development as well as the exercise of personal freedom. It reinforces the pluralism of structures and organizations within a society. It respects the organic networks of close human relationships, and prevents the government from being the all-controlling, oppressive bureaucracy.

The principle of subsidiarity is the most striking evidence of the enormous difference between Catholic social theory on the one hand, and both socialism and capitalism on the other. For capitalism and its socialist heresy both believe in centralization and bigness, whereas as Catholic social theory, along with the social theory of the anarchists and the syndicalists, the Buddhists, and, to some extent, the Moslems, believe in smallness and decentralization.

The late E. F. Schumacher, the English economist, became a cult hero in the last years of his life because of his extraordinary book, *Small Is Beautiful.* He argued that technology and industrialization did not of themselves require either centralization or large size. Indeed, greater efficiency could be obtained through decentralization and small size.

It was accidental in Schumacher's perspective that the capitalist theory of bigness and centralization happened to come historically at the same time as industrial science and technology were developed. One could have all the benefits of modern scientific technology without paying the price of excessive size and overcentralization.

There are a number of ironies in Schumacher's work. For example, in *Small Is Beautiful* there is an essay on Buddhist economics, which, it would seem, is relatively similar to the Catholic social theory.

In one part of the chapter there was a passage that struck me as being vaguely familiar. Somewhere I had read it before. Schumacher had it footnoted, so I flipped to the back of the book and discovered that in the middle of his essay on Buddhist economics he was quoting Pius XI and the encyclical letter *Quadragesimo Anno.*

Schmacher, searching for a religion in which his economic and social perspective would find an appropriate base, spent the middle years of his life as a Catholic. The most disappointing irony of all is that even though he was a cult hero on the college campuses and among progressive and radical social thinkers, Schumacher was utterly ignored by the American church.

The social activists at that time were "into" Marxism and Liberation. Indeed, most American Catholics were unaware that Schumacher was one of their own. A num-

ber of us found out about it only when we read an article about him in the Protestant journal, *The Christian
Century*.

In a bitter mood long ago, I formulated Greeley's
First Law: When Catholics abandon part of their heritage, other people discover it. The treatment of *Small Is
Beautiful* by American social thinkers and activists is a
tragic and stupid proof of how accurate that melancholy
law is.

Subsidiarity, local wisdom, decentralization, neighborhood control, small is beautiful—all of these things
are currently fashionable among some of America's
most advanced social theorists and planners. They are
also a rearticulation of the traditonal Catholic social
thinking.

As I noted, the American church and its peace and
justice enthusiasts are utterly ignorant of the convergence of the writings of the great papal encyclicals and
the current trend in thinking. It is much more popular to
be a Catholic Marxist and to posture as a radical than
to try to understand the profound human wisdom contained in the principle of subsidiarity. For all too many
Catholics, Marx is beautiful (popularized Marx, not the
real thing) and small is irrelevant.

An official of the Department of Health, Education
and Welfare once pointed out to me that federal and
state governments can spend up to $10,000 a year for
each citizen of the state of New York who passes the last
months or years of his or her life in a hospital bed. Can
you imagine, this official asked, how much care the
families of these older people would be able to provide if
the government gave them, rather than the hospitals,
even $7500 a year? And can you imagine the enormous
saving we would make in administrative overhead?

"Then why don't we do it?" I asked. "Accountants," he replied. Congress would demand that there be an accounting for every penny of the program, and accountants argue that it would be impossible to supervise such a program. I say that if we don't want to turn it over to the individual family, then at least we could have neighborhood delivery systems and let the neighborhoods supervise the money the government gives them to care for their aged. "The accountants won't buy that either."

I certainly wouldn't blame accountants either personally or as a profession. They are caught in bureaucratic rules and regulations which proclaim that bigness is better, centralization is cheaper.

The empirical evidence runs the other way, of course, but the basic social perspective that permeates American society rejects the evidence. The bigger the better; the more central control, the more efficiency. That is the way we Americans think and behave whether we are capitalists or socialists.

And yet, Catholic social theory responds in complete agreement with E. F. Schumacher: small is beautiful; add that small is more efficient, too. This perspective is far more radical, if radicalism is what you're looking for, than Marxism.

The tragedy is that American Catholics are almost unaware of the theory and American Catholic thinkers and scholars, with precious few exceptions, have not tried to reflect upon what such a theory might imply for the reorganization of American life. Perhaps in the years ahead they will.

The bottom line of Catholic social teaching is quite simple. Small is beautiful and, besides, it works better.

Chapter Eighteen

Temperance

**What does the Christian perspective add
to the virtue of temperance?**

TEMPERANCE is the virtue which inclines us to discretion and moderation in our consumption of the pleasures of this world. As it has frequently been described in Catholic writing, it may seem to be indistinguishable from the virtue practiced by the Greek Stoics or urged by the Old Testament Wisdom writers who provided catalogs of appropriate moral behavior—don't eat too much, don't drink too much, don't dance too much, don't enjoy too much sexual pleasure.

The principle underlying such exhortations to moderation and discretion was that excessive consumption of any pleasure caused both loss of self-control and destruction of the pleasure itself from an overdose.

The Greek philosophers and the Hebrew Wisdom writers were acute observers of the human condition. If there seems little new in the exhortations of today, the reason is that Western culture has been so profoundly shaped by their worldview.

Christianity has little to add to their pragmatic, wise advice. The Catholic Christian contribution, as we have insisted repeatedly in these notes, is not primarily moral but religious. Our perspective on the virtue of temperance, our bottom line, does not consist of new moral injunctions, but rather of a new religious insight (which is really a renewal and a revalidation of an old religious insight) on the position of humankind in creation.

251

The Catholic Christian believes the world and its plea-sures are a gift of a loving and gracious God. All that is good, all that is true, all that is beautiful, all that is en-joyable, all that is fun in this world is God's gift to us. Food, drink, sex are only good sacraments. That is to say, they reveal God's loving graciousness to us.

Food, drink, and sex, for example, also become Sac-raments, official channels which the church uses for the flow of grace. If some things are Sacraments, it is only because everything is a sacrament. God reveals himself to us through the whole of creation.

For the Catholic Christian, the virtue of temperance begins with this fundamental insight—the pleasures and joys of life are sacramental, that is to say, they reveal God's loving goodness.

Are worldly pleasures necessarily evil?

FROM the Catholic Christian viewpoint, there is no possibility of assuming a puritanical or pessimistic ap-proach to pleasure. Pleasure is not an evil, it is a good. Things of this world are not sinful, they are sacraments. The joys of this world are not to be fled as temptations but celebrated as presents. If we use them carefully and, on occasion, cautiously, the reason is not that we are afraid of them but that we value and respect them.

Therefore, by Catholic Christian standards, poverty is not a good thing in itself. Celibacy is not a good thing in itself; fasting and abstinence are not good things in themselves. They may be, as we shall see later, useful voluntary means to other ends. The Catholic Christians' practice of celibacy, poverty, abstinence is not observed because those pleasures that are given up are evil but rather because the free relinquishing of such goods —either permanent or temporary—can facilitate more important goods.

As a Christian, one may give up certain joys not because they are joys but because it is understood that for some people in some situations greater joys may be obtained (*in this life*) by giving up other joys.

Sacrifice in the Catholic Christian heritage is the exercise of an option to relinquish one good in preference for another. The free exercise of such an option, performed with the guidance of the Holy Spirit, is not caused by fear, guilt, prudery, or pessimism.

Priests and religious relinquish the joys of marriage and family life not because they think sex is evil, not because they are sexless, and surely not because they have a lower hormone level than other people. A committed, celibate person makes his/her choice because the choice frees him or her for more total service of God and God's people.

The choice is not made because the person is more virtuous and the choice does not make the person more virtuous; it bestows on the person a freedom, a mobility, a capacity for extensive as well as intensive commitment. It also makes the person a symbol of the love which is not so visible as are other human loves.

It may well be argued that celibacy does not and has not meant these things for many priests and religious in the present or even in the past. Motivations for the celibate choice have often been fear and guilt, and the arguments in favor of celibacy have often been based on prudery and puritanism and the conviction that sex is evil and that only weak men and women dirty themselves with such vile behavior.

Must celibacy be a requirement for priesthood?

AT one time, not so long ago, many young Catholics were told in school that if they really wanted to be good, they had to become priests and nuns. Now young people may hear from some purveyors of the conventional wisdom that if they want to be good, they have to marry.

Both positions are wrong. Neither the married nor the celibate state is in itself superior. The pertinent question is rather how one lives within the context of the choice one has made.

I have emphasized that decisions about celibacy, abstinence, and poverty are to be freely made. No one should be forced into marriage or forced not to marry; no one should be hassled into poverty or impeded in the practice of it. Once the free choice is made, however, it becomes a commitment which should not be easily abandoned.

I do not agree with those who say that the church has no right to require a commitment of celibacy of those who become priests in the Western Rite. One is under no compulsion to be a priest and one has no right to claim admission to the priesthood.

I also believe, however, that the choice of celibacy as a free option ought to be separated from a commitment to the priesthood. While I am personally committed to celibacy, I think (in theory) that the disengagement of the priestly commitment from celibate commitment would be an advantage to the church.

However, I must add quickly that the empirical evidence available to me does not indicate that celibacy is the reason for the vocation shortage today. I would also add that in the present circumstances I believe that obligatory celibacy should be continued.

I see no reason to believe that in Catholicism a voluntary celibacy of the clergy would mean anything more than the obligatory marriage that is expected of Protestant and Orthodox parish clergy.

In fact, I suspect that obligatory marriage is what

many of the advocates of "optional" celibacy want. I will become a supporter of optional celibacy in practice only when I am persuaded that it can be truly maintained in the church as an option.

Finally, I would note that whether celibacy is optional or obligatory, whether dispensations are easy or hard to come by, one should not lightly abandon a commitment one has made to a way of life.

Many of the opponents of celibacy cite all the bad arguments that have been advanced for it as evidence that celibacy (and poverty and abstinence too, though those are rarely discussed) is a mistake. But such a line of reasoning ignores the fact that the right thing may be done for the wrong reason and that the wrong reason may eventually be replaced by the right one.

What is the Catholic position on alcohol?

VOLUNTARY celibacy, voluntary poverty, voluntary abstinence have always been part of the Catholic tradition. However mixed the motivations may have been at certain times and however deficient in practice, in its best moments Catholic Christianity has known that sacrifice does not mean giving up that which is dirty, vile, evil, or sinful but rather exchanging that which is good for that which is better.

Catholic Christians may have made mistakes down through the years, but they were never Manichaean. They never argued (despite all the warnings about patent leather shoes) that sex, food, drink, or worldly possessions were evil. The bottom line on the pleasures of this world for a Catholic Christian is not that these pleasures should be avoided, but rather that these pleasures are sacraments.

One hardly need observe that most humans manage to

get themselves in trouble by becoming obsessed with food, drink, or sex. Throughout the course of Christianity, one virtually automatic response to this observation has been to forbid the enjoyment of those things which sometimes, for most of us, become problems and at all times cause some people problems.

In America the word "temperance" has come to stand for legislation against the use of alcoholic beverages (legislation pushed with enormous success by the Women's Christian Temperance Union). The "noble experiment" of Prohibition was, in retrospect, an incredible attempt to deny an entire population the use of alcohol. What was incredible about Prohibition was not that it failed and not that it was an enormous boost to big-time crime, but that anybody thought it would work.

However, neo-Prohibitionism is still alive and well (and flourishing at the Department of Health, Education and Welfare). Its arguments are almost the same as those of the WCTU a hundred years ago: "Look at the high rate of alcoholism, look at all the broken families caused by excessive drinking, look at all the auto deaths caused by drunken driving. We can eliminate all this trouble by putting heavier taxes on alcohol, limiting its sales, and restricting its usage."

It is not at all clear, of course, that any such tactics would work to reduce the amount of alcohol consumed in this country. Nor is it clear that reduced alcohol use would cure alcoholics and stop the lunacy of drunken driving.

Finally, it would hardly seem to be wise social policy to try to prevent and inhibit everyone from making use of alcohol because some people abuse it.

Thus does the Catholic Christian heritage oppose

puritanism, and thus did it resist the Eighteenth Amendment, which (and you will read this in very few history books) was in part directed at the drinking of Catholic immigrant groups by their Protestant "betters." The fruit of the vine (and its cousins) is meant to be used and enjoyed. It is a sacrament as well as the matter for a Sacrament. "Wherever the Catholic sun doth shine/there is music and laughter and good red wine./At least I've found it so./Benedicamus Domino," as Hilaire Belloc wrote in defiance of prohibitionism.

How is the fundamental perspective of sacramentality applied to temperance?

BUT the Catholic Christian tradition that supports drinking is vigorously opposed to drunkenness. On the one hand it does not accept the Prohibition argument that drinking inevitably leads to drunkenness, but it also warns that everyone should drink in moderation and that some, for reasons of physiology or personality would be much better advised not to drink at all.

There is nothing original or profound in such a warning, though the persistence of the Prohibitionist position is evidence that the "moderate use" approach is by no means self-evident. To this moderate stance, the Catholic Christian heritage adds its own special reason: one does not drink excessively because drink is a sacrament, and one does not misuse sacraments.

The Catholic Christian argument, then, for temperance and moderation is one rooted in sacramentality, the sacredness of things. The goods of the world are put here for our enjoyment and our use. We can enjoy them only when we also use them moderately, but we also use them moderately because we respect them, reverence them, and are grateful for them.

Temperance and moderation, rooted in a belief in sacramentality, take different shapes, depending on the particular worldly joy whose goodness we are celebrating.

Some people should not drink at all, others choose not to drink because of caution and the need to bear witness. (Neither of my parents drank, and my own personal abhorrence of drunkenness is no doubt powerfully influenced by that fact.)

Still others may voluntarily give up drinking for a certain period of time either to assure themselves of self-control or to bear witness to others that it is possible to have fun and to celebrate without drinking.

Many people fast and abstain (but they call it "dieting") for the purely secular though perfectly legitimate reason of improving their physical appearance. Others reduce their levels of eating (especially during Lent) as an exercise in the focus of energies and in the possession of the self.

Some people practice total poverty for the better service of God and his people (though the vow of poverty in a religious community does not necessarily mean a poor life). Others are very cautious in their collection of material goods, because, under the guidance of the Spirit, they believe in "hanging loose" and "traveling light." still others periodically divest themselves of excess possessions because they have become a barrier and a burden and an obstacle, an end rather than a means.

For married people temperance in sexuality is much more likely to mean improving the quality of sexual relationships instead of diminishing the quantity.

The point about all of these choices is respect for the sacramentality of wordly pleasures. They are highly personal choices, to be made under the inspiration and illumination of the spirit and in the context of a situation in which a given person finds himself or herself.

The general principle of moderation and the fundamental perspective of sacramentality do not dictate specific courses of action that are universally applicable. Freedom of choice of the individual Christian must be respected, and moralistic judgment about other people's choices, to say nothing of pressures and constraints to impose our choices on other people are to be resolutely rejected.

Why does too much of a good thing become a bad thing?

THE style of life of another person is between that person and the person's confessor, the Internal Revenue Service, and God. One's lifestyle is not anyone else's business. The person who appoints himself or herself a judge of someone else's lifestyle is preempting the role of the Holy Spirit and betraying his/her pathological envy.

If judgment of the lifestyle of others has been frequently made in the course of history, the reason is that the coming of Jesus of Nazareth did not eliminate envy.

If the things of this world are good and meant to be enjoyed—if they are, in fact, sacraments designed to reveal God's loving goodness—why should there be any problem in their use? If one Pontiac Phoenix is a sacrament, would not 10 be 10 sacraments? Are not 10 sacraments better than one? If one woman is a revelation of God's loving goodness, are not a half dozen women even more of a revelation? If one bottle of Chateau Lafite Rothschild is a hint of paradise, would not 100 bottles hint even more strongly?

The questions are absurd, of course, but they clearly

specify the problem. Too much of any good thing becomes a bad thing. Too much is more than we can handle, more than we can use, more than we need, more than we can enjoy, more than we can celebrate.

It may be hard to specify what is too much of any good thing for a specific individual, but for all of us there are levels beyond which it becomes excessive. We all know from bitter experience how easy it is to reach those levels.

The problem, then, is not in the good news of sacramental reality; the problem is in our inability to avoid excess. The Puritan and the Prohibitionist simply cannot see that. Neither, for that matter, can the Catholic enthusiast who wishes to make universally applicable rules.

Puritans and Prohibitionists wish to avoid the abuse by eliminating use; the Catholic enthusiast wishes to control the abuse by requiring that everyone do exactly the same thing. The Puritan abandons his/her faith in the goodness of this world's joys, while the Catholic enthusiast abandons his/her faith in the diversity of human nature and in the variety of the human condition.

Why do we destroy the sacramentality of things by overusing them? This question, at the heart of the discussion of the virtue of temperance, points again to the fundamental flaw in human nature which we call original sin. We misuse the goods of this world precisely because we are afraid we will lose them. We pile up treasures for ourselves so that we may build walls of protection around ourselves to defend against our own frailty, our own mortality, our own contingency.

What drives people to abuse and overuse pleasure?

IT is the fear of death, the terror of nonbeing which drives us to pile up possessions and pleasures, food and drink and sex objects as barriers to keep out the icy cold of nonbeing. The alcoholic, the miser, the spendthrift, the compulsive gambler, the Don Juan may not realize that they are trying to defend themselves against nonbeing. Various layers of psychological problems may intervene between existential fear and compulsive behavior.

Nonetheless we abuse and overuse the good things, the joys, the sacraments of this world because we are afraid, in the depths of our personality, that we will lose them. We ignore Jesus' warning, which is at the center of the gospel message, against the folly of relying on worldly joys as an insurance against nonbeing.

Often the warnings of Jesus have been interpreted as puritanical injunctions, as though Jesus were saying that the pleasures and joys of this world were wrong. But in fact what he says is that it is wrong for us to place our security in them; for no matter how many of them we have, they cannot protect us from death.

For Jesus, the critical question is whether the sacraments reveal the reality or interfere with it. As long as food, drink, and pleasure reveal to us and point us toward God's love for us, we should merrily celebrate their goodness.

Once these possessions become a means for protecting ourselves without the need of God or an effort to guaratee our personal security by our own efforts or merit, then we will have no time for God's love and their purpose will have been frustrated. That which was sacramental will have become sacrilegious.

From the Catholic Christian perspective, the bottom line on temperance is to keep the sacrament from turning into a sacrilege.

Both Jesus and St. Paul tell us that the material things of this world are also destined for salvation. Their salvation comes in and through us. Food, drink, natural resources, sexual pleasures are not merely sacramental and salvific; they are also destined in ways we do not fully understand to be caught up finally in God's mighty scheme, in his brilliant story of creation and salvation. They play their part in the story through us.

To the extent that God is revealed through created things and to the extent that we unite ourselves with them in the quest for God, then creation is redeemed. We participate in God's loving, redemptive story by living lives of loving goodness amidst the joys and pleasures which he uses to reveal himself to us.

Thus the pleasures of this world are not only sacramental, they are also destined as a sacred goal, caught up through us in a sacred story. To misuse them is not only sacrilege, it is an attempt to destroy the happy ending that has been plotted for the Story.

Where does the virtue of temperance place the Catholic Christian in the debate over the environment?

THE sacramental/sacred story approach that is the Catholic Christian bottom line for temperance puts the Catholic in a middle position in the current debate about "the environment."

The Catholic Christian cannot be an extreme capitalist or an extreme socialist in his/her approach to the physical world, because both attitudes are ruthless in their use of the environment. Neither can he/she approve the denuding of the topsoil, the tearing down of forests, the ripping open of the earth, the pollution of the air, the desecration of the landscape as important but inevitable consequences of material and human progress.

But neither can he/she advocate a return to the primitive simplicity in which humankind is expected merely to adapt to nature like the other animals instead of using its intelligence to adjust reasonably to nature.

Thus one writer says that the origin of our current environmental problems came with the monk who invented the metal-tipped plow in the 9th century. The writer, an anti-Catholic, took great joy in the fact that it was a monk who invented this idea for "ripping open the earth." Even the most simple and elementary forms of agricultural development, in other words, are to be condemned because they lead to the imposition of human order on the natural process.

Another writer has deplored the fact that the glories of the great American prairie have been blighted by the ugliness of grain fields. It did not occur to that writer that grain fields enable hundreds of millions of people to live longer and better and happier lives. (And that substantial segments of the prairie could have easily been preserved while still permitting us the grain fields.)

Still others blame the environmental problems of our era on the Christian-Jewish religion which taught in Genesis that humankind had dominion over the earth. These commentators did not feel any obligation to explain why it took thousands of years after the writing of Genesis for ruthless exploitation of the environment to occur. (Nor did they explain why just a decade or two ago they, or their intellectual predecessors, were damning Catholicism for being antiscientific. Now they are damning it for being proscientific.)

While there are few Americans who accept this kind of environmental extremism, the fact is that such a philosophy, particularly in popularized form, has a certain effect today. It illustrates how quickly humankind can go from one extreme to another—from abusing nature to wanting to surrender oneself to the natural dynamism, and caring not one bit about human nature's essential continuity with nature.

Both extremes are intellectually facile, though their implications are devastatingly destructive. An intermediate position—humankind living in intelligent and rational harmony with nature—may be intellectually difficult to describe, though it is the only way humankind has survived and will continue to survive on earth.

The Catholic position is, of course, the moderate, temperate one between the two extremes. But it says more than just that we must live in intelligent harmony with nature because that is the good and sensible and practical thing to do; it also says that we must live in intelligent harmony with nature because nature is a sacrament, a revelation of God's loving goodness.

Nature is part of the plot of the sacred Story, part of the divine love affair which we humans are caught in. All the good things of the material world around us are caught up in the story of the divine love affair together with us.

This is the religious bottom line with which we Catholic Christians approach the virtue of temperance.

Chapter Nineteen

Confidence & Prudence

Is there a virtue called confidence?

THE old moral virtue of fortitude was a characteristic of soldiers in combat, of kings in crisis, of slaves under oppression, and of Christians faced with persecution. Fortitude, or courage, was a thoroughly admirable virtue. While many of us may not be particularly disposed to be brave ourselves, we admired brave men and women.

Despite demythologization, heroes and heroines are still popular. The police and fire persons who save people, the astronauts, the missionaries, the underground freedom fighters are all men and women who have the strength and the conviction necessary to risk their lives for what they believe in. We sing their praises even if in our more sophisticated thoughts we may be suspicious about their motivations and eager to pick out the human faults and frailties that may appear when they show up on the "Tonight" show.

The Catholic Christian virtue which I call *confidence* is a parallel to the old moral virtue of fortitude. It adds nothing substantive to the qualities of this virtue but rather transforms it by providing a new motivation—or by revalidating an old motivation.

At the core of the gospel message are the parables of Jesus. Central to the parable collection is that group of stories that one scholar has called the tales of "the Great Assurance." They are the most dramatic of the parables, those that tell us of God's dizzying love: the parables of the crazy farmer, the indulgent father (or the prodigal son), and the woman taken in adultery.

The second most important group of parables are those that asssure us of the persistence of God's love and its absolute implacability. The Kingdom of God is like a grain seed which is planted in the fields and *will* come to fruition. It is like the mustard seed that turns into a tree. It is like a seed sown in the fields that resists thorns, rocks, and a lack of moisture and bears a harvest. However small, tiny, and powerless, it will triumph over all its enemies, all the obstacles and barriers that stand in its way.

Such an assertion is not the kind of triumphalism which has often characterized the church. The parables of the Great Assurance only promise us that the gospel will succeed. They do not tell of the glory and triumph of the church as an institution.

Indeed, these parables seem to hint that the more humble the church the more likely it is to succeed. It is not the institution or any ecclesiastical panoply that triumphs, but God's love. The astonishing love of the father for the prodigal son, of the farmer for his workers, of the compassionate judge for the woman taken in adultery—these parables of the Great Assurance tell us God's love is permanent, implacable, and victorious.

We have, therefore, nothing of which we need be afraid—at least not paralyzingly afraid. The only thing we need to fear, as Franklin Roosevelt said long ago, is fear itself—blind, unreasoning terror which paralyzes our every action. The Catholic Christian virtue of confidence tells us that we do not need to be afraid, because God loves us and because that love is stronger than any terror with which this world might threaten us.

The bottom line, then, of the Catholic Christian virtue of confidence is hope. Confidence is the old virtue of fortitude or courage transformed into the radiant power of hope. Confidence is hope applied to all the fears, little and big, and all the challenges, major and minor, that we encounter during our pilgrimage.

Many of us who were trained in Catholic schools tend to link the virtue of fortitude with "standing up for" or "not denying" our faith. In this perspective, confidence means asserting that you are Catholic when the civil authorities demand that you make sacrifice to pagan gods, or charging into an argument when a group of people are attacking the Catholic church at a dinner party, for example.

In both cases we learn that the easy and cowardly response is to go along, to toss the incense on the brazier, or to smile discreetly and politely and say nothing. The courageous Christian, however, refuses to sacrifice and takes on the opposition, effectively refuting (with appropriate historical quotes and references) all the falsehoods spoken about the church.

The civil authorities currently do not have incense braziers, and opportunities to engage in controversial donneybrooks are few and far between. However, there are still certain segments of American society in which you are better off in your career plans and expectations if you soft-pedal your Catholicism. In such environments—certain sections of the government and the academic world, for example—it is better to be a retiring, quiet Catholic than a clearly devout one, better to be a former Catholic than a practicing one, better to be an apostate than someone who still defends the church.

However, the virtue of confidence is something more than a stand-by mechanism ready to be activated in the relatively rare instances when our faith or our church is under unfair attack. Confidence, it seems to me, is the virtue which enables us to seize the opportunities for goodness that are offered us—whether they are big or small—and not be paralyzed by the fear of what will happen if the risk we take in seizing such opportunities doesn't pay off.

As we grow up and mature, we experience two kinds of love—the love that demands performance, requiring that we do certain things, on the one hand, and the love that loves us because we are lovable, on the other. Having experienced both kinds of love, we oscillate back and forth, sometimes responding to love narrowly, fearfully, rigidly, and at other times responding bravely, courageously, openly.

We are told that God is Love and we are prepared to believe it; but the question is, which kind of love is God? God has asserted, and Jesus has claimed, that he is the second kind of love—the love which adores us because we are lovable, the love to which it is safe to give ourselves in trust and fidelity.

Yet others have told us, and sometimes it seems easier to believe, that God is a harsh, demanding, punctilious lover who only loves us when we perform, and indeed, requires perfection in that performance. The Christian virtue of confidence, animated as it is by hope, tells us that God is generous, liberated love, and urges us to give up our fear, our timidity, our anxiety, our attempts to barter and negotiate, and surrender ourselves into his arms.

The Catholic Christian virtue of confidence is the virtue that demands less that we make a leap of faith (though that is involved) and more that we yield to God's passionate tenderness and let him do the worrying. It does not lead us into a life of wild and inconsiderate recklessness. On the contrary, it demands that we be prudent (as we shall see). But the virtue of confidence also enables us to take appropriate risks and to lead lives of excitement and adventure precisely because we know that whatever may go wrong—and all kinds of things may go wrong—the Father's love will never go wrong.

One of the most frequent experiences in any human life, especially in any intimate human relationship, is the experience of reconciliation. As my colleagues Marilyn and Kevin Ryan have put it, it is the experience of the rubber band pulling us back together again.

To attempt reconciliation or to respond to it requires courage, for in the reconciliation interlude, humans are vulnerable as they can ever be. Attempts at reconciliations are not only likely to result in hurt; on some occasions they will invariably do so.

A cautious, conservative, careful person will play the percentages and not run the risks of reconciliation. A confident person will cheerfully run those risks, knowing that sometimes reconciliation will work and the joy will be great, and at other times it will not work and God's healing love will provide consolation.

Make no mistake. Reconciliation is an art that requires skill, patience, senstivity, practice. Because of our confidence in God's love, we don't bumble clumsily into reconciliation attempts; rather, we wait for the proper time, the proper place, and use the proper language.

Confidence does not mean that we expect God to compensate for our own lack of effort; rather, it means we expect God to take over when our own frailties and weaknesses cause us to falter. Confidence does not justify presumptuousness, but entails justice, discipline, responsible, intelligent risk, the kind of risks without which a satisfying human life becomes quite impossible.

The ultimate enemy of confidence and courage is death. The final motivation for doing battle with death is life. We know we are going to die, but we still live. The very fact that we do live is a mystery, a gift of grace.

Is it not possible that the grace which is life—so sweet, so dear, so wonderful—might finally be stronger than the destruction of that grace in death? Such is the fundamental religious question which has bothered the human species since it has been able to think.

Intellectually, many humans have decided that death is stronger than life and that the only safe and prudent way to live is to carefully and cautiously protect and preserve life They do this, despite the evidence that a life which is obsessed with the need to avoid the dangers of death, strictly speaking, ceases to be any kind of life at all.

However, in our nervous systems, in our biology, in our preconscious and unconscious, life still asserts itself as stronger than death. So we hope, sometimes despite ourselves, and often hoping against hope. This hope, which is built into our genes and our nervous systems and our personalities, tells us that only when we live bravely, greatly, nobly, generously, defying death, asserting life in the teeth of death, does human life become worth living.

We oscillate between living lives dominated by fear of death and living lives which defy death. The revelation of Jesus confirmed the propriety of a stance which defies death. St. Paul put it bluntly, "Oh death, where is thy victory? Oh death, where is thy sting?"

The Christian virtue of confidence, then, is merely the death-defying propensity of our personalities, activated by the hope we have in God's love as revealed in Jesus. The seed will grow into a plant, the acorn will become a tree, the harvest will bear fruit, and God's love will conquer death.

In one of the more powerful episodes of the remarkable, short-lived television series, "United States," the husband and wife are preparing to go to the funeral of a brother-in-law. They must explain death to their children (which they do very well). Then they must explain death to themselves.

As they dress for the funeral, they bicker with each other, lament the loss of a man of whom they were fond, and then slowly come to reassert their own conviction that living is stronger than dying. As the program ends, they make love to each other while they wait for the funeral limousine to pick them up.

Deliberately or not, the authors of the episode touched upon a very old and primal human response to death. In the pre-Christian Irish wake (some vestiges of which survived long into the Christian era, although they have now ceased in Ireland), men and women would have sexual intercourse in the fields outside the house where the wake was taking place. It was the Irish culture's way of defying death, of laughing at it, of asserting that the life-giving power of human love is stronger than the destructiveness of death.

While the Irish cultural heritage might have carried this defiance further than other cultures because of the Irish love for wildness and grotesquery, the theme of sex in defiance of death is widespread, if not universal in human culture.

In moments of ecstatic joy and potential fruitfulness and in moments of renewed love, humankind experiences dramatically and devastatingly the vigor and power of life. It is as though, caught up in the power of passionate love, humans sense more forcefully than at any other time how strong life is and how determined is its defiance of death.

Courage, confidence, fortitude, whatever we call it, is finally grounded in the conviction that life is stronger than death and that while death may harm us and hurt us, it cannot do us in. The married couple in "United States," the manic early Irish, the Christian risking reconciliation because he or she believes the Great Assurance—all present human passion, human love, a human way of life defying the dark destructiveness of death.

The bottom line for the Catholic Christian virtue of confidence is, to repeat, forcefully stated by St. Paul: "Oh death, where is thy victory?" Oh death, where is thy sting?" We are confident in God's love; we can defy death.

What is the ultimate price of resisting God's love?

THE parables of prodigal love reveal to us Jesus' image of the Father in heaven who loves us the way an indulgent father loves a spoiled son, the way a reckless farmer loves lazy workers, the way a compassionate judge loves a guilty criminal caught in the act. The parables of the Great Assurance confirm for us that this love is implacable, that it will conquer all, that it will never turn its back on us.

Another set of parables—we might call them the "Urgency Parables"—sounds a very different note. They warn us of the need to choose, to act, to be decisive. They urge us to take advantage of the present moment, they exhort us to respond to God's love while we yet have time.

We are told to imitate the merchant who discovers the pearl of great price and sacrifices everything, if need be, to respond to God's invitation to love. We act like the peddler who discovers a treasure buried in the fields and gives everything he has to gain possession of that field.

We are warned that our opportunity to respond can be wiped out by a thief in the night. We are exhorted to make sure that we haven't built on shifting sands that will be swept away by wind and storms. We must be ready with fuel to keep our lamps lighted at night so the opportunity won't slip away from us.

We are like the fig tree or the vineyard which does not bear fruit and may eventually be cut down. Like the chaff separated from the wheat, we may be tossed into the rubbish fire, reserved for useless garbage.

If we delay or procrastinate in responding to the invitation to the Great Party that God is throwing, we risk being left out, standing outside, nose pressed to the window pane, teeth gnashing in frustration because we are not inside when we could have been.

Taken all together, these "Warning" or Urgency Parables present a terrifying picture. When combined with the Love Parables and the Assurance Parables, they seem paradoxical, if not contradictory. How could Jesus, who knew God's reckless love and implacable fidelity, think of us as excluded from the wedding feast? Would the loving Father ever exclude his children from a party? If the prodigal son not only got into a party but actually had one thrown in his honor, how can it be that others would be excluded?

The answer, of course, is that the prodigal son came back. Those who run the risk of missing the party exclude themselves by free and conscious choice. However much God wants us to seize the opportunity which he offers us, however much he passionately desires that we respond to his love, he still leaves us free not to respond, to turn our backs on his love and on him.

What is the virtue of prudence?

IT is not our concern to agonize over how many people finally and ultimately are able to resist love. The purpose of the parables is not to address the metaphysical or theological issues of the universality of salvation; rather, they are designed to be pragmatic, practical, to urge upon us the necessity of seizing the opportunity of the present moment.

No matter how many other opportunities may be offered during our life, the one at hand exists in the present moment, and as far as the challenge of God's love goes, it is already later than we think.

The parables of urgency, then, are exhortations to practice the virtue of prudence, the Christian descendant of the Old Testament virtue of wisdom, a virtue that gives us the discretion, the taste, the sensitivity, the practice, the "feel" of reacting appropriately to the challenges and opportunities, the dangers and the risks inherent in the situations in which we find ourselves.

The various books of Wisdom in the Old Testament describe in great detail how the wise and prudent person reacts to life's problems and promises. Christianity can offer very little in the way of new substance to these time-tested maxims. As in the other "moral" virtues, the Christian contribution is a new perspective and a new motivation.

For the Catholic Christian, prudence is the virtue which responds to the parables of urgency. It teaches us to seize the opportunities of each day, the graces and gifts as well as the trials, tragedies, and opportunities to respond to God's love. In the Catholic Christian worldview, prudence is that virtue which moves us to respond to the opportunity of the present moment precisely because we have seen in the present moment, however dimly, however obscurely, sometimes however painfully, an invitation to respond to God's love.

Does prudence demand perfection?

WHAT is the right thing to do at a given time? We have to rely on hunch, instinct, sensitivity, and practice. We get better (or some of us do) with the passage of time and repeated experience.

All the maxim books in the world will not necessarily provide us with the insight on how to behave in a given situation. Nor does it help us to be told that we must respond to God's love. In many circumstances, the exact kind of response that is required may not always be apparent. It takes long years of practice, listening for the inspiration of the Spirit, experience with bumbling mistakes and failed efforts to respond, to understand what the Spirit is saying to know how to react to a particular, specific, contingent situation.

To believe that the present moment is a challenge from God's love, however, helps us to continue despite our failures and to accept the blend of success and failure that marks most of human experience.

Human love can serve as both a paradigm and an illustration of the prudent response to life's difficulties and challenges. A man and woman learn slowly and often painfully to be sensitive to one another's moods, needs, fears, expectations and sensitivities. As they learn, they stumble and bumble, and sometimes fall. They are sometimes too slow, while at other times, too precipitous. Sometimes they are too passionate, and at other times, too casual.

While men and women may learn with time that it is better to risk than not to risk, they must still achieve skill in the delicate art of risking effectively, risking at the proper time. Despite their frustrations, their disappointments, mistakes, and failures, the power of love that binds them and the conviction that that love can survive the worst disappointments keeps them going.

Even after many years of being together, of growing in skill and competency and sensitivity within the intimate relationship, couples can still be surprised at what they did not know about each other and how many mistakes they are still capable of making. The mystery and excitement and romance of rediscovering one another over and over again has its own special thrill.

The prudent management of a relationship is an exercise that is bittersweet: bitter because one can so easily make a fool of oneself, and sweet because of the joy that comes from folly suffered and transcended for the sake of love.

So it is with our stumbling, bumbling attempts to respond to the divine lover. God does not demand perfection of us; he does not demand that we do everything in life well. In fact, he doesn't really seem to demand that we do anything well. All that he does require is that we try. And that is all that any lover can demand.

The woman taken in adultery was a sinner who was not even prepared to promise she would not sin again. The prodigal son was a ne'er-do-well, ready to eat crow only because it was better than eating swine food. The farmers of the eleventh hour were lazy and shiftless malcontents, hardly up to lifting a hoe a couple of times. But at least they made some effort and that was enough.

Jesus urges us through the Urgency Parables to enthusiastic response because, as in all love, the more enthusiastic our response, the more satisfying the love. However, he does not expect of us more than we are capable of. He will be satisfied, as a beginning, with a very hesitant and tentative response. Of course, that is the way it is with any lover. At first, a hint of a response is more than enough to satisfy the most passionate and eager of lovers.

The virtue of prudence, then, does not lay upon us an obligation to perfection in our efforts. It imposes on us something much more realistic—effort.

In their education, some Catholic Christians got the mistaken notion that it was necessary to be "perfect," or at least "practically perfect." They seem to have been told that responding to the situation at a given moment meant that they were not to make any mistakes at all. Even more demandingly, we should not only do the perfect thing, but we should do the "more perfect" thing.

Such a perspective is ludicrous given the fallibility, finitude, and frailty of human nature. In the New Testament, Jesus demanded not perfection but response, not total goodness but the beginning of goodness, not a life free of mistake and failure but a life of new beginnings and renewed efforts.

God is not a hanging judge or an accountant; he is a passionate lover who wants us back no matter how weak, inept, or stupid we are. The only imprudence is giving up, losing confidence in our own lovability, and doubting God's implacable fidelity.

The bottom line for the Catholic Christian virtue of prudence is that we must be prepared to start over again. This is what is demanded of us by the Urgency Parables, that we begin again—not next week, not tomorrow, not this afternoon, but now.

Chapter Twenty

Cherishing the Christian Life

Is the Christian life worth the effort?

THE Christian life requires faith in God's loving goodness, hope that that goodness will be stronger than death, loving response to God and those creatures which reveal him to us, generosity, confidence, patience, perserverance, sensitivity, discretion, resiliency. Like all love relationships, our love affair with God requires attention, practice, protection, and dedication.

Some people think that love does not require work and involves "doing what comes naturally." But anyone who has experienced intense love over a sustained period of time knows the enormous demands love makes and how much work it requires.

Asceticism—the discipline of the Christian life—is part of all intense and sustained love relationships, not merely of our love relationship with God. Responding well to another's love demands a focusing of energy and attention to detail, care, concern, and perceptiveness that requires an enormous amount of human effort.

St. Paul compared the Christian life to the conditioning of an Olympic athlete and Ignatius of Loyola compared it to the preparations of a soldier for battle. Both these comparisons may not be to the taste of some moderns, but they illustrate that while the Christian life is rewarding and produces happiness, it is not meant to be easy.

The bottom line of cherishing the Christian life is work—patient, persistent, dedicated work. Sometimes the work of the Christian life is wearisome, monotonous, seemingly unproductive; at other times it will be challenging and rewarding. So it is with the effort required of every human relationship that humans experience. Is the effort worth it? No lover hesitates for a moment in answering that question.

Why must our response to God be in a social context?

THE first observation that must be made about the Christian life is that it is communal in addition to being individual. Indeed, this is one of the major differences between what Father David Tracy calls the "Catholic imagination" and the "Protestant imagination."

The Catholic imagination does not at all deny individual responsibility; rather, it emphasizes, more strongly than the Protestant imagination, that this individual human effort occurs in a community context and with community support.

Our response to God's love is, of course, an individual response, but it is that of an individual living in a community which both challenges and comforts, sustains and urges us on. Our response to God is organized not for extrinsic reasons, such as political ideology, esthetic elegance, or ethical niceties; it is not that a communal response is "better" than an individual response.

We respond to God as members of communities because it is in our very nature to do so. We are social, communal animals who could no more detach ourselves from our backgrounds, our interaction networks, our rituals, images, or habits in responding to God than we could detach ourselves from our collectivity in any other human behavior.

It is not true to say, as some collectivistic enthusiasts have said, that the Christian life is not individual but social; rather, the Christian life is truly both individual and social precisely because we are social individuals (or gregarious individuals, if you wish). We can only act socially.

Our personalities are formed amidst other humans. Our language, our heritage are passed on to us. We learn to comprehend God and understand the meaning of love through the action of other human beings. We can no more deal with God only as individuals than we can fly by flapping our arms.

A community of believers, then, is not an option for the Christian life but a necessity. The church comes into being not because it is imposed on us as an extrinsic requirement but because it is a spontaneous response of our gregarious nature. The church is not an option, it is a necessity.

How important is the family to religion?

CHRISTIANITY came into existence as a small group and flourishes best in small group contexts—so long as the group does not turn in on itself, but rather points out toward the world beyond its boundaries.

The most powerful of the small group churches, of course, is the family. It is often said that the diocese or the parish is "the church in miniature." Without denying the theological accuracy of such a statement, one might say that, pragmatically, based on the evidence of the empirical resource, the family is also the church in miniature, and the most effective and most important "organ" the church has.

It is in the family that the basic religious images are acquired and reinforced; it is in the family that God is experienced through the love of parents for each other and in their love for their children; it is in the family that the man and woman encounter their primary "sacrament," where God reveals himself to most of us more powerfully, more persistently, and more pervasively through our spouse than he does through any other agent.

The religious life of parents and children, husband and wife, is shared—whether or nor they participate in the sharing explicitly and consciously. The correlations between parents and children, husbands and wives, to religious devotions are powerful. Furthermore, as the years of marriage go on, the religious imagination, the "religious stories" of husbands and wives converge: "your" religious story and "my" religious story become "our" religious story.

Indeed, the effects of parents and spouse on religious life are so massive that all the agencies of religious education and socialization are unimportant by comparison. It is therefore foolish to pretend that a man and woman living together in marriage are not having an important effect on the religious life of one another. Are they not, in fact, a "church" for each other?

It is possible, under extraordinary circumstances, to sustain a religious life and cherish the Christian life separately from one's spouse. But no one should think that such an isolation of religion from family life, of human love from divine love, does not involve tremendous difficulties.

In the ordinary course of human existence, sharing religion between a husband and wife can be a strong comfort and a stimulating challenge. It should be as natural as sharing the same bedroom. In fact, however, even when a man and woman are of the same faith, share the same values, and have a tremendous religious effect on each other, they are often even less likely to talk about their religious life than they are to talk about their sexual life—and most of the time they are strongly disinclined to talk about either.

The church, it must be confessed, is of no great help to them, for it only tells them repeatedly what they cannot do. The church provides husbands and wives with no patterns, no models, no suggestions, no motivations for creating a joint, explicitly religious life together other than an occasional, awkward suggestion that the family rosary was not such a bad idea after all.

How much do we need to pray?

THE first suggestion for cherishing the Christian life is to share the life with others in the church, of course, and if possible, with a small community of friends who share common goals and aspirations, and especially with that person who is God's primary "sacrament" in our lives.

Secondly, one must pray. Prayer is as essential in the Christian life as conversation is essential for human love. Indeed, in our divine love affair, prayer functions the same way that conversation does in our human love affair. We pray, not because God needs our prayer (though, if we are to believe the Scriptures, he seems to *want* it), but because we need to pray.

You may recall the story of one of my colleagues, an agnostic sociologist. When his little boy was sick, he prayed more than he had "in the forty-two misspent years of my life." (Years which were, from the point of view of an outsider, not all that misspent.) He prayed not because he was sure someone was listening—and he still isn't sure—but because he *needed* to pray. He had no choice but to pray. His father's love would not permit him not to pray.

I did not argue with him, and I will not argue here,

that this spontaneous impulse to pray (and the well-nigh universal practice of prayer—50 percent of Americans pray every day, 80 percent at least once a week) "proves" the existence of God. For my purposes, however, it does prove the human propensity to pray.

There was a period not so long ago when some of the elite groups in the Catholic church went on a "relevance" kick in which we were told by frantically activist clery and religious that group discussion was prayer, and that therefore they had no other need to pray. While those activities may be virtuous, they are not the same thing as prayer and, in fact, are no substitute for it.

At the time, these activities may have substituted for the ritualistic, routinized, empty prayer life which has been imposed on many priests and religious. Mechanically tolling the beads or ritualistically reciting the breviary in a foreign language and with a vacant mind caricatures prayer. Although such behavior allegedly contributes to the glory of God, one is hard put to see how God got much glory out of such compulsive, humanly meaningless behavior.

However, as with so many other things in the post-conciliar church, some enthusiastic priests and religious rejected authentic prayer because they had rarely experienced it.

The form and the style of prayer varies from individual to individual. Prayers of gratitude seem to be the most effective in promoting psychological well-being and personality adjustment. Perhaps it is because gratitude orients the human personality out toward others instead of in on itself.

We should not hesitate to pray for the things we need both because such prayer acknowledges our relationship with God and because God himself has urged us to pray that way. Yet prayers of gratitude should certainly be present in our prayer life because we have so much to be grateful for.

It also seems reasonable to suppose that in the lives of most Christians "reflective" prayer is essential. We may call it mental prayer, meditation, contemplation, or, in these ecumenical days, zen, yoga, or transcendental meditation. But it is under the influence of contemplative, reflective prayer that our dialogue with our divine lover truly becomes a dialogue.

Why is solitude the natural medium for prayer?

WE may complain that our prayer life is a one-way street in which we do all the talking and God does all the listening. It may be, however, that we lack the skills to shut up and listen to anybody, God included.

So, the second trait of cherishing the Christian life overlaps into the third, as prayer seeks solitude so that it may listen as well as talk. I said earlier in this book that the Christian life is both individual and social. When I urge the need for quiet I do not deny the social nature of human life, for we are social beings, who relate to other human beings even when we are alone, even when we are in the desert or in the forest by ourselves, even when we have temporarily sealed out the distractions of the world.

There is a reciprocity, an ebb and flow in our lives between solitude and action. If we seek solitude for reflection, the reason is, as Thomas Aquinas pointed out long ago, that we will return to our commitments in this world refreshed and renewed, able to engage in action which is more dedicated, more powerful, precisely because of the interlude of solitude which has intervened.

Blessed solitude may not in fact be the only blessedness, as the old Latin dictum put it, though we may often be tempted to think of it that way as the telephone rings off the hook. But it is a blessing, indeed an essential one, for the Christian life. There must be periods of solitude every day—or almost every day—as well as somewhat longer interludes of silent reflection.

There seems to be more sense in the church today than there was a decade ago. Meditation and contemplation are fashionable again. Indeed, there are Catholic counterparts to Outward Bound that turn people into hermits, living on mountains, in deserts and on islands for periods of time so that they might "get in touch" with themselves again.

This fashionable return to the eremetical state, however temporary it may be, makes it somewhat easier to urge on Catholic Christians the need for solitude in their lives. Yet, in fact, though contemplation may have become a fad, there is still very little of it in most of our lives. And, there is some reason to suspect that the "outward bound" hermits quickly lose touch with themselves when they return to the demands of ordinary daily life.

Make no mistake about it. Reflection, contemplation, solitude, thoughtful prayer require tremendous self-discipline. Yet there is no substitute for it, because conversation with the divine lover is a fundamental and essential "input" of the religious life.

What about the importance of spiritual reading?

FOR most of us, reading is also essential for the sustenance and growth of the religious life. It is not absolutely indispensable, as should be obvious from the fact that throughout much of the history of Christianity most Christians could not read. But, in an age like our own, with the endless input of images and ideas from the mass media, our minds and imaginations can easily be clogged with the trivial, the unimportant, the obscure, the distracting, and the foolish. It is important to balance this inundation with spiritual wisdom.

If we apply the paradigm of human love to our relationship with God, we will realize that it is essential to know all we can about our lover. Love requires not only knowledge but the increase in knowledge. The closer, the more intimate our love, the more powerful is our demand to know still more about the beloved. If there were books written about the one we love, we would certainly devour them, because though the printed word is no substitute for intimate communion, it helps to sustain our relationship, especially at those times when the beloved is, or seems to be, absent.

Spiritual reading provides us with the raw material of our prayer and our reflection and also pricks our conscience when we have permitted our prayer and reflection to become weak and infrequent. What matters with spiritual reading is not how many books we read, or how long it takes us to read a book or even what book we read. What counts is that we read regularly and that we read reflectively.

A few minutes of reflective reading every day or every other day or even once a week is far superior to devouring several books on vacation or during a retreat.

What are the benefits of making a retreat or having a spiritual director?

THE spiritual life also benefits enormously from a "retreat," a withdrawing from the world for prayer and reflection either by yourself or with your community (especially with your spouse). A retreat may be formal with a retreat master or informal where, in effect, you act as your own retreat master. Because a wide variety of retreat or quasi-retreat resources are available today, you must pick and choose in order to find the most appropriate format.

It seems to me that the twin dangers to be avoided in a retreat are, on the one hand, becoming so separated from your ordinary life that you will overestimate the ability to sustain the enthusiasm generated during the retreat to drastically and totally reform your life. On the other hand, you should not be so close to the outside world as to lose all possibility to achieve the perspective that distance and solitude provide.

The risk of many retreats, it seems to me, is that they become highly individualistic. Not merely do they take a person out of the network of his/her relationships, but they also forget the importance of that network. For not only is the network a challenge and an obligation, it is also a help and support. It would appear from research evidence that one of the reasons for the success of the marriage encounter movement is precisely that it does deal with spiritual problems in a relationship and does not isolate individuals.

However, marriage encounter is not necessarily for everyone, and it does not necessarily deal with every kind of spiritual problem. For some people, at certain times in their lives, only virtual isolation provides the spiritual environment that is needed for religious rest and rehabilitation. For myself—and I suspect for many, if not most, Americans—I am not able to make a retreat as long as there is a telephone nearby.

Most people find it useful to have a spiritual director. Indeed, the practice of having such a director, recently all but disappeared, has come back. Directors were unpopular with those of us who were oppressed by them in the seminary or in college or in the scholasticate precisely because they were as authoritarian as everyone else in the system and were, in fact, little more than auxiliary discipline officers, using their positions as monitors of our souls to keep tabs on us for those in authority.

The spiritual director should be neither an authoritarian giver of orders nor a psychiatric aid but someone who facilitates spiritual growth with wisdom, cautious advice, and discreet suggestion—all of which enhances rather than restricts our freedom.

Not everyone who claims to be a master or a mistress of the spiritual life is qualified to play the role, and there are a lot of phony gurus around, masquerading as prophets in Israel. Indeed, there are more people looking for spiritual guidance today than there are qualified guides available.

If you find someone who is sensitive to your personality and alert to the requirements of your growth in the love of God, hang onto that person. Such people are rare, especially if they are willing to let you make your own decisions, your own mistakes, and be content with helping to create a climate in which your spiritual growth becomes possible. Also keep in mind the profound advice of St. Teresa of Avila, who opined that she would much prefer to have a wise director than a holy one.

Is there an effective way to integrate life and liturgy?

THE rhythms of the liturgical year are theoretically an enormous asset to spiritual growth. Liturgical enthusiasts have spoken a good deal of nonsense about the power of the liturgy. Most of the nonsense is based on theoretical assumption and not practical experimentation.

I know of one priest who closed down his Catholic school because he thought it was better to spend the money on "the liturgy." Theoretically it sounded like a good idea. It turned out, however, that when he closed down the school, against the wishes of the laity, the money wasn't there, and his liturgical innovations did not educate very many people because the people didn't like them.

The Sunday liturgy, well done, can be a considerable help to us in our growth in the love of God. But Sunday liturgies are often not well done, and the format of the large congregational mass on Sundays (or Saturday afternoon) tends to minimize the psychological and spiritual impact of the liturgy.

Furthermore, while there is great grace in the rhythms of the liturgical year, it must be admitted that we have not yet found a way to integrate those rhythms (a product of a bygone era) into the lives of contemporary humans. The liturgy has enormous spiritual growth potential, but we do not yet understand how to achieve most of that potential.

A liturgical guidebook I read long ago (I believe it was one of the volumes of Pius Parsch) said that the Holy Week liturgy should ideally be celebrated in a monastery. This was so that the full rhythm of the sacred ritual, from the beginning to the end of Holy Week, could be appreciated. And the undivided attention of the participants was required. Most of us, however, do not have access to monasteries. What is more, the complicated schedules and demands of family life make it extremely difficult for most of us to give a whole week to such an activity, however valuable it might be for our spiritual growth.

A group of people with whom I work recently determined to spend Holy Week together, involving the children in the services. It was a great idea, but it never got off the ground because the adults were unable to coordinate their schedules, much less those of their offspring.

The problem of how to reintegrate liturgy and life has scarcely been addressed, much less solved. Many families and communities are going to have to experiment with trial and error until a new wisdom of liturgy and life is discovered. However, the new emphasis on the importance of our physical environment will at least provide motivation for such experimentation.

There are rich resources available to us for cherishing the Christian life. However, as was said at the beginning, it requires work—work to find the resources, work to adapt them to our present needs, and then, the hardest work of all, the work of actually cherishing the life of grace.

Chapter Twenty-One

The Presence of Grace

What is the ultimate question?

THE bottom line of all bottom lines is grace. The issue is not whether there is grace in the world. We all know that there is, for gracious events sprinkle our lives like spring rain.

Rather, the question is whether the moments of grace are pure chance, capricious tricks, genetic adjustments or revelations. Are the moments of grace random fluctuations in a cosmic buzz, or are they rumors of angels, rhythmic flapping of wings, melodic hints of an explanation?

The core question, then, is not whether there is a God but whether there is Grace behind the graces, whether reality is gracious, indeed whether Reality is Grace. The one we call God, unless and until he/she is corrupted by dogmas, legalisms, arguments, and philosophical questions, is nothing and no one more than the Assumed Other, who seems to be responsible for the gracious events in our life and therefore, it is reasonable to presume, might very well be Grace. The issue is whether God is Grace and Grace is God. Even more specifically, the issue is whether God is Love and Love is God.

The issue has to be phrased this way to escape the endless philosophical arguments about whether God exists. As philosophical discourse, the arguments are surely important. Both David Tracy and Hans Kung have addressed themselves brilliantly to these issues in recent years.

To the extent a human person is concerned about rational and philosophical discourse (and we all must be at least somewhat concerned about it), then the issue of the existence of God must be faced, as men like Kung and Tracy have faced it.

I submit, however, that there is, religiously speaking, a prior question. Can we trust our experiences of the present grace when they suggest to us that lurking behind those experiences there is Grace and even Loving Grace? Philosophical arguments do not produce faith. They may sustain faith intellectually after the leap; more rarely, they may anticipate and prepare the way for the act of faith.

But the act of faith, which is, indeed, an act of loving response to a loving grace revealing itself through gracious events and gracious persons is a very different form of human behavior than intellectual assent to the proposition that God exists.

Those who are pursuing a philosophical bottom line may well be content intellectually with the conclusion that God does exist; those who are pursuing a religious bottom line, according to which they may live, must ask a different question, one that demands more than intellectual assent in the commitment of the whole personality: is there really Loving Grace inviting me to respond?

Need it be said that this question is both more difficult and easier than a philosophical question of the existence of God? It is more difficult because it demands far more than just intellectual agreement; it demands total surrender of the self. It is easier because the rumors of angels are sometimes so loud that it is impossible to drown them out, and the experience of grace is sometimes so powerful that it seems fruitless to resist its inherent demand.

If one is finally to reject the Catholic Christian vision of faith, one should not do so on questions of ecclesiology, sexual ethics, or even the precise terms of Christology. In truth, if one turns one's back on Catholic Christianity, it should be because, in its best moments, it maintains with far too much confidence and far too much enthusiasm that Reality is indeed Loving Grace demanding response. This stance seems patently absurd, but the very absurdity of the claim provides a reason for turning away from Catholicism—the only reason that really matters.

The problem, then, is not whether there is a God, but whether there is Grace; for if there is Grace, then Grace is God and God is good, whatever things may be wrong with both life and the universe. If there should be a God and there is no Grace, then Ingmar Bergman is right, and God is a great ugly spider.

What makes grace and religion sacramental?

THE Catholic approach to the presence of grace is *sacramental,* that is to say, it assumes God reveals himself/herself (Grace manifests itself) through creatures, through the world, through the events of human life. Indeed, whatever one's Christological explanations might be, Catholics still must believe that while Jesus must be the most adequate, the most perfect, and the highest self-revelation of God, he is still a revelation which is made manifest through the created nature of Jesus and through the audible words and visible deeds of the Lord.

The Catholic approach to religion is sacramental not because the church has a system of seven sacraments; rather, the opposite is the case. There exist seven sacraments precisely because Catholicism, like prophetic Judaism, which is its ancestor, takes a sacramental view of the world, believes that God reveals himself/unveils herself through created things and the events of ordinary life.

Some things can be Sacraments only if one has a world-view that sees everything as having the potential for sacramentality. "Grace," Karl Rahner has said, "is everything," by which he meant that loving goodness tends to explode almost whenever it is given a chance. The Sacraments are those occasions and situations in which the explosion of grace is especially likely to occur.

Are there alternative approaches to sacramentality?

SACRAMENTALITY, as an approach to the relationship between God and world (or Grace and world) is sharply different from a number of alternatives:

Animism: direct divine intervention—does God direct the thunder?

This is the belief that God directly and literally controls the various forces of nature. Thunder is God's cry of anger, lightning is God's punishment from the sky, a destroyed harvest is God's judgment on the village, military defeat is the result of disloyalty to God, sickness is a punishment for sin. God is in the water, the sky, the air, the trees. Primitive people are especially likely to be animists, though even the Pygmies of Africa and the Australian aborigines seem to have some times and some places that are especially sacred.

But animism is not absent from the modern world. Many fundamentalists believe that God directly intervenes when one randomly opens a page of the Scriptures and speaks words spontaneously into one's mind in settings of religious enthusiasm. Indeed, one could detect traces of animism in some of the critics of my work on the papal elections of 1978. It was wrong, they said, to consider the election of a pope as a political process, for, after all, was not the Holy Spirit involved?

The question and the criticism both seem to assume that God's Spirit would somehow intervene directly, overriding, as it were, the human dynamics that were involved in the election process. However pious were the intentions of those who spoke of the Holy Spirit as working independently of the creature dynamics of the papal election, that position is not sacramental and not compatible with the Catholic tradition of sacramentality.

Dualism: The sacred versus the profane—is this world only an imitation?

If the animist sees God in everything, the dualist sees God only in certain things, or at least so powerfully present in special times and special places (temples, sacred groves, rituals, celebrations, etc.) that the rest of the world is profane by comparison.

For the dualist who draws sharp taboos around the sacred, the distinction between the sacred and the profane is precise and decisive. In sacred times and in sacred places the Real World is revealed, a world of which ours is only a pale imitation. The profane world imitates the sacred, just as the sacred imitates and re-presents the Real. But the profane has little value of its own, and even the sacred is but a pale shadow of the Real.

Most of the nature religions which preceded the great world religions were dualistic, though in the case of the Celts, for example, the dualism was drastically modified. The sacred and the profane, the present land and the multicolored land, were like two flowing rivers which frequently mingled one with another.

The Celts hedged their bets, they were open to the possibility that the many-colored land could impinge upon their world in the most unexpected times and places. One of the results of such modified dualism was to notably heighten the worth of the ordinary world, which, since it flowed parallel with the many-colored land was something more than its pale reflection.

Dualism is not unpopular today. It is much to be feared that most Americans are to some extent dualists, sharply distinguishing between the sacred events in life (most of which happen in church) and the profane events in life (most of which, however powerful and important they may be, would be quite unthinkable in church).

Secularism: Does everything occur by chance?

In this perspective there is no sacred and there is no grace. There is only one world, this one, and it has no meaning beyond itself. The gracious persons and events in our lives either occur by chance or, at best, point to nothing beyond themselves.

Despite the theory of some sociologists (not very good ones and certainly with no empirical data to back them up) and some theologians, there is no reason to think that the secularist propensity in the human personality has grown stronger or that the number of out-and-out secularists has increased in the human race over past eras. Each of us is often skeptical about Grace and some of us have always insisted that the apparent harmony of the flapping wings is in fact a meaningless buzz.

How does the sacramentalist respond to the alternative approaches?

THE *sacramental* approach shares something in common with all three of the other positions but also rejects a portion of each position. With the animist, the sacramentalist believes that God lurks everywhere.

With the dualist, however, the sacramentalist insists that God is distinct from that in which he reveals himself. God may well be immanent in the world and in every object and event and person in the world, but he also transcends the world and is distinct from it.

Finally, along with the secularist, the sacramentalist asserts the reality of all things in this world. They are not pale shadows or imitations, they are events, objects, and persons with value unto themselves. They did not acquire their worth as reflections of some other world which is unique and absolutely real.

Prophetic Judaism was profoundly secularist. It railed against the worship of idols, sacred groves, and mountain sanctuaries because it said the idols are merely statues created by human hands, the high sanctuaries are merely mountaintops, and the groves of trees merely forests. Yahweh is not to be identified with any of these creatures.

Indeed, precisely to protect the transcendence of Yahweh, the Jewish prophets were vigorous secularists. Yahweh could only transcend the ordinary when the ordinary was declared independent and endowed with a reality of its own.

The sacramentalist, then, will deny that thunder is God's voice (though if he/she has any imagination, he/she will enjoy the pyrotechnics of a thunderstorm); the sacramentalist will also deny that some places and events are so sacred as to reduce everything else to a profanity verging on unreality; but he/she will also deny that the ordinary world, the profane world, the secular world is devoid of grace.

Finally, for empirical reasons, if we encounter grace in the events, things and persons of our life, if there are so many hints of loving goodness in so many different life experiences, how, says the sacramentalist, can one deny the presence of Grace?

The sacramentalist comes almost full circle to the animist. Poet Richard Wilbur does not believe that the sun which creates the light on the brick wall is God, or contains God, or operates at the direct instruction of God. He merely says the sunlight reveals, manifests, declares that there is light and hence, inevitably, Light.

To put the matter in abstract philosophical terms, sacramentality is the position that holds that beings reveal Being in which they participate. Catholic sacramentality further insists that beings are analogous to Being. Beings are not Being, graces are not Grace, beings only participate in Being, beginning to exist precisely because they participate in Being and are not Being.

Beings are radically different from Being, and graces are radically different from Grace. However, beings in fact *are,* and they do reflect that Being in which they participate. Graces are graceful, and hence they do reflect the Grace in which they participate.

What part does imagination play in understanding sacramentality?

THE Catholic doctrine of sacramentality is based on what David Tracy calls "the analogical imagination," the ability to see beings and Being as both similar and dissimilar. To use less philosophical language, it is the ability to see that streams are like God and unlike him. Other forms of Christianity may stress the radical dichotomy between creatures and God so vigorously as to obscure, if not to deny completely, the similarity that persists despite the dichotomy.

The Catholic imagination, if it is faced in its sacramentality with a choice of succumbing on the one hand to dualism or, on the other hand, to animism will cheerfully err in the latter direction. With the animist, the Catholic imagination believes that Grace works everywhere, even if it has a very different idea of how it works.

This discussion may seem unnecessarily abstract. I want to be very clear in this concluding chapter to precisely state where the Catholic imagination stands. By way of illustration, let us consider the grace which is human sexual love.

The animist will see fertility gods and goddesses gamboling in the fields among the flocks and among the maidens and youths in the tribe. He/she will worship the forces of fertility, for it is through them that there are food, clothing, and children to keep the tribe alive.

The dualist will see in the union of male and female a sacred event which, for all its profane pleasures, does reenact the original creative behavior of the God in the Real World in Real Time. The sacred and the profane in sexuality are sharply distinguished in the marriage ritual, where the profane behavior of husband and wife is at least linked to the Real Events which happened in the age of the gods.

The secularist will see in human life pleasure, wonder, and surprise, but they offer no hints about the meaning of the human condition other than the absurdity which can be seen in the ebb and flow, the rise and fall of human romance.

The sacramentalist will say that in the passionate tenderness of human intimacy there is a hint of the passionate tenderness with which Grace loves us. Sex is a grace; it is gracious, it is graceful because it reveals, through human loving goodness, a loving goodness which indeed lurks in human love but also goes beyond human love.

And if the sacramentalist is a Catholic Christian, he/she will add that despite the radical distinction between the two loves, between God's passion and human passion, there is still a fundamental continuity. For while they are dissimilar, they are not totally dissimilar; and thus, in at least some respects, the two loves are similar. The Catholic Christian will also add that the difference between the passion of Grace and the passion to be found in the grace of human sexuality intimacy is not that Loving Grace is something "purer," "more spiritual," and "less passionate" but that it is indeed more demanding, more passionate, more consuming, and more pleasurable.

In other words, the sacramentalist with the analogical imagination will insist that the difference between graces and Grace can always be expressed in the following dictum: "Grace is like grace only better." God's passion is like human passion only more intense. The analogical imagination does not deny to God's Goodness any of the goodnesses we experience through creatures. It merely says that with God it is better.

There are a number of extremely important conclusions that may be drawn from the Catholic imagination view of analogical sacramentality:

1. However repressed, puritanical, dehumanized, anti-body, and pessimistic certain forms of Catholicism have become (most notably spiritualities and Catholic educational practice), the Catholic imagination insists, and must insist vigorously, on the goodness of material objects, human pleasures, and happy events in life. The Manichaean temptation, the temptation to pessimism has been persistent; Catholics have repeatedly regressed

into dualism (as many of us who were brought up as Catholics in the '30s, '40s and '50s can testify).

However, an anti-flesh, anti-joy dualism is both doctrinal and imaginative heresy which cannot be acceptable to the Catholic view of analogical sacramentality. If everything is grace, then everything is good. For one reason or another, we may relinquish certain graces, but whatever the reason, it cannot be that they are bad—not if our imagination is Catholic.

2. Again, despite frequent practice to the contrary, the Catholic Christian tradition is profoundly secular. It does not identify Grace with the graces that reveal it, but it does defend the continuity between Grace and graces as a precondition for the conviction that graces are sacraments of Grace.

Hence Catholic Christianity in its true genius has always believed that God can be found revealing himself/herself everywhere. While there are indeed sacred times and sacred places, these exist mainly to heighten the sacramentality of every time and of everyday life.

The self-revelation, the self-unveiling of God and the work of the Holy Spirit occurs in church, of course, particularly when the ecclesial community is assembled. But it is by no means limited to such circumstances. The Spirit blows whither he/she will, and the challenge to religious leadership is not merely to preside over those occasions when the Spirit is believed to be especially present, but also to discern his/her presence in non-official, non-public, ordinary circumstances in which the Spirit also appears to be at work.

The Catholic instinct for sacramentality, based as it is on the analogical imagination, is both profoundly secular, for it believes Grace is everywhere, and at the same time profoundly transcendental, for it insists that while

Grace is very like the graces which unveil it, it is also very unlike them and transcends them because it is so much better.

The Catholic sacramental imagination, therefore, can respond to both the Protestant fear that we may commit idolatry by identifying God with creatures by not distinguishing between graces and Grace, and also to the secularist fear that we will devalue the authentic importance of the things, persons, and events of secular life.

It may well be that many Catholics, including many Catholic leaders, will not understand the Catholic sacramental imagination. That may be unfortunately true, but it only means that many of those who are Catholics and, by their lights, good Catholics, do not understand the genius of Catholicism.

3. A third consequence is that Catholic Christianity, because it believes Grace is everywhere, is open, in principle at least, as St. Ignatius of Antioch put it long ago, to all that is good, all that is true, all that is beautiful, all that is fully human in any of the world's cultures and religions.

In the great burst of optimism which followed Easter, Catholicism absorbed the rites, the deities, the art, and the music of pagan cultures. The mother goddesses became Mary, the local deities became angels and patron saints, the fertility rituals were integrated into the liturgy. The liturgy was translated from Aramaic to Greek and from Greek to Latin and eventually from Latin to Slavonic.

During the course of Christian history many of the leaders of Catholic Christianity lost their sacramental nerve. In one of the great tragedies of Christian history, the Jesuit experiment of Christianizing Indian and Chinese culture was rejected by the Vatican. Surely there is a need for the discernment of the Spirit when those newly in contact with Catholicism do, indeed, respond to Ignatius of Antioch's criterion.

I confess I do not see, for example, how Catholic Christianity can accept the polygamy of Africa with its inevitable degradation of women. Nonetheless, the proper approach of Catholicism to non-Western and non-Christian cultures, given the sacramental imagination, is not to search for what can be excluded but for what can be included. Similarly, those who convert from other religions, whether the religion be Hindu or Baptist, should be told that they are not so much leaving behind their heritage as adding to it.

Can sacramentality be demonstrated in a modern context?

TWO modern parables demonstrate the Catholic sacramental imagination. The unintentional account of an experience of Grace is Bob Fosse's film *All That Jazz.* Joe Gideon (Fosse's surrogate in the movie) encounters death (as Fosse himself did, although, unlike the movie character, Fosse recovered). It turns out that death is not an ugly, evil, and destructive foe but a lovely, patiently amused woman called "Angelique."

Death is the angel of Yahweh, and as we know from contemporary Scripture scholars, the Angel of Yahweh is Yahweh himself. The gentle amusement of the "particular judgment" scene in the film is more than a little terrifying, but is also passionately loving. Even an encounter with death is Grace and, indeed, for Bob Fosse/ Joe Gideon, it is an overwhelming encounter with a passionately loving Grace.

Is Jessica Lang, in *All That Jazz,* a sacrament? Is she not too sensuous, too sexy, too passionate, too seductive? The Catholic sacramental imagination would reply that Jessica Lang is a revelation of God, a hint of God's passionate goodness. The difference between God and Jessica Lang, however, is not that God is less sensuous (less attractive to the human senses) but more. Ms. Lang's appeal, impressive as it is, is but a hint of the appeal of Ultimate Grace.

Far more deliberately Catholic is Walker Percy's dazzlingly brilliant novel, *The Second Coming,* in which the only sane and likable people are the hero and heroine, a middle-aged lawyer with a rare epileptic disorder and a young woman just breaking free of schizophrenia.

Will Barrett goes into a cave determined to die if God does not send some sign of his existence. God doesn't exactly send Barrett a sign, but does dump him into a greenhouse where Alison, the young woman, is hiding out. Is she a sacrament or not? Will Barrett hesitates and then decides that while God may not have sent quite the sign he expected, God nonetheless revealed himself (unveiled herself) in an offbeat, flaky, but appealing woman.

Is she not a gift and therefore a sign of the giver? Could it be that the Lord is here, masquerading behind that simple, silly, holy face? Am I crazy to love both, her and Him? I want . . . no, not want, I must have and will have them both.

That is the bottom line. We humans want and must have, indeed will have them both—our human loves and the Ultimate Love which human love discloses, reveals, unveils, and promises.